Instant Pot Pressure Cooker Cookbook #2020

600 Affordable, Quick and Delicious Instant Pot Recipes for Beginners and Advanced Users (1000-Day Meal Plan)

Maria Bradou

Table of contents

Introduction

Here in this book you will find healthy, delicious and tasty recipes. Pressure cooking is one of the healthy cooking methods used around the world. Smart and advanced cooking equipment's make your daily cooking easy. In this book of recipes, we have to use advanced pressure-cooking equipment popularly known as instant pot. It is not only pressure cooker it's a multifunctional cooking appliance which performs task of 7 different cooking appliances. The instant pot allows you to cook wide verity of delicious dishes including poultry, fish, meat, beans, vegetables, desserts, cakes, etc.

The instant pot comes with different smart functions which will help you to cook delicious food in very less time and gives you consistent cooking. In this book you have to cook different types of delicious dishes with your instant pot. You can use your instant pot as a pressure cooker, rice cooker, slow cooker, steamer, sauté pan, and more. It comes with automatic pre-programmed functions or you can also use it by manual functions to cook your food by perfections. It saves your time and kitchen space. Instant pot cooks your food at high pressure without compromising the food nutritional values. In this book you have to find the different varieties of delicious recipes from globally inspired dishes.

In this book each and every recipe is written by its exact preparation time, cooking time, ingredients require and step by step cooking instructions. This book covers all types of recipes from soup to deserts and meatless to meaty.

Chapter 1: Breakfast

Delicious French toast Casserole

Preparation Time: 10 minutes; Cooking Time: 25 minutes; Serve: 4

Ingredients:

- 2 eggs
- 1 cup of water
- 2 1/2 tbsp butter, melted
- 1/2 tsp vanilla extract
- 1/2 tsp cinnamon
- 6 tbsp brown sugar
- 1/4 tsp nutmeg
- 1 1/2 cups milk
- 1/2 bread loaf, cut into cubed
- 1/4 cup maple syrup

Directions:

1. In a large bowl, whisk together eggs, butter, vanilla, cinnamon, nutmeg, brown sugar, and milk.
2. Spray a 7-inch baking dish with cooking spray.
3. Add bread cubed into the egg mixture and stir to coat.
4. Pour 1 cup of water into the instant pot then place the trivet in the pot.
5. Pour bread mixture into the prepared baking dish and place dish on top of the trivet.
6. Seal pot with lid and cook on manual high pressure for 25 minutes.
7. Once done then release pressure using quick-release method than open the lid.
8. Carefully remove baking dish from the pot.
9. Pour maple syrup on top and serve.

Nutritional Value (Amount per Serving):

Calories 290; Fat 12.7 g; Carbohydrates 41.7 g; Sugar 33.2 g; Protein 4.1 g; Cholesterol 27 mg

Easy Breakfast Grits

Preparation Time: 10 minutes; Cooking Time: 15 minutes; Serve: 6

Ingredients:

- 1 cup ground white grits
- 1 cups of milk
- 3 cups of water
- 1/2 cup cheddar cheese, shredded
- 2 tbsp butter

Directions:

1. Add butter into the instant pot and set the pot on sauté mode.
2. Once butter is melted then add grits and cook for 1-2 minutes.
3. Add water and salt and stir everything well.
4. Seal pot with lid and cook on manual high pressure for 10 minutes.
5. Once done then allow to release pressure naturally for 10 minutes then release using quick-release method.
6. Open the lid. Stir in cheese and milk.
7. Serve and enjoy.

Nutritional Value (Amount per Serving):

Calories 116; Fat 7.9 g; Carbohydrates 7.5 g; Sugar 2 g; Protein 4.3 g; Cholesterol 23 mg

Pumpkin Oatmeal

Preparation Time: 10 minutes; Cooking Time: 5 minutes; Serve: 6

Ingredients:

- 1 1/2 cups steel-cut oats
- 1/2 tsp vanilla
- 1/2 tsp allspice
- 1 1/2 tsp cinnamon
- 14 oz can pumpkin puree
- 4 1/2 cups water

- 2 tbsp pecans, chopped
- 2 tbsp walnuts, chopped

Directions:
1. Add all ingredients except pecan and walnuts into the instant pot and stir well.
2. Seal pot with lid and cook on manual high pressure for 3 minutes.
3. Once done then allow to release pressure naturally then open the lid.
4. Stir well and top with pecan and walnuts.
5. Serve and enjoy.

Nutritional Value (Amount per Serving):
Calories 227; Fat 6.2 g; Carbohydrates 38.7 g; Sugar 9.8 g; Protein 6.2 g; Cholesterol 0 mg

Roasted Baby Potatoes

Preparation Time: 10 minutes; Cooking Time: 16 minutes; Serve: 4
Ingredients:
- 2 lbs baby potatoes, scrubbed, washed and pierce each potato
- 2 tbsp olive oil
- 1 cup vegetable broth
- 2 garlic cloves, peeled
- For seasoning:
- 1/2 tsp sage
- 1/2 tsp thyme
- 1/2 tsp oregano
- 1/2 tsp rosemary
- Pepper
- Salt

Directions:
1. Add garlic, potatoes, and broth into the instant pot and stir well.
2. Seal pot with lid and cook on manual high pressure for 11 minutes.
3. Once done then release pressure using quick-release method than open the lid.
4. Drain broth from pot and pat dry the potatoes.
5. Set pot on sauté mode. Add seasonings and oil into the pot and stir well.
6. Cook on sauté mode for 5 minutes.
7. serve and enjoy.

Nutritional Value (Amount per Serving):
Calories 205; Fat 7.6 g; Carbohydrates 29.3 g; Sugar 0.2 g; Protein 7.2 g; Cholesterol 0 mg

Easy Cinnamon Apples

Preparation Time: 10 minutes; Cooking Time: 3 minutes; Serve: 3
Ingredients:
- 4 medium apples, peel, core, and cubed
- 1 tbsp honey
- 1/8 cup water
- 3/4 tsp cinnamon

Directions:
1. Add all ingredients into the instant pot and stir well.
2. Seal pot with lid and cook on manual high pressure for 3 minutes.
3. Once done then release pressure using quick-release method.
4. Stir well and serve.

Nutritional Value (Amount per Serving):
Calories 177; Fat 0.5 g; Carbohydrates 47.3 g; Sugar 36.7 g; Protein 0.8 g; Cholesterol 0 mg

Ranch Potatoes

Preparation Time: 10 minutes; Cooking Time: 7 minutes; Serve: 4
Ingredients:
- 2 lbs potatoes, scrubbed and cut into 1-inch pieces
- 1/2 cup vegetable broth
- 1/2 cup water

- 3/4 cup parmesan cheese, shredded
- 1 oz ranch seasoning
- 1/2 tsp salt

Directions:
1. Add all ingredients except cheese into the instant pot and stir well.
2. Seal pot with lid and cook on manual high pressure for 7 minutes.
3. Once done then release pressure using quick-release method than open the lid.
4. Add cheese and stir until cheese is melted.
5. Serve and enjoy.

Nutritional Value (Amount per Serving):
Calories 200; Fat 1.5 g; Carbohydrates 35.9 g; Sugar 2.7 g; Protein 6.1 g; Cholesterol 4 mg

Quick & Easy Oatmeal

Preparation Time: 10 minutes; Cooking Time: 6 minutes; Serve: 12
Ingredients:
- 2 cups rolled oats
- 1/3 cup maple syrup
- 1/3 cup brown sugar
- ¼ tsp cinnamon
- 3 ½ cups water
- Pinch of salt

Directions:
1. Add all ingredients into the instant pot and stir well.
2. Seal pot with lid and cook on manual high pressure for 6 minutes.
3. Once done then allow to release pressure naturally then open the lid.
4. Stir everything well and serve.

Nutritional Value (Amount per Serving):
Calories 90; Fat 0.9 g; Carbohydrates 19.1 g; Sugar 9.3 g; Protein 1.8 g; Cholesterol 0 mg

Creamy Mashed Potatoes

Preparation Time: 10 minutes; Cooking Time: 8 minutes; Serve: 6
Ingredients:
- 6 medium potatoes, peeled and sliced
- ½ tsp garlic powder
- ¼ cup milk
- ¼ cup sour cream
- ¼ cup butter
- 5 cups of water
- ½ tsp pepper
- 2 tsp salt

Directions:
1. Add potatoes, water, and 1 tsp salt into the instant pot and stir well.
2. Seal pot with lid and cook on manual high pressure for 8 minutes.
3. Once done then release pressure using quick-release method than open the lid.
4. Drain potatoes well and place in a large bowl.
5. Add remaining ingredients and mashed potatoes until smooth.
6. Serve and enjoy.

Nutritional Value (Amount per Serving):
Calories 242; Fat 10.1 g; Carbohydrates 34.7 g; Sugar 3 g; Protein 4.4 g; Cholesterol 25 mg

Delicious Chocolate Oatmeal

Preparation Time: 10 minutes; Cooking Time: 4 minutes; Serve: 6
Ingredients:
- 1 ½ cups rolled oats
- 2 tbsp maple syrup
- 2 tbsp cocoa powder
- 2 cups of water
- 2 ¾ cups almond milk
- ½ tsp vanilla

Directions:

1. Spray instant pot from inside with cooking spray.
2. Add all ingredients into the instant pot stir well.
3. Seal pot with lid and cook on manual high pressure for 4 minutes.
4. Once done then allow to release pressure naturally then open the lid.
5. Stir well and serve.

Nutritional Value (Amount per Serving):
Calories 353; Fat 27.8 g; Carbohydrates 25.4 g; Sugar 7.9 g; Protein 5.5 g; Cholesterol 0 mg

Hearty Polenta Porridge

Preparation Time: 10 minutes; Cooking Time: 9 minutes; Serve: 4
Ingredients:

- ½ cup polenta
- 1 cup of water
- ½ tsp vanilla
- 3 tbsp maple syrup
- 2 cups almond milk
- 3 tbsp milk

Directions:
1. Spray oven-safe dish with cooking spray.
2. Add polenta, vanilla, maple syrup, and 2 cups almond milk into the prepared dish and stir well.
3. Pour water into the instant pot then place trivet into the pot.
4. Place dish on top of the trivet.
5. Seal pot with lid and cook on manual high pressure for 9 minutes.
6. Once done then allow to release pressure naturally then open the lid.
7. Carefully remove the dish from the pot. Add 3 tbsp milk into the polenta mixture and whisk polenta until creamy.
8. Serve and enjoy.

Nutritional Value (Amount per Serving):
Calories 392; Fat 29 g; Carbohydrates 32.6 g; Sugar 13.7 g; Protein 4.6 g; Cholesterol 1 mg

Peach Oatmeal

Preparation Time: 10 minutes; Cooking Time: 6 minutes; Serve: 8
Ingredients:

- 4 cups rolled oats
- 2 cups peaches
- 1/3 cup sugar
- 1/2 tsp cinnamon
- 3 1/2 cups milk
- 2 1/2 cups water
- Pinch of salt

Directions:
1. Add all ingredients into the instant pot and stir well.
2. Seal pot with lid and cook on manual high pressure for 6 minutes.
3. Once done then allow to release pressure naturally then open the lid.
4. Stir well and serve with milk.

Nutritional Value (Amount per Serving):
Calories 255; Fat 5 g; Carbohydrates 44.9 g; Sugar 17.1 g; Protein 9.2 g; Cholesterol 9 mg

Apple Cinnamon Oatmeal

Preparation Time: 10 minutes; Cooking Time: 4 minutes; Serve: 4
Ingredients:

- 2 cups steel-cut oats
- 1/4 tsp nutmeg
- 1 1/2 tsp cinnamon
- 2 apples, diced
- 4 1/2 cups water

Directions:
1. Add all ingredients into the instant pot and stir well.
2. Seal pot with lid and cook on manual high pressure for 4 minutes.
3. Once done then allow to release pressure naturally for 10 minutes then release using quick-release method. Open the lid.
4. Stir well and serve.

Nutritional Value (Amount per Serving):
Calories 216; Fat 2.9 g; Carbohydrates 43.9 g; Sugar 12.1 g; Protein 5.7 g; Cholesterol 0 mg

Choco Banana Oatmeal

Preparation Time: 10 minutes; Cooking Time: 9 minutes; Serve: 4
Ingredients:
- 1 cup steel-cut oats
- 3 1/2 cups water
- 3 tbsp cocoa powder
- 3 medium bananas, mashed

Directions:
1. Add water, cocoa powder, and oats into the instant pot and stir well.
2. Add mashed banana on top. Do not stir.
3. Seal pot with lid and cook on manual high pressure for 9 minutes.
4. Once done then allow to release pressure naturally then open the lid.
5. Stir well and serve.

Nutritional Value (Amount per Serving):
Calories 165; Fat 2.2 g; Carbohydrates 36.3 g; Sugar 11.1 g; Protein 4.4 g; Cholesterol 0 mg

Healthy Almond Oatmeal

Preparation Time: 10 minutes; Cooking Time: 7 minutes; Serve: 4
Ingredients:
- 1 1/4 cups steel-cut oats
- 2 1/3 cups water
- 4 tbsp honey
- 2 tbsp chia seeds
- 1 tsp cinnamon
- 1/2 cup almonds, chopped
- Pinch of salt

Directions:
1. Add all ingredients into the instant pot and stir well.
2. Seal pot with lid and cook on manual high pressure for 9 minutes.
3. Once done then allow to release pressure naturally then open the lid.
4. Stir well and serve.

Nutritional Value (Amount per Serving):
Calories 300; Fat 12 g; Carbohydrates 43.6 g; Sugar 18 g; Protein 8.3 g; Cholesterol 0 mg

Spinach Frittata

Preparation Time: 10 minutes; Cooking Time: 5 minutes; Serve: 6
Ingredients:
- 6 eggs, lightly beaten
- 1/2 onion, chopped
- 2 tomatoes, peeled and chopped
- 1 cup fresh spinach, chopped
- 1 cup of water
- Pepper
- Salt

Directions:
1. Spray a baking dish with cooking spray and set aside.
2. Pour one cup water into the instant pot then place trivet into the pot.
3. In a bowl, whisk eggs with onion, tomatoes, spinach, pepper, and salt.

4. Pour egg mixture into the prepared baking dish and place dish on top of the trivet.
5. Seal pot with lid and cook on manual high pressure for 5 minutes.
6. Once done then allow to release pressure naturally then open the lid.
7. Remove dish carefully from the pot.
8. Serve and enjoy.

Nutritional Value (Amount per Serving):
Calories 113; Fat 6.7 g; Carbohydrates 4.5 g; Sugar 2.7 g; Protein 9.2 g; Cholesterol 246 mg

Broccoli Frittata

Preparation Time: 10 minutes; Cooking Time: 10 minutes; Serve: 4
Ingredients:

- 6 eggs
- 1/2 cup cheddar cheese, shredded
- 1/4 cup onions, chopped
- 8 oz broccoli florets, chopped
- Pepper
- Salt

Directions:
1. Pour 1 cup water into the instant pot then place the trivet in the pot.
2. In a bowl, whisk eggs with pepper and salt.
3. Add onion, cheese, and broccoli into the eggs and stir well.
4. Spray a 7-inch baking dish with cooking spray.
5. Pour egg mixture into the prepared dish and place dish on top of the trivet.
6. Seal pot with lid and cook on manual high pressure for 10 minutes.
7. Once done then allow to release pressure naturally for 10 minutes then release using quick-release method. Open the lid.
8. Carefully remove the dish from the pot.
9. Serve and enjoy.

Nutritional Value (Amount per Serving):
Calories 174; Fat 11.4 g; Carbohydrates 5.1 g; Sugar 1.8 g; Protein 13.5 g; Cholesterol 238 mg

Quinoa Porridge

Preparation Time: 10 minutes; Cooking Time: 12 minutes; Serve: 4
Ingredients:

- 1 cup quinoa, uncooked
- 1 1/2 tsp cinnamon
- 1 tsp vanilla
- 4 dates, pitted and chopped
- 1/4 cup raisins
- 1 apple, cored and chopped
- 1 cup almond milk
- 2 cups of water

Directions:
1. Add quinoa, water, vanilla, cinnamon, raisins, dates, apple, and milk into the instant pot and stir well.
2. Seal pot with lid and cook on manual high pressure for 12 minutes.
3. Once done then allow to release pressure naturally then open the lid.
4. Stir well and serve.

Nutritional Value (Amount per Serving):
Calories 379; Fat 17.1 g; Carbohydrates 52.5 g; Sugar 18.6 g; Protein 8 g; Cholesterol 0 mg

Creamy Walnut Grits

Preparation Time: 10 minutes; Cooking Time: 4 minutes; Serve: 6
Ingredients:

- 2 cups instant cook grits
- 1/2 cup walnuts, chopped
- 1/4 cup maple syrup
- 1 tsp vanilla

- 2 tsp cinnamon
- 1/2 cup brown sugar
- 1 cup milk
- 2 cups of water
- 2 tbsp butter
- Pinch of salt

Directions:
1. Add butter into the instant pot and set the pot on sauté mode.
2. Once butter is melted then add grits and cook for 2 minutes.
3. Add water and salt and stir well.
4. Seal pot with lid and cook on manual high pressure for 2 minutes.
5. Once done then release pressure using quick-release method than open the lid.
6. Add remaining ingredients and stir everything well.
7. Serve and enjoy.

Nutritional Value (Amount per Serving):
Calories 235; Fat 11 g; Carbohydrates 31.8 g; Sugar 21.6 g; Protein 4.7 g; Cholesterol 14 mg

Healthy Wheat Porridge

Preparation Time: 10 minutes; Cooking Time: 13 minutes; Serve: 6
Ingredients:
- 1 cup cracked wheat
- 1 tbsp coconut oil
- 1 tbsp raisins
- 2 tbsp almonds, chopped
- 1 tsp ground cardamom
- 1/4 cup sugar
- 3 1/2 cups almond milk

Directions:
1. Add coconut oil into the instant pot and set the pot on sauté mode.
2. Add cracked wheat to the pot and cook for 2-3 minutes.
3. Add 2 1/2 cups almond milk, almonds, raisins, and cardamom and stir well.
4. Add sugar and stir well. Seal pot with lid and cook on high pressure for 10 minutes.
5. Once done then allow to release pressure naturally then open the lid.
6. Add remaining milk and stir well.
7. Serve and enjoy.

Nutritional Value (Amount per Serving):
Calories 403; Fat 36.9 g; Carbohydrates 20.4 g; Sugar 14 g; Protein 4.2 g; Cholesterol 0 mg

Quinoa Pumpkin Porridge

Preparation Time: 10 minutes; Cooking Time: 11 minutes; Serve: 3
Ingredients:
- 1 cup quinoa, uncooked
- 1 tsp vanilla
- 3/4 cup coconut milk
- 3/4 cup water
- 1/3 cup brown sugar
- 1 tsp pumpkin pie spice
- 1/2 cup pumpkin puree
- 1/4 tsp salt

Directions:
1. Add quinoa, vanilla, coconut milk, water, sugar, pumpkin pie spice, pumpkin puree, and salt into the instant pot and stir well.
2. Seal pot with lid and cook on manual high pressure for 1 minute.
3. Once done then allow to release pressure naturally then open the lid.
4. Stir well and serve with milk.

Nutritional Value (Amount per Serving):
Calories 428; Fat 17.9 g; Carbohydrates 59.4 g; Sugar 19.2 g; Protein 9.9 g; Cholesterol 0 mg

Blueberry Oatmeal

Preparation Time: 10 minutes; Cooking Time: 13 minutes; Serve: 4

Ingredients:
- 1 cup steel-cut oats
- 1 tbsp chia seeds
- 1/2 cup blueberries
- 1 1/2 cups water
- 1 1/2 cups milk
- 1 tsp vanilla
- 2 tbsp sugar
- 1 tbsp coconut oil
- Pinch of salt

Directions:
1. Add oil into the instant pot and set the pot on sauté mode.
2. Add oats to the pot and toast for 2-3 minutes.
3. Add remaining ingredients except for blueberries and stir well.
4. Seal pot with lid and cook on high pressure for 10 minutes.
5. Once done then allow to release pressure naturally for 10 minutes then release using quick-release method. Open the lid.
6. Add blueberries and stir well.
7. Serve and enjoy.

Nutritional Value (Amount per Serving):
Calories 223; Fat 8.8 g; Carbohydrates 30.1 g; Sugar 12.3 g; Protein 7 g; Cholesterol 8 mg

Mushroom Frittata

Preparation Time: 10 minutes; Cooking Time: 30 minutes; Serve: 4

Ingredients:
- 4 large eggs
- 1 tsp dried thyme
- 1/2 cup heavy cream
- 8 oz mushrooms, sliced
- 1 cup cheddar cheese, shredded
- 1 tbsp butter
- 1 tsp salt

Directions:
1. Spray a 7-inch baking dish with cooking spray and set aside.
2. Add butter into the instant pot and set the pot on sauté mode.
3. Add mushrooms and cook until softened, about 5 minutes.
4. Transfer mushroom to a prepared baking dish.
5. Pour 1 1/2 cups of water into the instant pot then place the trivet in the pot.
6. In a bowl, whisk eggs with thyme, heavy cream, 1/2 cup cheese, and salt.
7. Pour egg mixture over mushrooms into the baking dish and place dish on top of the trivet.
8. Seal pot with lid and cook on high pressure for 25 minutes.
9. Once done then allow to release pressure naturally then open the lid.
10. Carefully remove the dish from the pot.
11. Slice and serve.

Nutritional Value (Amount per Serving):
Calories 275; Fat 22.9 g; Carbohydrates 3.2 g; Sugar 1.5 g; Protein 15.5 g; Cholesterol 244 mg

Quick Brussels Sprouts

Preparation Time: 10 minutes; Cooking Time: 5 minutes; Serve: 4

Ingredients:
- 15 oz Brussels sprouts, trimmed and cut in half
- 5 bacon slices, chopped
- 1/2 onion, chopped
- 2 tsp garlic, minced
- 1 tbsp olive oil

- 1/4 tsp pepper
- 1/2 tsp salt

Directions:
1. Add 1 1/2 cups of water into the instant pot then place a steamer basket into the pot.
2. Add Brussels sprouts into the steamer basket.
3. Seal pot with lid and cook on manual high pressure for 3 minutes.
4. Once done then release pressure using the quick-release method than open the lid.
5. Drain Brussels sprouts well and place in a bowl.
6. Set instant pot on sauté mode. Add oil, garlic, and onion and sauté for 2 minutes.
7. Add bacon and cook until crisp. Add Brussels sprouts and stir for a minute.
8. Serve and enjoy.

Nutritional Value (Amount per Serving):
Calories 212; Fat 13.8 g; Carbohydrates 11.8 g; Sugar 2.9 g; Protein 12.7 g; Cholesterol 26 mg

Oatmeal Porridge

Preparation Time: 10 minutes; Cooking Time: 5 minutes; Serve: 6
Ingredients:
- 2 cups coarse oatmeal
- 2 tbsp maple syrup
- 1/2 tbsp cinnamon
- 1 apple, cored, peeled and chopped
- 1/4 cup raisins
- 2 cups almond milk
- 2 1/2 cups water

Directions:
1. Add all ingredients into the instant pot and stir well.
2. Seal pot with lid and cook on manual high pressure for 5 minutes.
3. Once done then release pressure using quick-release method than open the lid.
4. Stir well and serve.

Nutritional Value (Amount per Serving):
Calories 295; Fat 20.4 g; Carbohydrates 28.6 g; Sugar 14.3 g; Protein 4.1 g; Cholesterol 0 mg

Healthy Breakfast Porridge

Preparation Time: 10 minutes; Cooking Time: 3 minutes; Serve: 2
Ingredients:
- 1/4 cup pepitas, shelled
- 1 tbsp honey
- 2 tsp coconut oil, melted
- 1 cup of water
- 1/2 cup shredded coconut
- 1/2 cup pecan
- 1/2 cup cashews

Directions:
1. Add pepitas, coconut, pecan, and cashes into the blender and blend for 30 seconds.
2. Transfer blended mixture into the instant pot.
3. Add honey, oil, and water and stir well.
4. Seal pot with lid and cook on manual mode for 3 minutes.
5. Once done then release pressure using the quick release method than open the lid.
6. Stir well and serve.

Nutritional Value (Amount per Serving):
Calories 359; Fat 28.9 g; Carbohydrates 23.6 g; Sugar 11.6 g; Protein 6.9 g; Cholesterol 0 mg

Strawberry Oatmeal

Preparation Time: 10 minutes; Cooking Time: 20 minutes; Serve: 4
Ingredients:
- 1 cup steel-cut oats
- 1/4 cup sugar

- 1 1/2 cup strawberries, chopped
- 3 cups of water
- 2 tsp vanilla
- 2 tbsp butter
- Pinch of salt

Directions:
1. Add butter into the instant pot and set the pot on sauté mode.
2. Once butter is melted then add oats, vanilla, and salt and stir well.
3. Add water and stir. Seal pot with lid and cook on manual high pressure for 5 minutes.
4. Once done then allow to release pressure naturally for 10 minutes then release using quick-release method. Open the lid.
5. Mix together strawberries and sugar and add into the oatmeal.
6. Stir well and serve.

Nutritional Value (Amount per Serving):
Calories 199; Fat 7.3 g; Carbohydrates 30.8 g; Sugar 15.6 g; Protein 3.1 g; Cholesterol 15 mg

Berry Oatmeal

Preparation Time: 10 minutes; Cooking Time: 4 minutes; Serve: 4
Ingredients:
- 1 cup steel-cut oats
- 1/4 tsp cinnamon
- 1/2 tsp vanilla
- 2 tbsp honey
- 4 oz mix berries
- 1 cup almond milk
- 14 oz coconut milk

Directions:
1. Add all ingredients into the instant pot and stir well.
2. Seal pot with lid and cook on manual high pressure for 4 minutes.
3. Once done then allow to release pressure naturally for 10 minutes then release using quick-release method. Open the lid.
4. Stir well and serve.

Nutritional Value (Amount per Serving):
Calories 355; Fat 19.4 g; Carbohydrates 44.6 g; Sugar 19.3 g; Protein 5.8 g; Cholesterol 0 mg

Perfect Breakfast Casserole

Preparation Time: 10 minutes; Cooking Time: 25 minutes; Serve: 8
Ingredients:
- 10 eggs
- 1 cup cheddar cheese, shredded
- 1 bell pepper, diced
- 1 small onion, diced
- 2 cups frozen hash browns
- 1 cup of water
- 8 bacon slices, cooked and crumbled
- 1/4 tsp pepper
- 1/2 tsp salt

Directions:
1. Spray a 6*4-inch baking dish with cooking spray and set aside.
2. Whisk eggs in a large bowl with pepper and salt. Add cheese, onion, bell pepper, hash browns, and bacon into the egg and stir well.
3. Pour 1 cup of water into the instant pot then place trivet into the pot.
4. Pour egg mixture into the prepared baking dish and place dish on top of the trivet.
5. Seal pot with lid and cook on manual high pressure for 25 minutes.
6. Once done then allow to release pressure naturally for 10 minutes then release using quick-release method. Open the lid.
7. Serve and enjoy.

Nutritional Value (Amount per Serving):

Calories 350; Fat 23 g; Carbohydrates 16.6 g; Sugar 2.2 g; Protein 18.9 g; Cholesterol 240 mg

Delicious Breakfast Casserole

Preparation Time: 10 minutes; Cooking Time: 20 minutes; Serve: 6
Ingredients:

- 6 eggs
- 1 cup cheddar cheese, grated
- 3/5 cup bacon, cooked and diced
- 1/4 cup green onion, chopped
- 1 bell pepper, chopped
- 1 cup cauliflower florets, chopped
- 1/2 tsp paprika
- 1/2 cup milk
- 1/2 tsp dried oregano
- Pinch of salt

Directions:

1. In a bowl, whisk eggs with paprika, oregano, milk, and salt.
2. Spray baking dish with cooking spray. Arrange cauliflower, bell pepper, green onion, cheese, and bacon into the prepared dish.
3. Pour egg mixture over cauliflower mixture and cover baking dish with aluminum foil.
4. Pour 1 cup of water into the instant pot then place the trivet in the pot.
5. Place baking dish on top of the trivet. Seal pot with lid and cook on manual high pressure for 20 minutes.
6. Once done then allow to release pressure naturally for 10 minutes then release using quick-release method. Open the lid.
7. Carefully remove the dish from the instant pot.
8. Serve and enjoy.

Nutritional Value (Amount per Serving):
Calories 172; Fat 11.9 g; Carbohydrates 4.5 g; Sugar 2.9 g; Protein 12.3 g; Cholesterol 187 mg

Sweet Potato Breakfast

Preparation Time: 10 minutes; Cooking Time: 16 minutes; Serve: 4
Ingredients:

- 3 sweet potatoes, washed
- 1 cup of water
- 1 tbsp maple syrup
- 1/4 tsp cinnamon
- 2 tbsp milk
- Pinch of salt

Directions:

1. Pour water into the instant pot then place rack in the pot.
2. Place sweet potatoes on top of the rack. Seal pot with lid and cook on manual mode for 16 minutes.
3. Once done then release pressure using quick-release method than open the lid.
4. Remove sweet potato skin and place sweet potatoes in a large bowl.
5. Add remaining ingredients and mash sweet potatoes until getting desired consistency.
6. Serve and enjoy.

Nutritional Value (Amount per Serving):
Calories 150; Fat 0.4 g; Carbohydrates 35.2 g; Sugar 3.9 g; Protein 2 g; Cholesterol 1 mg

Banana Peanut Butter Oats

Preparation Time: 10 minutes; Cooking Time: 10 minutes; Serve: 3
Ingredients:

- 1 cup steel-cut oats
- 1/4 cup honey
- 1/4 tsp nutmeg
- 1 tsp cinnamon
- 1 tsp vanilla
- 1/4 cup peanut butter
- 2 bananas, mashed
- 2 cups almond milk

- Pinch of salt

Directions:
1. In a bowl, mix together mashed banana, honey, nutmeg, cinnamon, vanilla, peanut butter, and salt.
2. Spray instant pot from inside with cooking spray.
3. Add almond milk and oats into the instant pot and stir well. Add banana mixture on top. Do not stir.
4. Seal pot with lid and cook on porridge mode for 10 minutes.
5. Once done then allow to release pressure naturally for 10 minutes then release using quick-release method. Open the lid.
6. Stir well and serve.

Nutritional Value (Amount per Serving):
Calories 760; Fat 51.1 g; Carbohydrates 73.7 g; Sugar 40.7 g; Protein 2 g; Cholesterol 0 mg

Jalapeno Cheddar Grits

Preparation Time: 10 minutes; Cooking Time: 12 minutes; Serve: 8
Ingredients:
- 1 cup stone-ground grits
- 2 oz cream cheese
- 8 oz cheddar cheese, shredded
- 1 cup heavy cream
- 3 cups of water
- 1 tbsp butter
- 2 jalapeno peppers, chopped
- 3 bacon slices, cooked and chopped
- Salt

Directions:
1. Add butter into the instant pot and set the pot on sauté mode.
2. Add jalapeno to the pot and cook for 2 minutes or until softened.
3. Add grits and stir for 15 seconds.
4. Add water, heavy cream, and salt and stir everything well.
5. Seal pot with lid and cook on manual high pressure for 10 minutes.
6. Once done then allow to release pressure naturally for 10 minutes then release using quick-release method. Open the lid.
7. Stir in cream cheese and cheddar cheese.
8. Top with bacon and serve.

Nutritional Value (Amount per Serving):
Calories 324; Fat 22.9 g; Carbohydrates 18.6 g; Sugar 0.3 g; Protein 12.7 g; Cholesterol 70 mg

Fruit Compote

Preparation Time: 10 minutes; Cooking Time: 3 minutes; Serve: 6
Ingredients:
- 12 oz cranberries
- 1/2 cup walnuts, chopped
- 1/2 cup raisins
- 1/2 cup dried apricots, chopped
- 2 tbsp vinegar
- 1/4 cup orange juice
- 2/3 cup brown sugar

Directions:
1. Add cranberries, vinegar, orange juice, and brown sugar into the instant pot and stir well.
2. Seal pot with lid and cook on high pressure for 3 minutes.
3. Once done then allow to release pressure naturally for 5 minutes then release using quick-release method. Open the lid.
4. Stir in walnuts, raisins, and apricots.
5. Serve over pancakes and waffles.

Nutritional Value (Amount per Serving):
    Calories 205; Fat 6.3 g; Carbohydrates 34.1 g; Sugar 27 g; Protein 3.1 g; Cholesterol 0 mg

Carrot Oatmeal

Preparation Time: 10 minutes; Cooking Time: 10 minutes; Serve: 8
Ingredients:

- 1 cup steel-cut oats
- 1/2 tsp pumpkin pie spice
- 1 1/2 tsp cinnamon
- 1/2 cup raisins
- 2 cup shredded carrots
- 20 oz pineapple, crushed
- 4 1/2 cups water

Directions:

1. Add all ingredients into the instant pot and stir well.
2. Seal pot with lid and cook on manual high pressure for 10 minutes.
3. Once done then allow to release pressure naturally for 10 minutes then release using quick-release method. Open the lid.
4. Stir well and serve.

Nutritional Value (Amount per Serving):
    Calories 114; Fat 0.8 g; Carbohydrates 26.5 g; Sugar 13.8 g; Protein 2.3 g; Cholesterol 0 mg

Slow Cook Cherry Oatmeal

Preparation Time: 10 minutes; Cooking Time: 7 hours; Serve: 6
Ingredients:

- 1 cup steel-cut oats
- 1/4 tsp cinnamon
- 1/3 cup brown sugar
- 3/4 cup dried cherries
- 4 cups almond milk
- Pinch of salt

Directions:

1. Spray instant pot from inside with cooking spray.
2. Add all ingredients into the instant pot and stir well.
3. Seal the pot with a lid and cook on slow cook mode for 7 hours.
4. Once done then release pressure using quick-release method than open the lid.
5. Stir well and serve.

Nutritional Value (Amount per Serving):
    Calories 451; Fat 39 g; Carbohydrates 28.7 g; Sugar 13.3 g; Protein 5.5 g; Cholesterol 0 mg

Ham Cheese Breakfast Casserole

Preparation Time: 10 minutes; Cooking Time: 35 minutes; Serve: 6
Ingredients:

- 6 eggs
- 1 cup of water
- 2 cups cheddar cheese, shredded
- 1/2 onion, chopped
- 3/4 cup ham, cubed and cooked
- 4 cups hash brown potatoes, shredded
- 1/2 cup milk
- 1/4 tsp pepper
- 1/2 tsp salt

Directions:

1. In a bowl, whisk eggs with pepper and salt.
2. In a round baking dish, mix together hash brown potatoes, cheese, onion, and ham. Pour egg mixture on top.
3. Pour 1 cup of water into the instant pot then place the trivet in the pot.
4. Cover baking dish with foil and place on top of the trivet.
5. Seal pot with lid and cook on manual high pressure for 35 minutes.

6. Once done then allow to release pressure naturally for 10 minutes then release using quick-release method. Open the lid.
7. Serve and enjoy.

Nutritional Value (Amount per Serving):
Calories 532; Fat 31.8 g; Carbohydrates 39.9 g; Sugar 3.4 g; Protein 21.6 g; Cholesterol 215 mg

Cranberry Apple Breakfast Grains

Preparation Time: 10 minutes; Cooking Time: 25 minutes; Serve: 10
Ingredients:
- 2 apples, peeled and chopped
- 6 cups of water
- 1 1/2 tsp cinnamon
- 1/2 cup brown sugar
- 1/2 cup walnuts, chopped
- 1/2 cup pearl barley
- 1/2 cup oat bran
- 1/2 cup quinoa
- 1/2 cup wheat berries
- 1 cup cranberries
- 1 cup of sugar

Directions:
1. Add all ingredients into the instant pot and stir well.
2. Seal pot with lid and cook on manual high pressure for 25 minutes.
3. Once done then allow to release pressure naturally for 10 minutes then release using quick-release method. Open the lid.
4. Stir well and serve.

Nutritional Value (Amount per Serving):
Calories 252; Fat 4.6 g; Carbohydrates 51.3 g; Sugar 32.4 g; Protein 4.4 g; Cholesterol 0 mg

Sausage Casserole

Preparation Time: 10 minutes; Cooking Time: 30 minutes; Serve: 6
Ingredients:
- 4 eggs
- 2.5 oz cheddar cheese, grated
- 2/3 cup chicken broth
- 1 lb ground Italian sausage
- Pepper
- Salt

Directions:
1. Add sausage into the instant pot and cook on sauté mode until sausage meat is no longer pink.
2. In a large bowl, whisk eggs with pepper and salt. Add cheese and sausage and stir well.
3. Add cooked sausage mixture into the egg mixture and stir well.
4. Spray 7-inch baking pan with cooking spray and set aside.
5. Pour 1 cup of water into the instant pot then place the trivet in the pot.
6. Pour egg mixture into the baking pan and place pan on top of the trivet.
7. Seal pot with lid and cook on manual mode for 28 minutes.
8. Once done then allow to release pressure naturally for 10 minutes then release using quick-release method. Open the lid.
9. Carefully remove the pan from the pot.
10. Slice and serve.

Nutritional Value (Amount per Serving):
Calories 321; Fat 24.3 g; Carbohydrates 1.8 g; Sugar 1.7 g; Protein 20.5 g; Cholesterol 175 mg

Blueberry French Toast Casserole

Preparation Time: 10 minutes; Cooking Time: 15 minutes; Serve: 4
Ingredients:

- 3 eggs
- 1 French bread loaf, cut into cubed
- 1/2 cup blueberries
- 1/2 tsp vanilla
- 1/2 tbsp cinnamon
- 1/2 cup milk
- 1 cup half and half

Directions:
1. Spray instant pot from inside with cooking spray.
2. Add bread cubed into the instant pot.
3. In a bowl, whisk eggs with vanilla, cinnamon, half and half, and milk.
4. Pour egg mixture over bread cubes then sprinkle blueberries on top.
5. Seal pot with lid and cook on manual high pressure for 15 minutes.
6. Once done then allow to release pressure naturally then open the lid.
7. Serve and enjoy.

Nutritional Value (Amount per Serving):
Calories 201; Fat 11.2 g; Carbohydrates 16.8 g; Sugar 4 g; Protein 9 g; Cholesterol 148 mg

Oat Millet Porridge

Preparation Time: 10 minutes; Cooking Time: 12 minutes; Serve: 8
Ingredients:
- 1/2 cup rolled oats
- 3/4 cup dry millet
- 1/2 tsp ground ginger
- 1/2 tsp cinnamon
- 3 cups of water
- 2 apples, diced
- Pinch of salt

Directions:
1. Add millet into the instant pot and toast on sauté mode for 1-2 minutes.
2. Add remaining ingredients and stir well.
3. Seal pot with lid and cook on high pressure for 10 minutes.
4. Once done then allow to release pressure naturally then open the lid.
5. Stir well and serve.

Nutritional Value (Amount per Serving):
Calories 120; Fat 1.2 g; Carbohydrates 25 g; Sugar 5.9 g; Protein 2.9 g; Cholesterol 0 mg

Baked Apples

Preparation Time: 10 minutes; Cooking Time: 8 minutes; Serve: 6
Ingredients:
- 6 apples, wash, and core
- 1 1/2 tbsp cinnamon
- 1/2 cup sugar
- 1 cup of orange juice

Directions:
1. Place apples into the instant pot then pour orange juice over apples.
2. Sprinkle cinnamon and sugar over apples.
3. Seal pot with lid and cook on manual high pressure for 8 minutes.
4. Once done then allow to release pressure naturally then open the lid.
5. Serve and enjoy.

Nutritional Value (Amount per Serving):
Calories 201; Fat 0.5 g; Carbohydrates 53.1 g; Sugar 43.4 g; Protein 1 g; Cholesterol 0 mg

Quinoa Blueberry Bowl

Preparation Time: 10 minutes; Cooking Time: 1 minute; Serve: 4
Ingredients:
- 1 1/2 cup quinoa, rinsed
- 1/4 cup pistachios, chopped

- 1 cup plain yogurt
- 1 cup of orange juice
- 1/2 cup apple, grated
- 1 tbsp honey
- 3 tbsp raisins
- 1/2 tsp cinnamon
- 1 1/2 cups water

Directions:
1. Add water, quinoa, and cinnamon into the instant pot and stir well.
2. Seal pot with lid and cook on manual mode for 1 minute.
3. Once done then allow to release pressure naturally for 10 minutes then release using the quick-release method. Open the lid.
4. Transfer quinoa in a medium bowl. Add orange juice, apple, honey, and raisins into the quinoa and stir to combine.
5. Place quinoa into the refrigerator for 1 hour.
6. Add yogurt and stir to combine.
7. Serve and enjoy.

Nutritional Value (Amount per Serving):
Calories 378; Fat 6.6 g; Carbohydrates 66.5 g; Sugar 21 g; Protein 14 g; Cholesterol 4 mg

Savory Barley

Preparation Time: 10 minutes; Cooking Time: 18 minutes; Serve: 4
Ingredients:
- 1 cup pearl barley
- 4 oz baby kale
- 4 cups vegetable broth
- 1/4 cup onion, chopped
- 1 tbsp olive oil
- 1/2 tsp sea salt

Directions:
1. Add oil into the instant pot and set the pot on sauté mode.
2. Add onion and barley and sauté for 3 minutes.
3. Add broth and salt and stir everything well.
4. Seal pot with lid and cook on manual high pressure for 15 minutes.
5. Once done then allow to release pressure naturally then open the lid.
6. Add kale and stir until kale is wilted.
7. Serve and enjoy.

Nutritional Value (Amount per Serving):
Calories 262; Fat 5.6 g; Carbohydrates 43.4 g; Sugar 1.4 g; Protein 10.9 g; Cholesterol 0 mg

Fajita Casserole

Preparation Time: 10 minutes; Cooking Time: 7 minutes; Serve: 2
Ingredients:
- 4 eggs
- 1 tbsp olive oil
- 1 1/2 cups bell peppers, sliced
- 1/2 medium onion, sliced
- Pepper
- Salt

Directions:
1. Add oil into the instant pot and set the pot on sauté mode.
2. Add bell peppers and onions and sauté for 5 minutes. Transfer bell peppers and onion mixture into the baking dish.
3. Crack eggs and place them on top of onion and bell pepper mixture. Season with pepper and salt.
4. Pour 1 cup of water into the instant pot then place the trivet in the pot.
5. Place baking dish on top of the trivet.
6. Seal pot with lid and cook on high pressure for 2 minutes.

7. Once done then release pressure using the quick-release method than open the lid.
8. Serve and enjoy.

Nutritional Value (Amount per Serving):

Calories 225; Fat 16 g; Carbohydrates 10 g; Sugar 6.4 g; Protein 12.3 g; Cholesterol 327 mg

Latte Oatmeal

Preparation Time: 10 minutes; Cooking Time: 10 minutes; Serve: 4

Ingredients:

- 1 cup steel-cut oats
- 1 1/2 tsp vanilla
- 1 tsp espresso powder
- 2 tbsp sugar
- 1 cup milk
- 2 1/2 cups water
- 1/4 tsp salt

Directions:

1. Add oats, espresso powder, sugar, milk, water, and salt into the instant pot and stir well.
2. Seal pot with lid and cook on high pressure for 10 minutes.
3. Once done then allow to release pressure naturally for 10 minutes then release using the quick-release method. Open the lid.
4. Stir in vanilla and serve.

Nutritional Value (Amount per Serving):

Calories 135; Fat 2.6 g; Carbohydrates 23 g; Sugar 9.2 g; Protein 4.7 g; Cholesterol 5 mg

Coconut Blueberry Oatmeal

Preparation Time: 10 minutes; Cooking Time: 30 minutes; Serve: 6

Ingredients:

- 2 1/4 cups oats
- 1 cup blueberries
- 1/4 cup gluten-free flour
- 1/2 tsp vanilla
- 3 cups of water
- 14 oz coconut milk
- 6 tbsp brown sugar
- 1/8 tsp salt

Directions:

1. Add all ingredients into the instant pot and stir well.
2. Seal pot with lid and cook on manual mode for 30 minutes.
3. Once done then release pressure using the quick-release method than open the lid.
4. Stir well and serve.

Nutritional Value (Amount per Serving):

Calories 337; Fat 18.1 g; Carbohydrates 40.3 g; Sugar 13.7 g; Protein 6.4 g; Cholesterol 0 mg

Pumpkin Cranberry Oatmeal

Preparation Time: 10 minutes; Cooking Time: 3 minutes; Serve: 4

Ingredients:

- 1 cup steel-cut oats
- 2 tbsp honey
- 1/2 cup dried cranberries
- 3/4 cup pumpkin puree
- 1 cup milk
- 2 cups of water
- 1 1/2 tsp pumpkin pie spice
- Pinch of salt

Directions:

1. Add oats, cranberries, pumpkin puree, milk, water, pumpkin pie spice, and salt and stir well.
2. Seal pot with lid and cook on manual high pressure for 3 minutes.
3. Once done then release pressure using the quick-release method than open the lid.
4. Add honey and stir well.

5. Serve and enjoy.

Nutritional Value (Amount per Serving):
    Calories 165; Fat 2.8 g; Carbohydrates 30.9 g; Sugar 13.6 g; Protein 5.3 g; Cholesterol 5 mg

Cranberry Farro

Preparation Time: 10 minutes; Cooking Time: 20 minutes; Serve: 8

Ingredients:

- 15 oz farro
- 1/2 cup dried cranberries
- 1 tsp lemon extract
- 1/2 cup brown sugar
- 4 1/2 cups water
- 1/4 tsp salt

Directions:
1. Add farro, lemon extract, brown sugar, water, and salt into the instant pot and stir well.
2. Seal pot with lid and cook on high pressure for 20 minutes.
3. Once done then allow to release pressure naturally for 10 minutes then release using the quick-release method. Open the lid.
4. Add cranberries and stir well.
5. Serve and enjoy.

Nutritional Value (Amount per Serving):
    Calories 130; Fat 3.9 g; Carbohydrates 21.2 g; Sugar 10.4 g; Protein 3.9 g; Cholesterol 6 mg

Tropical Oatmeal

Preparation Time: 10 minutes; Cooking Time: 4 minutes; Serve: 4

Ingredients:

- 1 cup steel-cut oats
- 3 tbsp hemp seeds
- 1/2 papaya, chopped
- 1/2 cup coconut cream
- 2 cups of water

Directions:
1. Add oats, coconut cream, and water into the instant pot and stir well.
2. Seal pot with lid and cook on manual high pressure for 4 minutes.
3. Once done then allow to release pressure naturally for 10 minutes then release using the quick-release method. Open the lid.
4. Stir in hemp seeds and papaya.
5. Serve and enjoy.

Nutritional Value (Amount per Serving):
    Calories 195; Fat 11.2 g; Carbohydrates 20.1 g; Sugar 4.3 g; Protein 5.5 g; Cholesterol 0 mg

Simple & Easy Breakfast Casserole

Preparation Time: 10 minutes; Cooking Time: 20 minutes; Serve: 4

Ingredients:

- 2 1/2 cups egg whites
- 1/2 cup Mexican blend cheese
- 1/4 cup cream cheese
- 1/2 cup onion, chopped
- 1 cup bell pepper, chopped
- 1/2 tsp onion powder
- 1/4 tsp garlic powder
- 1/4 tsp pepper
- 1/4 tsp salt

Directions:
1. Spray instant pot from inside with cooking spray.
2. Add onion and bell pepper to the pot and cook until softened, about 5 minutes.
3. Transfer onion and bell pepper to the baking dish.

4. Add egg whites, seasonings, and cream cheese and stir well. Top with Mexican blend cheese.
5. Pour 1 cup of water into the instant pot then place the trivet in the pot.
6. Place baking dish on top of the trivet.
7. Seal pot with lid and cook on manual mode for 15 minutes.
8. Once done then release pressure using the quick-release method than open the lid.
9. Slice and serve.

Nutritional Value (Amount per Serving):
Calories 208; Fat 10.4 g; Carbohydrates 6.3 g; Sugar 4.1 g; Protein 21.7 g; Cholesterol 33 mg

Creamy Mac n Cheese

Preparation Time: 10 minutes; Cooking Time: 5 minutes; Serve: 8
Ingredients:
- 15 oz elbow macaroni
- 1 cup milk
- 1/2 cup parmesan cheese, shredded
- 1 cup mozzarella cheese, shredded
- 2 cups cheddar cheese, shredded
- 1 tsp garlic powder
- 1 tsp hot pepper sauce
- 2 tbsp butter
- 4 cups vegetable broth
- 1/4 tsp pepper
- 1/2 tsp salt

Directions:
1. Add macaroni, garlic powder, hot sauce, butter, broth, pepper, and salt into the instant pot and stir well.
2. Seal pot with lid and cook on manual high pressure for 5 minutes.
3. Once done then release pressure using the quick-release method than open the lid.
4. Add cheese and milk and stir until cheese is melted.
5. Serve and enjoy.

Nutritional Value (Amount per Serving):
Calories 388; Fat 15.3 g; Carbohydrates 42.5 g; Sugar 3.4 g; Protein 19 g; Cholesterol 43 mg

Cherry Risotto

Preparation Time: 10 minutes; Cooking Time: 10 minutes; Serve: 4
Ingredients:
- 1 1/2 cups Arborio rice
- 1/2 cup dried cherries
- 3 cups of milk
- 1 cup apple juice
- 1/3 cup brown sugar
- 1 1/2 tsp cinnamon
- 2 apples, cored and diced
- 2 tbsp butter
- 1/4 tsp salt

Directions:
1. Add butter into the instant pot and set the pot on sauté mode.
2. Add rice and cook for 3-4 minutes.
3. Add brown sugar, spices, apples, milk, and apple juice and stir well.
4. Seal pot with lid and cook on manual high pressure for 6 minutes.
5. Once done then release pressure using the quick-release method than open the lid.
6. Stir in dried cherries and serve.

Nutritional Value (Amount per Serving):
Calories 544; Fat 10.2 g; Carbohydrates 103.2 g; Sugar 37.6 g; Protein 11.2 g; Cholesterol 30 mg

Almond Coconut Risotto

Preparation Time: 10 minutes; Cooking Time: 5 minutes; Serve: 4

Ingredients:
- 1 cup Arborio rice
- 1 cup of coconut milk
- 3 tbsp almonds, sliced and toasted
- 2 tbsp shredded coconut
- 2 cups almond milk
- 1/2 tsp vanilla
- 1/3 cup coconut sugar

Directions:
1. Add coconut and almond milk in instant pot and set the pot on sauté mode.
2. Once the milk begins to boil then add rice and stir well.
3. Seal pot with lid and cook on manual high pressure for 5 minutes.
4. Once done then allow to release pressure naturally then open the lid.
5. Add remaining ingredients and stir well.
6. Serve and enjoy.

Nutritional Value (Amount per Serving):
Calories 425; Fat 20.6 g; Carbohydrates 53.7 g; Sugar 9.6 g; Protein 6.8 g; Cholesterol 0 mg

Creamy Polenta

Preparation Time: 10 minutes; Cooking Time: 5 minutes; Serve: 3
Ingredients:
- 1/2 cup polenta
- 1 cup of coconut milk
- 1 cup of water
- 1/2 tbsp butter
- 1/4 tsp salt

Directions:
1. Set instant pot on sauté mode.
2. Add milk, water, and salt in a pot and stir well.
3. Once milk mixture begins to boil then add polenta and stir to combine.
4. Seal pot with lid and cook on high pressure for 5 minutes.
5. Once done then allow to release pressure naturally then open the lid.
6. Stir and serve.

Nutritional Value (Amount per Serving):
Calories 293; Fat 21.2 g; Carbohydrates 24.7 g; Sugar 2.9 g; Protein 3.8 g; Cholesterol 5 mg

Sweet Cherry Chocolate Oat

Preparation Time: 10 minutes; Cooking Time: 15 minutes; Serve: 4
Ingredients:
- 2 cups steel cuts oats
- 3 tbsp honey
- 2 cups of water
- 2 cups of milk
- 3 tbsp chocolate chips
- 1 1/2 cups cherries
- 1/4 tsp cinnamon
- Pinch of salt

Directions:
1. Spray instant pot from inside with cooking spray.
2. Add all ingredients into the pot and stir everything well.
3. Seal pot with lid and cook on high pressure for 15 minutes.
4. Once done then allow to release pressure naturally then open the lid.
5. Stir well and serve.

Nutritional Value (Amount per Serving):
Calories 503; Fat 10.9 g; Carbohydrates 85.5 g; Sugar 22.5 g; Protein 16.8 g; Cholesterol 12 mg

Coconut Lime Breakfast Quinoa

Preparation Time: 10 minutes; Cooking Time: 1 minute; Serve: 5
Ingredients:

- 1 cup quinoa, rinsed
- 1/2 tsp coconut extract
- 1 lime juice
- 1 lime zest
- 2 cups of coconut milk
- 1 cup of water

Directions:

1. Add all ingredients into the instant pot and stir well.
2. Seal pot with lid and cook on manual high pressure for 1 minute.
3. Once done then allow to release pressure naturally for 10 minutes then release using the quick-release method. Open the lid.
4. Stir well and serve.

Nutritional Value (Amount per Serving):

Calories 350; Fat 25 g; Carbohydrates 28.1 g; Sugar 3.5 g; Protein 7.1 g; Cholesterol 0 mg

Quick & Easy Farro

Preparation Time: 5 minutes; Cooking Time: 10 minutes; Serve: 4
Ingredients:

- 1 cup pearl farro
- 1 tsp olive oil
- 2 cups vegetable broth
- 1/4 tsp salt

Directions:

1. Add all ingredients into the instant pot and stir well.
2. Seal pot with lid and cook on manual mode for 10 minutes.
3. Once done then allow to release pressure naturally for 5 minutes then release using the quick-release method. Open the lid.
4. Stir well and serve.

Nutritional Value (Amount per Serving):

Calories 169; Fat 1.9 g; Carbohydrates 30.5 g; Sugar 0.4 g; Protein 8.4 g; Cholesterol 0 mg

Farro Breakfast Risotto

Preparation Time: 10 minutes; Cooking Time: 12 minutes; Serve: 4
Ingredients:

- 1 cup farro
- 1 tsp Italian seasoning
- 1/2 cup parmesan cheese, grated
- 1/2 cup mozzarella cheese, grated
- 2 tbsp heavy whipping cream
- 2 cups vegetable stock
- 1 tbsp butter

Directions:

1. Add butter into the instant pot and set the pot on sauté mode.
2. Add farro and cook for 2 minutes. Add stock and stir everything well.
3. Seal pot with lid and cook on manual high pressure for 10 minutes.
4. Once done then allow to release pressure naturally for 10 minutes then release using the quick-release method. Open the lid.
5. Add remaining ingredients and stir well.
6. Serve and enjoy.

Nutritional Value (Amount per Serving):

Calories 206; Fat 13.7 g; Carbohydrates 13.4 g; Sugar 1.8 g; Protein 9.9 g; Cholesterol 37 mg

Tapioca Pudding

Preparation Time: 10 minutes; Cooking Time: 7 minutes; Serve: 4
Ingredients:

- 1/2 cup tapioca
- 2 cups of water
- 2 egg yolks
- 1/2 tsp vanilla
- 1/2 cup sugar
- 1/2 cup milk

Directions:
1. Add water and tapioca into the instant pot and stir well.
2. Seal pot with lid and cook on high pressure for 5 minutes.
3. Once done then release pressure using the quick-release method than open the lid.
4. Set pot on sauté mode. In a small bowl, whisk together milk and egg yolks
5. Slowly pour egg mixture into the pot and stir constantly.
6. Add vanilla and sugar and stir until sugar is dissolved.
7. Transfer pudding to a bowl and let it cool completely.
8. Place in refrigerator until pudding thickens.
9. Serve and enjoy.

Nutritional Value (Amount per Serving):
Calories 206; Fat 2.9 g; Carbohydrates 43.7 g; Sugar 27.1 g; Protein 2.4 g; Cholesterol 107 mg

Sweetened Breakfast Oats

Preparation Time: 10 minutes; Cooking Time: 7 minutes; Serve: 4
Ingredients:

- 1 cup steel-cut oats
- 3/4 cup shredded coconut
- 1/4 tsp ground ginger
- 1/4 tsp ground nutmeg
- 1/2 tsp ground cinnamon
- 1/4 cup raisins
- 1 large apple, chopped
- 2 large carrots, grated
- 1 cup of coconut milk
- 3 cups of water

Directions:
1. Add oats, nutmeg, ginger, cinnamon, raisins, apple, carrots, milk, and water into the instant pot and stir to combine.
2. Seal pot with lid and cook on manual mode for 4 minutes.
3. Once done then allow to release pressure naturally for 20 minutes then release using the quick-release method. Open the lid.
4. Top with coconut and serve.

Nutritional Value (Amount per Serving):
Calories 341; Fat 20.8 g; Carbohydrates 38.2 g; Sugar 16.1 g; Protein 5.3 g; Cholesterol 0 mg

Cauliflower Mash

Preparation Time: 10 minutes; Cooking Time: 3 minutes; Serve: 6
Ingredients:

- 1 large cauliflower head, cut into florets
- 1/2 cup parmesan cheese, shredded
- 1/2 tsp garlic powder
- 2 tbsp butter
- 2 cups vegetable stock
- 1/4 tsp salt

Directions:
1. Pour the stock into the instant pot then place a steamer basket into the pot.
2. Add cauliflower florets into the steamer basket.
3. Seal pot with lid and cook on high pressure for 3 minutes.

4. Once done then release pressure using the quick-release method than open the lid.
5. Transfer cauliflower into the food processor along with remaining ingredients and blend until smooth.
6. Serve and enjoy.

Nutritional Value (Amount per Serving):
Calories 102; Fat 6 g; Carbohydrates 8.2 g; Sugar 3.7 g; Protein 6 g; Cholesterol 17 mg

Chia Oatmeal

Preparation Time: 10 minutes; Cooking Time: 15 minutes; Serve: 6

Ingredients:
- 1 cup steel-cut oatmeal
- 1/2 tsp vanilla
- 2 tbsp chia seeds
- 1 1/2 cups coconut milk
- 1 1/2 cup water
- 1/4 tsp sea salt

Directions:
1. Spray instant pot from inside with cooking spray.
2. Add all ingredients into the instant pot and stir well.
3. Seal pot with lid and cook on porridge mode for 15 minutes.
4. Once done then allow to release pressure naturally for 10 minutes then release using the quick-release method. Open the lid.
5. Stir well and serve.

Nutritional Value (Amount per Serving):
Calories 210; Fat 17.7 g; Carbohydrates 11.8 g; Sugar 2 g; Protein 3.8 g; Cholesterol 0 mg

Blueberry Lemon Oatmeal

Preparation Time: 10 minutes; Cooking Time: 10 minutes; Serve: 6

Ingredients:
- 1 cup steel-cut oats
- 1/4 cup chia seeds
- 1 cup blueberries
- 1/2 tbsp lemon zest
- 2 tbsp sugar
- 1/2 cup half and half
- 3 cups of water
- 1 tbsp butter
- Salt

Directions:
1. Add butter into the instant pot and set the pot on sauté mode.
2. Add oats into the pot and stir well.
3. Add remaining ingredients and stir everything well.
4. Seal pot with lid and cook on manual high pressure for 10 minutes.
5. Once done then allow to release pressure naturally then open the lid.
6. Stir well and serve.

Nutritional Value (Amount per Serving):
Calories 130; Fat 5.6 g; Carbohydrates 18.2 g; Sugar 6.6 g; Protein 2.8 g; Cholesterol 13 mg

Breakfast Cobbler

Preparation Time: 10 minutes; Cooking Time: 15 minutes; Serve: 2

Ingredients:
- 2 tbsp sunflower seeds
- 1/4 cup pecan
- 1/4 cup shredded coconut
- 1/2 tsp cinnamon
- 2 1/2 tbsp coconut oil
- 2 tbsp honey
- 1 plum, diced
- 1 apple, diced
- 1 pear, diced

Directions:
1. Add fruits, cinnamon, coconut oil, and honey into the instant pot and stir well.
2. Seal pot with a lid and select steam mode and set timer for 10 minutes.
3. Once done then release pressure using the quick-release method than open the lid.
4. Transfer fruit mixture into the serving bowl.
5. Add sunflower seeds, pecans, and coconut into the pot and cook on sauté mode for 5 minutes.
6. Pour sunflower seed, pecans and coconut mixture on top of fruit mixture.
7. Serve and enjoy.

Nutritional Value (Amount per Serving):
Calories 426; Fat 27.2 g; Carbohydrates 50.9 g; Sugar 40.1 g; Protein 2.6 g; Cholesterol 0 mg

Tomato Corn Risotto

Preparation Time: 10 minutes; Cooking Time: 13 minutes; Serve: 4

Ingredients:
- 1 1/2 cups Arborio rice
- 1 cup cherry tomatoes, halved
- 1/4 cup basil, chopped
- 1/4 cup parmesan cheese, grated
- 1/4 cup half and half
- 32 oz vegetable broth
- 1 cup sweet corn
- 3 garlic cloves, minced
- 1/2 cup onion, chopped
- 2 tbsp olive oil
- 4 tbsp butter
- 1 tsp salt

Directions:
1. Add butter into the instant pot and set the pot on sauté mode.
2. Add garlic and onion and sauté for 5 minutes.
3. Add rice and cook for 2-3 minutes.
4. Add broth, corn, pepper, and salt and stir well.
5. Seal pot with lid and cook on high pressure for 6 minutes.
6. Once done then release pressure using the quick-release method than open the lid.
7. Stir in cherry tomatoes, basil, parmesan, and a half and half.
8. Serve and enjoy.

Nutritional Value (Amount per Serving):
Calories 548; Fat 24 g; Carbohydrates 69.6 g; Sugar 3.8 g; Protein 14.1 g; Cholesterol 41 mg

Chapter 2: Vegan and Vegetarian

Flavourful Ramen

Preparation Time: 10 minutes; Cooking Time: 1 minute; Serve: 4
Ingredients:
- 1 lb ramen noodles
- 1 1/2 tbsp soy sauce
- 1 tsp garlic puree
- 1 tsp ginger puree
- 1/4 cup green onions, sliced
- 1/2 cup snow peas, cut into quarters
- 2 cups mushrooms, sliced
- 5 cups vegetable stock

Directions:
1. Add all ingredients into the instant pot and stir everything well.
2. Seal pot with lid and cook on low pressure for 1 minute.
3. Once done then release pressure using the quick-release method than open the lid.
4. Stir well and serve.

Nutritional Value (Amount per Serving):
Calories 530; Fat 19.3 g; Carbohydrates 71.3 g; Sugar 2.5 g; Protein 16.1 g; Cholesterol 0 mg

Delicious Black Eyed Peas Curry

Preparation Time: 10 minutes; Cooking Time: 20 minutes; Serve: 4
Ingredients:
- 1 cup dried black-eyed peas, soaked for 4-6 hours and drain
- 2 1/2 cups vegetable broth
- 1/2 tsp cumin
- 1/2 tsp turmeric
- 1 1/2 tbsp curry powder
- 1/2 tsp dried thyme
- 1 medium tomato, chopped
- 1 tsp ginger, grated
- 2 tbsp green onions, chopped
- 2 garlic cloves, minced
- 1 small onion, chopped
- 2 tbsp olive oil
- 1/2 tsp salt

Directions:
1. Add oil into the instant pot and set the pot on sauté mode.
2. Add garlic, ginger, green onion, and onion to the pot and sauté for 3 minutes.
3. Add tomatoes, cumin, turmeric, curry powder, thyme, black eye peas, and broth and stir well.
4. Seal pot with lid and cook on manual high pressure for 20 minutes.
5. Once done then allow to release pressure naturally for 10 minutes then release using the quick-release method. Open the lid.
6. Stir well and serve.

Nutritional Value (Amount per Serving):
Calories 201; Fat 8.4 g; Carbohydrates 29.2 g; Sugar 3.2 g; Protein 13.1 g; Cholesterol 0 mg

Rich & Creamy Alfredo Sauce

Preparation Time: 10 minutes; Cooking Time: 3 minutes; Serve: 6
Ingredients:
- 1 lb fettuccine pasta, cooked
- 3 cups vegetable stock
- 1/2 cup cashews
- 5 1/2 cup cauliflower florets
- 6 garlic cloves, minced
- 2 tbsp olive oil
- 1/2 tsp salt

Directions:
1. Add oil into the instant pot and set the pot on sauté mode.

2. Add garlic and cook for a minute.
3. Add cauliflower, broth, and cashews and stir well.
4. Seal pot with lid and cook on manual high pressure for 3 minutes.
5. Once done then allow to release pressure naturally for 10 minutes then release using the quick-release method. Open the lid.
6. Transfer pot mixture to the blender and blend until smooth.
7. Pour blended mixture over cooked pasta and stir well.
8. Serve and enjoy.

Nutritional Value (Amount per Serving):
Calories 351; Fat 11.8 g; Carbohydrates 51.4 g; Sugar 3.2 g; Protein 12.5 g; Cholesterol 55 mg

Indian Curried Cauliflower Potato

Preparation Time: 10 minutes; Cooking Time: 10 minutes; Serve: 4
Ingredients:
- 1 small cauliflower head, chopped
- 2 potatoes, cubed
- 1/2 tsp paprika
- 1/2 tsp garam masala
- 1 tsp ground cumin
- 1/2 tsp turmeric
- 1 tsp olive oil
- 1/2 green chili, chopped
- 1 tbsp ginger
- 6 garlic cloves
- 2 tomatoes
- 1/2 small onion
- 3/4 tsp salt

Directions:
1. Add tomatoes, green chili, ginger, garlic, and onion into the blender and blend until smooth.
2. Add oil into the pot and set the pot on sauté mode.
3. Add blended mixture to the pot and sauté for 2-3 minutes.
4. Add potato and spices and cook for 4-5 minutes.
5. Add cauliflower and stir well. Seal pot with lid and cook on manual low pressure for 2 minutes.
6. Once done then release pressure using the quick-release method than open the lid.
7. Stir well and serve.

Nutritional Value (Amount per Serving):
Calories 131; Fat 1.8 g; Carbohydrates 26.7 g; Sugar 5.1 g; Protein 4.3 g; Cholesterol 0 mg

Carrot Potato Medley

Preparation Time: 10 minutes; Cooking Time: 15 minutes; Serve: 6
Ingredients:
- 2 lbs carrots, sliced
- 4 lbs potatoes, cut into chunks
- 2 garlic cloves, chopped
- 1 tsp spike seasoning
- 1 tsp Italian seasoning
- 1 1/2 cups vegetable broth
- 1 onion, diced
- 2 tbsp olive oil

Directions:
1. Add oil into the instant pot and set the pot on sauté mode.
2. Add onion and sauté for 5 minutes.
3. Add carrots and cook for 4-5 minutes.
4. Add remaining ingredients and stir everything well.
5. Seal pot with lid and cook on manual mode for 5 minutes.

6. Once done then allow to release pressure naturally for 10 minutes then release using the quick-release method. Open the lid.
7. Stir well and serve.

Nutritional Value (Amount per Serving):
Calories 331; Fat 5.6 g; Carbohydrates 64.7 g; Sugar 12 g; Protein 7.8 g; Cholesterol 1 mg

Lentil Chickpea Curry

Preparation Time: 10 minutes; Cooking Time: 22 minutes; Serve: 5
Ingredients:

- 15 oz can chickpeas, rinsed and drained
- 1/2 cup water
- 1 cup dry lentils, rinsed and drained
- 14 oz coconut milk
- 14 oz can tomatoes, diced
- 1 tbsp red curry paste
- 2 garlic cloves, minced
- 1 tbsp fresh ginger, grated
- 1/4 cup green onion, chopped
- 1 tbsp coconut oil
- 1/2 tsp kosher salt

Directions:
1. Add oil into the pot and set the pot on sauté mode.
2. Add ginger, green onion, and garlic and sauté for 2-3 minutes.
3. Add tomatoes and curry paste and stir for 2-3 minutes.
4. Add water, chickpeas, lentils, coconut milk, and salt and stir well.
5. Seal pot with lid and cook on manual high pressure for 6 minutes.
6. Once done then allow to release pressure naturally for 10 minutes then release using the quick-release method. Open the lid.
7. Stir well and serve.

Nutritional Value (Amount per Serving):
Calories 479; Fat 24 g; Carbohydrates 52.9 g; Sugar 6.3 g; Protein 16.9 g; Cholesterol 0 mg

Creamy Sweet Potato Curry

Preparation Time: 10 minutes; Cooking Time: 6 minutes; Serve: 4
Ingredients:

- 2 medium sweet potatoes, peeled and diced
- 1 cup tomato sauce
- 1 1/3 cup coconut milk
- 1/4 tsp ground ginger
- 1/2 tsp red pepper flakes
- 1/2 tsp smoked paprika
- 1 tsp ground cumin
- 1 tsp turmeric
- 1/2 tbsp curry powder
- 1 tbsp fresh ginger, minced
- 2 garlic cloves, minced
- 1 medium onion, chopped
- 1/2 tbsp olive oil
- 2 cups fresh spinach, chopped
- 1/4 tsp pepper
- 3/4 tsp salt

Directions:
1. Add oil into the instant pot and set the pot on sauté mode.
2. Add onion and sauté for 3 minutes.
3. Add ginger and garlic and sauté for a minute. Add all spices and stir well.
4. Add coconut milk, sweet potato, and tomato sauce. Stir.
5. Seal pot with lid and cook on manual mode for 2 minutes.
6. Once done then release pressure using the quick-release method than open the lid.
7. Add spinach and stir until spinach is wilted.
8. Serve over rice and enjoy.

Nutritional Value (Amount per Serving):

Calories 328; Fat 21.5 g; Carbohydrates 33.7 g; Sugar 7 g; Protein 4.9 g; Cholesterol 0 mg

Steamed Broccoli

Preparation Time: 10 minutes; Cooking Time: 1 minute; Serve: 4
Ingredients:
- 1 lb broccoli florets
- 1 cup of water
- Pepper
- Salt

Directions:
1. Pour water into the instant pot then place steamer basket in the pot.
2. Add broccoli into the steamer basket.
3. Seal pot with lid and cook on low pressure for 1 minute.
4. Once done then release pressure using the quick-release method than open the lid.
5. Season with pepper and salt.
6. Serve and enjoy.

Nutritional Value (Amount per Serving):
Calories 39; Fat 0.4 g; Carbohydrates 7.6 g; Sugar 1.9 g; Protein 3.2 g; Cholesterol 0 mg

Curried Spinach Quinoa

Preparation Time: 10 minutes; Cooking Time: 7 minutes; Serve: 4
Ingredients:
- 2 cups spinach, chopped
- 1 1/2 cups water
- 1 cup quinoa, rinsed and drained
- 1 sweet potato, peeled and diced
- 1/2 tsp paprika
- 1 tsp coriander powder
- 1 tsp turmeric
- 1 tsp cumin seeds
- 1 tsp ginger, grated
- 2 garlic cloves, chopped
- 1 onion, chopped
- 2 tbsp olive oil
- Pepper
- Salt

Directions:
1. Add oil into the instant pot and set the pot on sauté mode.
2. Add onion and sauté for 2 minutes.
3. Add garlic, ginger, spices, and quinoa and stir for 3-4 minutes.
4. Add spinach, water, and sweet potatoes and stir well.
5. Seal pot with lid and cook on manual high pressure for 2 minutes.
6. Once done then allow to release pressure naturally then open the lid.
7. Stir well and serve.

Nutritional Value (Amount per Serving):
Calories 265; Fat 10 g; Carbohydrates 37.9 g; Sugar 3.2 g; Protein 7.6 g; Cholesterol 0 mg

Healthy Vegan Chili

Preparation Time: 10 minutes; Cooking Time: 8 minutes; Serve: 8
Ingredients:
- 15 oz can corn, rinsed and drained
- 15 oz can kidney beans, rinsed and drained
- 1/2 cup quinoa
- 8 oz tomato sauce
- 2 1/2 cups vegetable broth
- 1 tsp ground cumin
- 1/2 tbsp paprika
- 1 tbsp chili powder
- 2 garlic cloves, minced
- 1/2 jalapeno pepper, minced
- 1/2 onion, diced
- 2 bell peppers, diced
- 2 tsp salt

Directions:

1. Add quinoa, tomato sauce, spices, garlic, jalapeno, onion, and bell peppers into the instant pot. Stir well.
2. Seal pot with lid and cook on manual high pressure for 8 minutes.
3. Once done then release pressure using the quick-release method than open the lid.
4. Add corn and beans and stir well. Let sit for 5-10 minutes.
5. Stir and serve.

Nutritional Value (Amount per Serving):
Calories 169; Fat 2 g; Carbohydrates 31.3 g; Sugar 5.4 g; Protein 8.7 g; Cholesterol 0 mg

Cabbage with Coconut

Preparation Time: 10 minutes; Cooking Time: 10 minutes; Serve: 4
Ingredients:
- 1 medium cabbage, shredded
- 1 tbsp olive oil
- 1/2 cup desiccated coconut
- 2 tbsp fresh lemon juice
- 1 carrot, peeled and sliced
- 1 tbsp turmeric
- 1 tbsp curry powder
- 1/2 red chili, sliced
- 1/3 cup water
- 2 garlic cloves, chopped
- 1 onion, sliced
- 1 tbsp coconut oil
- 1 1/2 tsp salt

Directions:
1. Add coconut oil into the instant pot and set the pot on sauté mode.
2. Add onion and 1/2 tsp salt and sauté until onion is softened.
3. Add spices, chili, and garlic and sauté for a minute.
4. Add coconut, olive oil, lemon juice, carrots, cabbage, and water and stir well.
5. Seal pot with lid and cook on manual high pressure for 5 minutes.
6. Once done then release pressure using the quick-release method than open the lid.
7. Stir well and serve.

Nutritional Value (Amount per Serving):
Calories 172; Fat 9.9 g; Carbohydrates 20.8 g; Sugar 9.7 g; Protein 4.1 g; Cholesterol 0 mg

Roasted Baby Potatoes

Preparation Time: 10 minutes; Cooking Time: 13 minutes; Serve: 4
Ingredients:
- 1 lb baby potatoes
- 1/2 tbsp garlic, minced
- 1 tbsp olive oil
- 1/4 tsp pepper
- 1/2 tsp salt

Directions:
1. Add oil into the instant pot and set the pot on sauté mode.
2. Add garlic and potatoes and sauté for 4-5 minutes.
3. Remove potatoes from pot and place in baking dish. Season with pepper and salt.
4. Pour 1 cup of water into the instant pot then place the trivet in the pot.
5. Place baking dish on top of the trivet and cook on manual high pressure for 8 minutes.
6. Once done then allow to release pressure naturally for 5 minutes then release using the quick-release method. Open the lid.
7. Serve and enjoy.

Nutritional Value (Amount per Serving):
Calories 98; Fat 3.6 g; Carbohydrates 14.5 g; Sugar 0 g; Protein 3 g; Cholesterol 0 mg

Spicy Chickpea Curry

Preparation Time: 10 minutes; Cooking Time: 18 minutes; Serve: 4

Ingredients:

- 2 cans chickpeas, rinsed and drained
- 14 oz coconut milk
- 3 tomatoes, diced
- 1 tsp chili powder
- 1 tsp turmeric
- 1 1/2 tsp cumin
- 2 tsp garam masala
- 1 1/2 tsp coriander
- 1 tbsp olive oil
- 2 garlic cloves, chopped
- 1 onion, chopped
- 1 tsp salt

Directions:

1. Add oil into the instant pot and set the pot on sauté mode.
2. Add onion and garlic and sauté until onion is softened.
3. Add remaining ingredients and stir everything well.
4. Seal pot with lid and cook on manual high pressure for 15 minutes.
5. Once done then allow to release pressure naturally for 10 minutes then release using the quick-release method. Open the lid.
6. Stir well and serve over rice.

Nutritional Value (Amount per Serving):

Calories 659; Fat 33.8 g; Carbohydrates 73.9 g; Sugar 17.7 g; Protein 23.1 g; Cholesterol 0 mg

Tasty Mushroom Stroganoff

Preparation Time: 10 minutes; Cooking Time: 12 minutes; Serve: 4

Ingredients:

- 8 oz pasta, uncooked
- 1 tbsp flour
- 2 tbsp mustard
- 2 cups vegetable broth
- 1/4 cup white wine
- 15 oz mushrooms, sliced
- 2 garlic cloves, chopped
- 1/2 onion, diced
- 3 tbsp olive oil
- 1/2 tsp pepper
- 3/4 tsp salt

Directions:

1. Add oil into the instant pot and set the pot on sauté mode.
2. Add mushrooms, garlic, onion, pepper, and salt and cook for 5-8 minutes.
3. Add flour, mustard, broth, wine, and pasta and stir well.
4. Seal pot with lid and cook on high pressure for 4 minutes.
5. Once done then release pressure using the quick-release method than open the lid.
6. Stir well and serve.

Nutritional Value (Amount per Serving):

Calories 349; Fat 14.4 g; Carbohydrates 40.8 g; Sugar 3.3 g; Protein 14.1 g; Cholesterol 41 mg

Quick & Healthy Kale

Preparation Time: 5 minutes; Cooking Time: 3 minutes; Serve: 6

Ingredients:

- 10 oz kale, chopped
- 1 cup vegetable broth

Directions:

1. Add kale and broth into the instant pot.
2. Seal pot with lid and cook on manual high pressure for 3 minutes.
3. Once done then release pressure using the quick-release method than open the lid.

4. Stir well and serve.

Nutritional Value (Amount per Serving):

Calories 30; Fat 0.2 g; Carbohydrates 5.1 g; Sugar 0.1 g; Protein 2.2 g; Cholesterol 0 mg

Perfect & Healthy Carrots

Preparation Time: 5 minutes; Cooking Time: 2 minutes; Serve: 8

Ingredients:

- 2 lbs carrots, washed and cut into 1-inch chunks
- 1 tbsp ghee, melted
- 1 tsp dried thyme
- 1 cup of water

Directions:

1. Add carrots and water into the instant pot and stir well.
2. Seal pot with lid and cook on manual high pressure for 2 minutes.
3. Once done then release pressure using the quick-release method than open the lid.
4. Drain carrots well and place in a serving bowl. Add ghee and thyme into the carrots and toss well.
5. Serve and enjoy.

Nutritional Value (Amount per Serving):

Calories 61; Fat 1.6 g; Carbohydrates 11.2 g; Sugar 5.6 g; Protein 0.9 g; Cholesterol 4 mg

Vegan Collard Greens

Preparation Time: 10 minutes; Cooking Time: 28 minutes; Serve: 6

Ingredients:

- 1 1/2 lbs collard green, diced
- 1 tbsp maple syrup
- 1/4 cup water
- 1/4 cup vinegar
- 1/2 tsp red pepper flakes
- 1/2 tsp paprika
- 2 garlic cloves, minced
- 1 onion, diced
- 2 tbsp olive oil
- 1 tsp sea salt

Directions:

1. Add oil into the instant pot and set the pot on sauté mode.
2. Add collard greens and onion and sauté for 5-8 minutes.
3. Add red pepper flakes, paprika, and garlic and sauté for a minute.
4. Stir in maple syrup, water, vinegar, and salt.
5. Seal pot with lid and cook on high pressure for 20 minutes.
6. Once done then release pressure using the quick-release method than open the lid.
7. Stir well and serve.

Nutritional Value (Amount per Serving):

Calories 92; Fat 5.6 g; Carbohydrates 10.8 g; Sugar 2.9 g; Protein 2.8 g; Cholesterol 0 mg

Potato Curry

Preparation Time: 10 minutes; Cooking Time: 5 minutes; Serve: 4

Ingredients:

- 3 potatoes, cut into cubes
- 1 tbsp lime juice
- 1/2 tsp garam masala
- 1 cup of water
- 1 cup tomato, chopped
- 1 tbsp ginger, minced
- 1/4 tsp asafoetida
- 1 tsp cumin seeds
- 2 tbsp olive oil
- 1/2 tsp chili powder
- 1/4 tsp turmeric
- 2 tsp coriander powder
- 1/2 tsp salt

Directions:
1. Add oil into the instant pot and set the pot on sauté mode.
2. Add cumin seeds, ginger, asafoetida and sauté for 30 seconds.
3. Spices and tomatoes and sauté for 2-3 minutes.
4. Add water and potatoes and stir well.
5. Seal pot with lid and cook on high pressure for 2 minutes.
6. Once done then release pressure using the quick-release method than open the lid.
7. Stir well and serve.

Nutritional Value (Amount per Serving):
Calories 189; Fat 7.5 g; Carbohydrates 29.2 g; Sugar 3.3 g; Protein 3.4 g; Cholesterol 0 mg

Garlic Mushrooms

Preparation Time: 10 minutes; Cooking Time: 17 minutes; Serve: 2
Ingredients:
- 1 lb button mushrooms
- 1/8 tsp dried thyme
- 3 garlic cloves, minced
- 2 tbsp butter
- 2 tbsp olive oil
- Salt

Directions:
1. Add oil into the instant pot and set the pot on sauté mode.
2. Add mushrooms and cook for 5 minutes.
3. Add thyme, garlic, butter, and salt and toss well.
4. Seal pot with lid and cook on manual high pressure for 12 minutes.
5. Once done then allow to release pressure naturally for 5 minutes then release using the quick-release method. Open the lid.
6. Stir well and serve.

Nutritional Value (Amount per Serving):
Calories 277; Fat 26.2 g; Carbohydrates 9 g; Sugar 4 g; Protein 7.5 g; Cholesterol 31 mg

Parmesan Broccoli

Preparation Time: 10 minutes; Cooking Time: 1 minute; Serve: 4
Ingredients:
- 1 lb broccoli florets
- 1/4 cup parmesan cheese, shredded
- 2 tbsp ghee, melted
- Pepper
- Salt

Directions:
1. Pour 1 1/2 cups of water into the instant pot then place steamer basket in the pot.
2. Add broccoli florets into the steamer basket.
3. Seal pot with lid and cook on high pressure for 1 minute.
4. Once done then release pressure using the quick-release method than open the lid.
5. Pour melted ghee on top of broccoli then sprinkle with shredded cheese.
6. Season with pepper and salt.
7. Serve and enjoy.

Nutritional Value (Amount per Serving):
Calories 117; Fat 8.2 g; Carbohydrates 7.8 g; Sugar 1.9 g; Protein 5.5 g; Cholesterol 21 mg

Perfect Green Beans

Preparation Time: 10 minutes; Cooking Time: 1 minute; Serve: 4
Ingredients:
- 1 lb green beans, washed and trimmed
- 1 cup of water

- 1 tbsp lemon juice
- 1 tsp lemon zest
- 2 tbsp butter, melted
- Pepper
- Salt

Directions:
1. Pour 1 cup of water into the instant pot then place steamer basket in the pot.
2. Add green beans into the steamer basket.
3. Seal pot with lid and cook on low pressure for 1 minute.
4. Once done then release pressure using the quick-release method than open the lid.
5. Transfer green beans into the mixing bowl. Add remaining ingredients over green beans and toss well.
6. Serve and enjoy.

Nutritional Value (Amount per Serving):
Calories 87; Fat 5.9 g; Carbohydrates 8.3 g; Sugar 1.7 g; Protein 2.2 g; Cholesterol 15 mg

Perfect Instant Pot Cabbage

Preparation Time: 10 minutes; Cooking Time: 3 minutes; Serve: 4
Ingredients:
- 1 cabbage head, cut into quarters
- 2 tbsp butter, melted
- 1 cup of water
- Pepper
- Salt

Directions:
1. Pour 1 cup of water into the instant pot then place steamer basket in the pot.
2. Add cabbage into the steamer basket.
3. Seal pot with lid and cook on high pressure for 3 minutes.
4. Once done then release pressure using the quick-release method than open the lid.
5. Pour melted butter over cabbage. Season with pepper and salt.
6. Serve and enjoy.

Nutritional Value (Amount per Serving):
Calories 96; Fat 5.9 g; Carbohydrates 10.4 g; Sugar 5.7 g; Protein 2.3 g; Cholesterol 15 mg

Delicious Cheesy Cauliflower

Preparation Time: 10 minutes; Cooking Time: 3 minutes; Serve: 5
Ingredients:
- 1 cauliflower head, cut into florets
- 1/2 tsp garlic salt
- 1 1/2 cup cheddar cheese, shredded
- 1 1/2 tsp Dijon mustard
- 2 oz cream cheese
- 3/4 cup heavy cream
- Salt

Directions:
1. Pour 1 cup of water into the instant pot then place steamer basket in the pot.
2. Add cauliflower florets into the steamer basket.
3. Seal pot with lid and cook on high pressure for 2 minutes.
4. Once done then release pressure using the quick-release method than open the lid.
5. Remove steamer basket from instant pot. Set pot on sauté mode.
6. Add remaining ingredients and stir until cheese is melted.
7. Add cauliflower and stir well and cook for 1-2 minutes.
8. Serve and enjoy.

Nutritional Value (Amount per Serving):
Calories 253; Fat 22 g; Carbohydrates 4.3 g; Sugar 1.6 g; Protein 10.8 g; Cholesterol 73 mg

Healthy & Easy Instant Pot Zucchini

Preparation Time: 10 minutes; Cooking Time: 5 minutes; Serve: 4

Ingredients:

- 4 zucchinis, cut into 1/2-inch pieces
- 1 cup of water
- 1/2 tsp Italian seasoning
- 1/2 tsp red pepper flakes
- 1 tsp garlic, minced
- 2 tsp olive oil
- 1/2 cup tomato sauce
- 1/2 tsp salt

Directions:

1. Add water and zucchini into the instant pot and stir well.
2. Seal pot with lid and cook on manual high pressure for 2 minutes.
3. Once done then release pressure using the quick-release method than open the lid. Drain zucchini well.
4. Add oil into the instant pot and set the pot on sauté mode.
5. Add garlic and sauté for a minute.
6. Add zucchini, Italian seasoning, red pepper flakes, tomato sauce, and salt and stir well and cook for 2 minutes.
7. Serve and enjoy.

Nutritional Value (Amount per Serving):

Calories 62; Fat 3 g; Carbohydrates 8.6 g; Sugar 4.8 g; Protein 2.8 g; Cholesterol 0 mg

Sweet & Sour Red Cabbage

Preparation Time: 10 minutes; Cooking Time: 10 minutes; Serve: 6

Ingredients:

- 2 lbs red cabbage, shredded
- 2 apples, peeled, cored and diced
- 1 tbsp sugar
- 1/3 cup apple cider vinegar
- 1/4 tsp allspice
- 1 onion, sliced
- 4 tbsp butter
- 1/8 tsp pepper
- 1/2 tsp kosher salt

Directions:

1. Add butter into the instant pot and set the pot on sauté mode.
2. Add onion to the pot and sauté until softened.
3. Add cabbage and stir for 2-3 minutes. Add allspice, pepper, and salt and stir well.
4. Add sugar, vinegar, and apples and stir well.
5. Seal pot with lid and cook on high pressure for 5 minutes.
6. Once done then release pressure using the quick-release method than open the lid.
7. Stir well and serve.

Nutritional Value (Amount per Serving):

Calories 162; Fat 8 g; Carbohydrates 23 g; Sugar 15.4 g; Protein 2.4 g; Cholesterol 20 mg

Sugar Snap Peas

Preparation Time: 10 minutes; Cooking Time: 1 minute; Serve: 2

Ingredients:

- 2 cups sugar snap peas
- 2 tbsp water
- 2 tsp olive oil
- Pepper
- Salt
- For topping:
- 1/4 tsp garlic powder
- 1 tsp sesame seeds, toasted
- 1 1/2 tbsp peanuts, toasted and crushed
- 1 tbsp lemon juice

Directions:

1. Add sugar snap peas, water, oil, pepper, and salt into the instant pot and stir well.
2. Seal pot with lid and cook on manual low pressure for 1 minute.
3. Once done then release pressure using the quick-release method than open the lid.
4. Transfer sugar snaps peas on a serving plate and top with garlic powder, sesame seeds, peanuts, and lemon juice.
5. Serve and enjoy.

Nutritional Value (Amount per Serving):

Calories 117; Fat 9 g; Carbohydrates 6.7 g; Sugar 3 g; Protein 3.9 g; Cholesterol 0 mg

Southern Okra & Tomatoes

Preparation Time: 10 minutes; Cooking Time: 30 minutes; Serve: 4
Ingredients:

- 2 cups okra, diced
- 1 cup of water
- 3 tsp Cajun seasoning
- 14 oz can tomatoes, diced
- 1/2 cup onion, diced
- Pepper
- Salt

Directions:
1. Add all ingredients into the instant pot and stir everything well.
2. Seal pot with lid and cook on manual mode for 30 minutes.
3. Once done then allow to release pressure naturally for 10 minutes then release using the quick-release method. Open the lid.
4. Stir well and serve.

Nutritional Value (Amount per Serving):

Calories 47; Fat 0.1 g; Carbohydrates 10.2 g; Sugar 4.7 g; Protein 2.1 g; Cholesterol 0 mg

Garlic Mushrooms

Preparation Time: 10 minutes; Cooking Time: 10 minutes; Serve: 4
Ingredients:

- 8 oz mushrooms, sliced
- 3 garlic cloves, minced
- 1 tbsp olive oil
- 1 cup of water

Directions:
1. Add mushrooms and water into the instant pot.
2. Seal pot with lid and cook on manual mode for 5 minutes.
3. Once done then release pressure using the quick-release method than open the lid.
4. Drain mushrooms well and return to the pot. Set pot on sauté mode.
5. Add garlic and oil and stir well and cook for 5 minutes.
6. Serve and enjoy.

Nutritional Value (Amount per Serving):

Calories 46; Fat 3.7 g; Carbohydrates 2.6 g; Sugar 1 g; Protein 1.9 g; Cholesterol 0 mg

Tasty Tikka Masala Chickpeas

Preparation Time: 10 minutes; Cooking Time: 10 minutes; Serve: 6
Ingredients:

- 15 oz can chickpeas, rinsed and drained
- 1 cup bell pepper, chopped
- 1/2 cup onion, chopped
- 3 tbsp garam masala
- 4 garlic cloves, chopped
- 1 cup of coconut milk
- 15 oz can tomatoes, chopped
- Pepper
- Salt

Directions:

1. Add all ingredients into the instant pot and stir everything well.
2. Seal pot with lid and cook on manual high pressure for 10 minutes.
3. Once done then release pressure using the quick-release method than open the lid.
4. Stir well and serve.

Nutritional Value (Amount per Serving):
Calories 205; Fat 10.4 g; Carbohydrates 24.9 g; Sugar 5.2 g; Protein 5.6 g; Cholesterol 0 mg

Cheesy & Creamy Ziti

Preparation Time: 10 minutes; Cooking Time: 6 minutes; Serve: 4

Ingredients:
- 8 oz dry ziti pasta
- 1/2 cup mozzarella cheese, shredded
- 3/4 cup parmesan cheese, shredded
- 1 cup pasta sauce
- 3 garlic cloves, minced
- 1 cup heavy cream
- 1 1/2 cups vegetable broth
- Pepper
- Salt

Directions:
1. Add vegetables broth, heavy cream, garlic, pepper, salt, and pasta into the instant pot.
2. Seal pot with lid and cook on manual mode for 6 minutes.
3. Once done then allow to release pressure naturally for 5 minutes then release using quick-release method. Open the lid.
4. Add pasta sauce and stir everything well.
5. Add cheese and stir until cheese is melted and sauce thicken.
6. Serve and enjoy.

Nutritional Value (Amount per Serving):
Calories 372; Fat 16.7 g; Carbohydrates 42 g; Sugar 5.8 g; Protein 13.4 g; Cholesterol 91 mg

Classic Mac n Cheese

Preparation Time: 10 minutes; Cooking Time: 4 minutes; Serve: 6

Ingredients:
- 1 lb shells pasta
- 4 oz parmesan cheese, grated
- 8 oz Monterey jack cheese, grated
- 1 cup heavy cream
- 2 tbsp butter
- 1/4 tsp cayenne
- 1/2 tsp garlic powder
- 2 garlic cloves, minced
- 4 cups of water

Directions:
1. Add pasta, butter, cayenne, garlic powder, garlic, and water into the instant pot and stir well.
2. Seal pot with lid and cook on manual high pressure for 4 minutes.
3. Once done then release pressure using the quick-release method than open the lid.
4. Add cheeses and heavy cream and stir until cheese is melted.
5. Serve and enjoy.

Nutritional Value (Amount per Serving):
Calories 591; Fat 28.1 g; Carbohydrates 57.4 g; Sugar 3 g; Protein 25.3 g; Cholesterol 85 mg

Sticky Noodles

Preparation Time: 10 minutes; Cooking Time: 3 minutes; Serve: 4

Ingredients:
- 8 oz rice noodles
- 2 cups of water
- 1/4 tsp garlic powder
- 1/4 tsp ground ginger

- 1 tbsp hot sauce
- 2 tbsp apple cider vinegar
- 2 tbsp coconut oil
- 3 tbsp maple syrup
- 1/4 tsp salt

Directions:
1. Add all ingredients into the instant pot and stir well.
2. Seal pot with lid and cook on manual high pressure for 3 minutes.
3. Once done then release pressure using the quick-release method than open the lid.
4. Stir well and serve.

Nutritional Value (Amount per Serving):
Calories 163; Fat 7 g; Carbohydrates 24.5 g; Sugar 9.1 g; Protein 0.6 g; Cholesterol 0 mg

Crispy Roasted Potatoes

Preparation Time: 10 minutes; Cooking Time: 16 minutes; Serve: 4
Ingredients:
- 2 lbs baby potatoes, scrubbed and pierce with a fork
- 2 tbsp olive oil
- 1 cup vegetable broth
- 4 garlic cloves, peeled
- Pepper
- Salt
- For seasoning:
- 1/8 tsp nutmeg
- 1/2 tsp sage
- 1/2 tsp thyme
- 1/2 tsp oregano
- 1 tsp rosemary
- 1/8 tsp pepper

Directions:
1. Add potatoes, broth, and garlic into the instant pot.
2. Seal pot with lid and cook on steam mode for 11 minutes.
3. Once done then release pressure using the quick-release method than open the lid.
4. Drain potatoes well and pat dry the potatoes.
5. Add oil into the pot and set the pot on sauté mode.
6. Add potatoes and seasoning to the pot and cook on sauté mode for 5 minutes.
7. Serve and enjoy.

Nutritional Value (Amount per Serving):
Calories 208; Fat 7.7 g; Carbohydrates 29.9 g; Sugar 0.2 g; Protein 7.3 g; Cholesterol 0 mg

Sweet Potato Mash

Preparation Time: 10 minutes; Cooking Time: 10 minutes; Serve: 6
Ingredients:
- 3 lbs sweet potatoes, peeled and cut into chunks
- 1 cup vegetable stock
- 1/2 tsp pepper
- 1/2 tsp kosher salt

Directions:
1. Add all ingredients into the instant pot and stir well.
2. Seal pot with lid and cook on manual high pressure for 10 minutes.
3. Once done then allow to release pressure naturally for 5 minutes then release using the quick-release method. Open the lid.
4. Using masher mash the sweet potatoes until smooth.
5. Serve and enjoy.

Nutritional Value (Amount per Serving):
Calories 269; Fat 0.4 g; Carbohydrates 63.5 g; Sugar 1.3 g; Protein 3.6 g; Cholesterol 0 mg

Cheesy Spaghetti

Preparation Time: 10 minutes; Cooking Time: 6 minutes; Serve: 6
Ingredients:

- 8 oz spaghetti, cut in half
- 2/3 cup parmesan cheese, grated
- 1 tsp dried oregano
- 4 tbsp butter
- 3 garlic cloves, minced
- 2/3 cup heavy cream
- 2 cups vegetable stock
- Pepper
- Salt

Directions:

1. Add all ingredients except cheese into the instant pot.
2. Seal pot with lid and cook on manual high pressure for 6 minutes.
3. Once done then allow to release pressure naturally for 6 minutes then release using quick-release method. Open the lid.
4. Stir in cheese and serve.

Nutritional Value (Amount per Serving):

Calories 258; Fat 15.6 g; Carbohydrates 22.4 g; Sugar 0.3 g; Protein 7.9 g; Cholesterol 73 mg

Sautéed vegetables

Preparation Time: 10 minutes; Cooking Time: 11 minutes; Serve: 3
Ingredients:

- 1 zucchini, diced
- 2 bell pepper, sliced
- 3 tbsp feta cheese, crumbled
- 1/2 cup mushrooms, sliced
- 1/4 tsp dried oregano
- 1 onion, sliced
- 1/4 tsp dried thyme
- 2 tbsp olive oil
- 1 1/2 tbsp tamari sauce
- 1/2 cup sour cream
- 1 tsp sea salt

Directions:

1. Add oil into the instant pot and set the pot on sauté mode.
2. Add zucchini and salt and cook for 5 minutes.
3. Add onion, bell peppers, tamari sauce, oregano, thyme, and salt. Stir well.
4. Add mushrooms and cheese and cook for 2-3 minutes.
5. Add 3 tbsp of water and stir well and cook for 3 minutes.
6. Add cream and stir well.
7. Serve and enjoy.

Nutritional Value (Amount per Serving):

Calories 246; Fat 19.8 g; Carbohydrates 14.6 g; Sugar 7.5 g; Protein 5.9 g; Cholesterol 25 mg

Healthy Veggie Curry

Preparation Time: 10 minutes; Cooking Time: 10 minutes; Serve: 6
Ingredients:

- 2 zucchini, peeled and diced
- 1 onion, diced
- 1 bell pepper, diced
- 1 cup cherry tomatoes, cut in half
- 1/2 cup vegetable stock
- 5 carrots, diced
- 1 1/2 tbsp curry powder
- 1/2 tsp sea salt

Directions:

1. Add all ingredients except tomatoes into the instant pot and stir well.
2. Seal pot with lid and cook on manual high pressure for 10 minutes.
3. Once done then release pressure using the quick-release method than open the lid.
4. Add tomatoes and stir well.

5. Serve and enjoy.

Nutritional Value (Amount per Serving):

Calories 56; Fat 0.5 g; Carbohydrates 12.6 g; Sugar 6.3 g; Protein 2.1 g; Cholesterol 0 mg

Braised Parsnips

Preparation Time: 10 minutes; Cooking Time: 3 minutes; Serve: 4

Ingredients:

- 2 lbs parsnips, peeled and sliced
- 1 1/2 tbsp maple syrup
- 3 tbsp vinegar
- 1/4 cup vegetable stock
- 1/8 tsp pepper
- 1/2 tsp salt

Directions:

1. Add parsnips, vinegar, and stock into the instant pot.
2. Seal pot with lid and cook on manual high pressure for 3 minutes.
3. Once done then release pressure using the quick-release method than open the lid.
4. Add maple syrup, pepper, and salt and stir well.
5. Serve and enjoy.

Nutritional Value (Amount per Serving):

Calories 193; Fat 0.7 g; Carbohydrates 46 g; Sugar 15.4 g; Protein 2.8 g; Cholesterol 0 mg

Healthy Ratatouille

Preparation Time: 10 minutes; Cooking Time: 7 minutes; Serve: 8

Ingredients:

- 12 oz red pepper, roasted, drained and sliced
- 28 oz can tomatoes, crushed
- 3 large zucchini, sliced
- 2 eggplants, peeled and sliced
- 4 garlic cloves, crushed
- 1 onion, sliced
- 1 tbsp olive oil
- 1 tsp salt

Directions:

1. Add oil into the instant pot and set the pot on sauté mode.
2. Add vegetables into the pot and cook for 3-4 minutes. Season with salt.
3. Add tomatoes and stir well.
4. Seal pot with lid and cook on manual high pressure for 4 minutes.
5. Once done then release pressure using the quick-release method than open the lid.
6. Stir well and serve.

Nutritional Value (Amount per Serving):

Calories 155; Fat 2.7 g; Carbohydrates 32.5 g; Sugar 19.2 g; Protein 5.8 g; Cholesterol 0 mg

Herb Mushrooms

Preparation Time: 10 minutes; Cooking Time: 4 minutes; Serve: 4

Ingredients:

- 24 oz mushrooms, cleaned
- 1/2 tsp dried basil
- 2 garlic cloves, minced
- 3 tbsp parsley, chopped
- 2 tbsp butter
- 1/4 cup half and half
- 1 cup vegetable stock
- 1 bay leaf
- 1/2 tsp dried thyme
- 1/2 tsp dried oregano
- Pepper
- Salt

Directions:

1. Add all ingredients except parsley, butter, and half and half into the instant pot and stir everything well.

2. Seal pot with lid and cook on manual high pressure for 4 minutes.
3. Once done then release pressure using the quick-release method than open the lid.
4. Add remaining ingredients and stir well.
5. Serve and enjoy.

Nutritional Value (Amount per Serving):
Calories 113; Fat 8.1 g; Carbohydrates 7.5 g; Sugar 3.2 g; Protein 6.2 g; Cholesterol 21 mg

Creamy Squash Puree

Preparation Time: 10 minutes; Cooking Time: 20 minutes; Serve: 6
Ingredients:
- 2 lbs butternut squash, peeled and diced
- 1 1/2 tbsp honey
- 1 sprig sage
- 1/2 cup vegetable stock
- 1/2 tsp baking soda
- 4 tbsp ghee
- 1 tsp salt

Directions:
1. Add ghee into the instant pot and set the pot on sauté mode.
2. Add squash, baking soda, water, sage, and salt and stir well.
3. Seal pot with lid and cook on manual high pressure for 20 minutes.
4. Once done then release pressure using the quick-release method than open the lid.
5. Remove sage. Using immersion blender puree squash until smooth.
6. Add honey and stir well.
7. Serve and enjoy.

Nutritional Value (Amount per Serving):
Calories 113; Fat 8.1 g; Carbohydrates 7.5 g; Sugar 3.2 g; Protein 6.2 g; Cholesterol 21 mg

Cheesy Cauliflower Rice

Preparation Time: 10 minutes; Cooking Time: 5 minutes; Serve: 3
Ingredients:
- 2 cups cauliflower rice
- 1/2 cup half and half
- 2 tbsp cream cheese
- 3/4 cup cheddar cheese, shredded
- Pepper
- Salt

Directions:
1. Add all ingredients into the baking dish and cover with foil.
2. Pour 1 1/2 cups water into the instant pot then place the trivet in the pot.
3. Place baking dish on top of the trivet.
4. Seal pot with lid and cook on manual high pressure for 5 minutes.
5. Once done then allow to release pressure naturally for 10 minutes then release using quick-release method. Open the lid.
6. Stir well and serve.

Nutritional Value (Amount per Serving):
Calories 190; Fat 16.3 g; Carbohydrates 2.3 g; Sugar 0.2 g; Protein 8.7 g; Cholesterol 52 mg

Delicious Baby Carrots

Preparation Time: 10 minutes; Cooking Time: 3 minutes; Serve: 4
Ingredients:
- 15 oz baby carrots
- 2 tbsp fresh mint leaves, chopped
- 1 tbsp ghee
- 1 cup of water
- Sea salt

Directions:

1. Add carrots and water into the instant pot.
2. Seal pot with lid and cook on manual high pressure for 2 minutes.
3. Once done then release pressure using the quick-release method than open the lid.
4. Drain carrots well and set aside.
5. Add ghee into the instant pot and set the pot on sauté mode.
6. Add mint, carrots, and salt sauté for a minute.
7. Stir well and serve.

Nutritional Value (Amount per Serving):
Calories 66; Fat 3.3 g; Carbohydrates 9.9 g; Sugar 5.1 g; Protein 0.8 g; Cholesterol 9 mg

Macaroni with Cauliflower Broccoli

Preparation Time: 10 minutes; Cooking Time: 9 minutes; Serve: 6
Ingredients:
- 8 oz macaroni
- 1 cup cheddar cheese, shredded
- 1 1/2 cups broccoli florets
- 1 1/2 cups cauliflower florets
- 3/4 cup milk
- 3 cups of water
- 1/2 tsp salt

Directions:
1. Add water, macaroni, cauliflower, broccoli, and salt into the instant pot and stir well.
2. Seal pot with lid and cook on manual high pressure for 4 minutes.
3. Once done then release pressure using the quick-release method than open the lid.
4. Set instant pot on sauté mode.
5. Add milk and cheddar cheese. Stir well and cook for 5 minutes.
6. Serve and enjoy.

Nutritional Value (Amount per Serving):
Calories 245; Fat 7.5 g; Carbohydrates 32.8 g; Sugar 3.5 g; Protein 11.8 g; Cholesterol 22 mg

Spicy Cabbage

Preparation Time: 10 minutes; Cooking Time: 6 minutes; Serve: 6
Ingredients:
- 1 cabbage head, chopped
- 3/4 tsp chili powder
- 2 tbsp soy sauce
- 1 cup of water
- 2 tbsp olive oil
- 1/2 onion, diced
- 1/2 tsp paprika
- 1/4 tsp garlic salt
- 1/2 tsp salt

Directions:
1. Add oil into the instant pot and set the pot on sauté mode.
2. Add cabbage and stir for 2-3 minutes.
3. Add remaining ingredients and stir to combine.
4. Seal pot with lid and cook on manual high pressure for 3 minutes.
5. Once done then release pressure using the quick-release method than open the lid.
6. Stir well and serve.

Nutritional Value (Amount per Serving):
Calories 78; Fat 4.9 g; Carbohydrates 8.5 g; Sugar 4.4 g; Protein 2 g; Cholesterol 0 mg

Instant Pot Artichokes

Preparation Time: 10 minutes; Cooking Time: 10 minutes; Serve: 4
Ingredients:

- 4 artichokes, wash, trim, and discard outer leaves
- 3 garlic cloves, minced
- 1/2 cup water
- 1/4 cup parmesan cheese, grated
- 1 tbsp olive oil

Directions:
1. Pour half cup of water into the instant pot then place the trivet in the pot.
2. Place artichokes on top of the trivet. Add garlic on top.
3. Drizzle oil over artichokes and sprinkle with cheese.
4. Seal pot with lid and cook on steam mode for 10 minutes.
5. Once done then release pressure using quick-release method than open the lid.
6. Serve and enjoy.

Nutritional Value (Amount per Serving):
   Calories 132; Fat 5.3 g; Carbohydrates 18 g; Sugar 1.6 g; Protein 7.7 g; Cholesterol 5 mg

Flavorful Ranch Cauliflower Mashed

Preparation Time: 10 minutes; Cooking Time: 15 minutes; Serve: 4
Ingredients:
- 1 cauliflower head, cut into florets
- 1 cup of water
- 2 1/2 tbsp heavy cream
- 4 tbsp ghee
- 1 tbsp ranch seasoning

Directions:
1. Pour water into the instant pot then place steamer basket in the pot.
2. Add cauliflower florets into the steamer basket.
3. Seal pot with lid and cook on manual high pressure for 15 minutes.
4. Once done then release pressure using quick-release method than open the lid.
5. Transfer cauliflower florets into the large bowl.
6. Add remaining ingredients and mash until smooth.
7. Serve and enjoy.

Nutritional Value (Amount per Serving):
   Calories 169; Fat 16.3 g; Carbohydrates 3.8 g; Sugar 1.6 g; Protein 1.5 g; Cholesterol 46 mg

Kale Curry

Preparation Time: 10 minutes; Cooking Time: 6 hours; Serve: 6
Ingredients:
- 2 cups butternut squash, cubed
- 1/2 tbsp garlic powder
- 1 cup kale, chopped
- 3/4 tsp chili powder
- 1/2 tbsp cumin powder
- 2 cups vegetable stock
- 1 tsp garlic, chopped
- 2 cups of coconut milk
- 1 cup chickpeas, soaked overnight and drained
- 1 onion, chopped
- 3 tbsp olive oil
- 1 tsp pepper

Directions:
1. Add oil into the instant pot and set the pot on sauté mode.
2. Add onion and garlic and sauté for 1-2 minutes.
3. Add remaining ingredients and stir well.
4. Seal the pot with a lid and cook on slow cook mode for 6 hours.
5. Once done then release pressure using quick-release method than open the lid.
6. Stir well and serve.

Nutritional Value (Amount per Serving):
   Calories 408; Fat 28.4 g; Carbohydrates 34.6 g; Sugar 8.5 g; Protein 9.7 g; Cholesterol 0 mg

Buttery Carrots & Parsnips

Preparation Time: 10 minutes; Cooking Time: 2 minutes; Serve: 4

Ingredients:

- 2 lbs parsnips, peeled and sliced
- 2 lbs carrots, peeled and sliced
- 1/4 cup butter
- 1 cup of water
- Pepper
- Salt

Directions:

1. Add parsnips, carrots, and water into the instant pot and stir well.
2. Seal pot with lid and cook on manual high pressure for 2 minutes.
3. Once done then allow to release pressure naturally for 10 minutes then release using quick release method. Open the lid.
4. Drain parsnips and carrots well and set aside.
5. Add butter into the instant pot and set the pot on sauté mode.
6. Add parsnips, carrots, pepper, and salt to the pot and stir well.
7. Serve and enjoy.

Nutritional Value (Amount per Serving):

Calories 365; Fat 12.2 g; Carbohydrates 63.1 g; Sugar 22.1 g; Protein 4.7 g; Cholesterol 31 mg

Creamy Parsnip Mash

Preparation Time: 10 minutes; Cooking Time: 12 minutes; Serve: 6

Ingredients:

- 1 lb parsnips, sliced
- 3 lbs potatoes, peeled and cubed
- 1/4 cup half and half
- 3 tbsp butter
- 1/4 tsp pepper
- 1 tsp salt

Directions:

1. Add 2 cups of water into the instant pot then place a steamer basket into the pot.
2. Add parsnips and potatoes into the steamer basket.
3. Seal pot with lid and cook on manual high pressure for 7 minutes.
4. Once done then release pressure using quick-release method than open the lid.
5. Transfer potatoes and parsnips into the large bowl.
6. Add remaining ingredients. Using the masher mash potatoes and parsnips until smooth.
7. Serve and enjoy.

Nutritional Value (Amount per Serving):

Calories 221; Fat 7.2 g; Carbohydrates 36.1 g; Sugar 2.6 g; Protein 4.2 g; Cholesterol 19 mg

Chapter 3: Beans & Grains

Red Bean Rice

Preparation Time: 10 minutes; Cooking Time: 25 minutes; Serve: 4
Ingredients:
- 1 1/4 cup red kidney beans, soaked for 4-5 hours and drained
- 2 cups of water
- 3 cups vegetable broth
- 1/4 cup cilantro, chopped
- 1 cup of salsa
- 1 1/2 cups brown rice, uncooked

Directions:
1. Add all ingredients into the instant pot and stir well.
2. Seal pot with lid and cook on manual high pressure for 25 minutes.
3. Once done then allow to release pressure naturally for 10 minutes then release using the quick-release method. Open the lid.
4. Stir well and serve.

Nutritional Value (Amount per Serving):
Calories 498; Fat 3.7 g; Carbohydrates 94.3 g; Sugar 3.7 g; Protein 23 g; Cholesterol 0 mg

Tender Pinto Beans

Preparation Time: 10 minutes; Cooking Time: 47 minutes; Serve: 8
Ingredients:
- 1 lb pinto beans, rinsed and drained
- 1/4 tsp cayenne pepper
- 1/2 tsp paprika
- 1/2 tsp coriander
- 1/4 tsp cumin
- 1/2 tsp chili powder
- 1 tsp garlic powder
- 1 1/2 cups water
- 4 cups vegetable broth
- 1 small onion, diced
- 1/4 tsp pepper
- 1 1/4 tsp sea salt

Directions:
1. Add all ingredients into the instant pot and stir well.
2. Seal pot with lid and cook on manual high pressure for 47 minutes.
3. Once done then allow to release pressure naturally for 10 minutes then release using the quick-release method. Open the lid.
4. Stir well and serve.

Nutritional Value (Amount per Serving):
Calories 222; Fat 1.5 g; Carbohydrates 37.3 g; Sugar 2 g; Protein 14.8 g; Cholesterol 0 mg

Tomatillo White Beans

Preparation Time: 10 minutes; Cooking Time: 40 minutes; Serve: 6
Ingredients:
- 1 1/2 cups dried great northern beans, soaked for overnight and drained
- 2 tsp dried oregano
- 1 1/2 cups water
- 1 1/4 tsp ground cumin
- 1/2 jalapeno pepper, chopped
- 1 cup onion, chopped
- 1 cup poblano, chopped
- 1 1/2 cups tomatillos, chopped
- Pepper
- Salt

Directions:
1. Add tomatillos, jalapeno, onion, and poblano into the food processor and process until just tiny pieces formed.

2. Pour blended mixture into the instant pot and set the pot on sauté mode.
3. Add cumin and stir well and cook tomatillo mixture for 4-5 minutes.
4. Add beans, oregano, and water and stir to combine.
5. Seal pot with lid and cook on high pressure for 35 minutes.
6. Once done then allow to release pressure naturally then open the lid.
7. Stir well and serve.

Nutritional Value (Amount per Serving):
Calories 177; Fat 1 g; Carbohydrates 32.8 g; Sugar 1.9 g; Protein 10.7 g; Cholesterol 0 mg

Flavorful Refried Beans

Preparation Time: 10 minutes; Cooking Time: 30 minutes; Serve: 12
Ingredients:
- 6 cups dry pinto beans, soaked in water for overnight, rinsed and drained
- 2 tsp chili powder
- 1 1/4 tsp onion powder
- 1 tsp garlic powder
- 2 tsp ground cumin
- 12 cups vegetable broth
- 2 tsp salt

Directions:
1. Add beans and broth into the instant pot.
2. Seal pot with lid and cook on manual high pressure for 30 minutes.
3. Once done then allow to release pressure naturally for 10 minutes then release using the quick-release method. Open the lid.
4. Reserve two cups of beans liquid.
5. Add 1 cup liquid into the pot along with seasonings and stir well.
6. Add beans and mash beans using the masher until smooth. Add remaining liquid if needed.
7. Serve and enjoy.

Nutritional Value (Amount per Serving):
Calories 378; Fat 2.7 g; Carbohydrates 62 g; Sugar 2.9 g; Protein 25.7 g; Cholesterol 0 mg

Delicious Beans & Rice

Preparation Time: 10 minutes; Cooking Time: 43 minutes; Serve: 10
Ingredients:
- 1 lb dry red kidney beans
- 10 cups rice, cooked
- 1 lb sausage, cut into slices
- 7 cups chicken stock
- 1 bay leaf
- 1/2 tsp dried thyme
- 1 tsp hot sauce
- 2 garlic cloves, minced
- 2 celery stalks, diced
- 1 bell pepper, diced
- 1 onion, diced
- 1/2 tsp pepper
- 1 tsp salt

Directions:
1. Add all ingredients except rice and sausage into the instant pot and stir well.
2. Seal pot with lid and cook on manual high pressure for 28 minutes.
3. Once done then release pressure using the quick-release method than open the lid.
4. Add sausage and stir well.
5. Again seal the pot with a lid and cook on manual high pressure for 15 minutes.
6. Once done then allow to release pressure naturally then open the lid.
7. Stir everything well and serve over cooked rice.

Nutritional Value (Amount per Serving):

Calories 999; Fat 15 g; Carbohydrates 178.6 g; Sugar 2.8 g; Protein 33 g; Cholesterol 38 mg

Indian Red Kidney Beans

Preparation Time: 10 minutes; Cooking Time: 30 minutes; Serve: 6
Ingredients:

- 1 cup dried red kidney beans, soaked in hot water for 1-2 hours
- 2 cups of water
- For masala:
- 1/3 cup water
- 1/2 tsp ground coriander
- 3/4 tsp ground cumin
- 1 tsp garam masala
- 1 tsp turmeric
- 1 tsp cayenne
- 1 cup can tomatoes
- 3 garlic cloves, minced
- 1 tbsp ginger, minced
- 1 large onion, diced
- 1 tbsp olive oil
- 1 tsp salt

Directions:
1. Add all masala ingredients into the instant pot and stir well.
2. Place trivet in the pot. Add beans into the oven-safe bowl with 2 cups of water and cover bowl with foil.
3. Place bowl on top of the trivet.
4. Seal pot with lid and cook on bean mode for 30 minutes.
5. Once done then allow to release pressure naturally for 10 minutes then release using the quick-release method. Open the lid.
6. Carefully remove the bowl from the pot and mash beans lightly with a fork.
7. Set instant pot on sauté mode.
8. Pour beans into the pot and stir well.
9. Serve over rice and enjoy.

Nutritional Value (Amount per Serving):
Calories 150; Fat 2.9 g; Carbohydrates 24.8 g; Sugar 3.1 g; Protein 7.9 g; Cholesterol 0 mg

Mexican Black Beans

Preparation Time: 10 minutes; Cooking Time: 25 minutes; Serve: 4
Ingredients:

- 1/2 lb dry black beans
- 1 tbsp olive oil
- 1/2 tsp paprika
- 2 garlic cloves, minced
- 1/2 onion, diced
- 1/2 cup vegetable broth
- 1 cup of water
- 1/4 tsp pepper
- 1/2 tsp salt

Directions:
1. Add all ingredients into the instant pot and stir well.
2. Seal pot with lid and cook on manual mode for 25 minutes.
3. Once done then allow to release pressure naturally then open the lid.
4. Stir well and serve.

Nutritional Value (Amount per Serving):
Calories 237; Fat 4.5 g; Carbohydrates 37.5 g; Sugar 1.9 g; Protein 13.2 g; Cholesterol 0 mg

Ham & Pinto Beans

Preparation Time: 10 minutes; Cooking Time: 60 minutes; Serve: 8
Ingredients:

- 32 oz pinto beans, rinsed
- 3 tbsp dried onion, minced
- 2 cups ham
- Pepper

- Salt

Directions:
1. Add all ingredients into the instant pot and stir well.
2. Pour enough water to the pot to cover the beans.
3. Seal pot with lid and cook on manual mode for 60 minutes.
4. Once done then allow to release pressure naturally for 10 minutes then release using the quick-release method. Open the lid.
5. Stir well and serve.

Nutritional Value (Amount per Serving):
Calories 450; Fat 4.3 g; Carbohydrates 72.6 g; Sugar 2.6 g; Protein 29.9 g; Cholesterol 19 mg

Sweet Baked Beans

Preparation Time: 10 minutes; Cooking Time: 40 minutes; Serve: 12
Ingredients:
- 15 oz dry pinto beans
- 1/2 cup water
- 1 tbsp olive oil
- 1/2 cup brown sugar
- 1/2 tsp liquid smoke
- 3 tbsp apple cider vinegar
- 1 1/2 tbsp brown mustard
- 1/2 cup ketchup
- 2/3 cup BBQ sauce
- 1/2 bell pepper, chopped
- 1 onion, chopped
- 6 bacon slices, cooked and chopped
- 8 cups of water
- 1 tsp salt

Directions:
1. Add water, beans, and salt into the instant pot.
2. Seal pot with lid and cook on manual high pressure for 25 minutes.
3. Once done then allow to release pressure naturally then open the lid.
4. Drain beans well and set aside.
5. Add oil into the instant pot and set the pot on sauté mode.
6. Add onion and bell pepper and cook until tender.
7. Add BBQ sauce, liquid smoke, vinegar, mustard, ketchup, water, brown sugar, and beans and stir everything well.
8. Seal pot with lid and cook on manual high pressure for 15 minutes.
9. Once done then allow to release pressure naturally then open the lid.
10. Add bacon and stir well.
11. Serve and enjoy.

Nutritional Value (Amount per Serving):
Calories 244; Fat 5.7 g; Carbohydrates 37.1 g; Sugar 13.2 g; Protein 11.4 g; Cholesterol 10 mg

Easy Baked Beans

Preparation Time: 10 minutes; Cooking Time: 40 minutes; Serve: 20
Ingredients:
- 1 lb navy beans, soak in water for overnight
- 3/4 cup maple syrup
- 1 cup of water
- 1 onion, chopped
- 1 lb bacon, cut into small pieces
- 8 tbsp brown sugar
- 3/4 tsp mustard
- 2 tbsp apple cider vinegar
- 1 cup ketchup

Directions:
1. Add all ingredients into the instant pot and stir well.
2. Seal pot with lid and cook on manual high pressure for 40 minutes.

3. Once done then allow to release pressure naturally then open the lid.
4. Stir well and serve.

Nutritional Value (Amount per Serving):
    Calories 258; Fat 9.9 g; Carbohydrates 29.1 g; Sugar 14.4 g; Protein 13.8 g; Cholesterol 25 mg

Sweet & Tender Lima Beans

Preparation Time: 10 minutes; Cooking Time: 7 minutes; Serve: 10
Ingredients:
- 28 oz fresh lima beans
- 1 bay leaf
- 2 tbsp butter
- 3 cups of water
- 1/4 tsp pepper
- 1/2 tsp salt

Directions:
1. Add all ingredients into the instant pot and stir well.
2. Seal pot with lid and cook on manual high pressure for 7 minutes.
3. Once done then release pressure using the quick-release method than open the lid.
4. Stir well and serve.

Nutritional Value (Amount per Serving):
    Calories 110; Fat 3 g; Carbohydrates 16.1 g; Sugar 1.2 g; Protein 5.5 g; Cholesterol 6 mg

Flavorful Onion Rice

Preparation Time: 10 minutes; Cooking Time: 3 minutes; Serve: 6
Ingredients:
- 2 cups white rice, uncooked and rinsed
- 1/4 cup ghee, melted
- 2 garlic cloves, minced
- 1 tbsp fresh parsley, chopped
- 1/2 onion, sliced
- 4 oz mushrooms, sliced
- 1/4 cup water
- 1 1/4 cups chicken broth
- 10 oz can onion soup
- 1/4 tsp pepper
- 1/4 tsp kosher salt

Directions:
1. Add all ingredients into the instant pot and stir well.
2. Seal pot with lid and cook on manual high pressure for 3 minutes.
3. Once done then allow to release pressure naturally for 5 minutes then release using the quick-release method. Open the lid.
4. Fluff rice using a fork and serve.

Nutritional Value (Amount per Serving):
    Calories 335; Fat 9.8 g; Carbohydrates 53.7 g; Sugar 2.5 g; Protein 7 g; Cholesterol 24 mg

Black Bean Rice

Preparation Time: 10 minutes; Cooking Time: 33 minutes; Serve: 6
Ingredients:
- 1 1/2 cups dry black beans, soaked in water for 2-3 hours and drained
- 3 cups of water
- 2 cups vegetable broth
- 14 oz can tomatoes, diced
- 1 1/2 cups brown rice, rinsed
- 1 tsp olive oil
- 1/4 tsp cayenne
- 1/2 tsp oregano
- 1 tsp chili powder
- 1 tsp cumin
- 2 garlic cloves, minced
- 1 onion, diced
- 1/2 tsp salt

Directions:

1. Add oil into the instant pot and set the pot on sauté mode.
2. Add garlic and onion and sauté for 2-3 minutes.
3. Add rice, beans, tomatoes, seasonings, broth, and water and stir to combine.
4. Seal pot with lid and cook on manual high pressure for 30 minutes.
5. Once done then allow to release pressure naturally for 10 minutes then release using the quick-release method. Open the lid.
6. Stir well and serve.

Nutritional Value (Amount per Serving):
Calories 383; Fat 3.4 g; Carbohydrates 72.7 g; Sugar 4.4 g; Protein 16.7 g; Cholesterol 0 mg

Nutritious Lentils Rice

Preparation Time: 10 minutes; Cooking Time: 24 minutes; Serve: 6
Ingredients:
- 1 1/2 cups brown rice
- 3 1/2 cups vegetable broth
- 1 cup dry brown lentils
- 1 1/2 tsp curry powder
- 1 1/2 tsp ground cumin
- 1/2 tbsp garlic powder
- 2 tbsp olive oil
- 1/2 cup mushrooms, chopped
- 1/2 cup bell pepper, chopped
- 1/2 cup onion, chopped

Directions:
1. Add oil into the instant pot and set the pot on sauté mode.
2. Add onion, mushrooms, and bell pepper and sauté until vegetables are translucent.
3. Add spices and stir well.
4. Add rice, lentils, and broth and stir well.
5. Seal pot with lid and cook on manual high pressure for 24 minutes.
6. Once done then allow to release pressure naturally for 15 minutes then release using the quick-release method. Open the lid.
7. Stir well and serve.

Nutritional Value (Amount per Serving):
Calories 261; Fat 7.1 g; Carbohydrates 41.2 g; Sugar 1.8 g; Protein 7.9 g; Cholesterol 0 mg

Cheesy Beef Rice

Preparation Time: 10 minutes; Cooking Time: 17 minutes; Serve: 4
Ingredients:
- 1 lb lean ground beef
- 2 cups cheddar cheese, shredded
- 8 oz can corn
- 10 oz can tomato soup
- 2 cups long-grain rice
- 1 1/2 tsp garlic powder
- 1 1/2 tsp onion powder
- 2 1/2 cups milk
- 10 oz chicken broth
- 1/2 tsp pepper
- 1 1/2 tsp salt

Directions:
1. Spray instant pot from inside with cooking spray.
2. Add beef into the pot and cook until meat is no longer pink.
3. Add broth, garlic powder, onion powder, milk, pepper, and salt and stir well.
4. Add rice and stir everything well.
5. Add corn and tomato soup. Do not stir.
6. Seal pot with lid and cook on manual high pressure for 7 minutes.
7. Once done then release pressure using the quick-release method than open the lid.
8. Add cheese and stir until cheese is melted.
9. Serve and enjoy.

Nutritional Value (Amount per Serving):

Calories 970; Fat 31.4 g; Carbohydrates 104.8 g; Sugar 15.7 g; Protein 64.5 g; Cholesterol 173 mg

Coconut Beans & Rice

Preparation Time: 10 minutes; Cooking Time: 10 minutes; Serve: 6

Ingredients:

- 15 oz can red kidney beans
- 1/2 tsp allspice
- 3/4 cup water
- 3/4 cup coconut milk
- 2 cups long-grain rice, rinsed
- 1/4 cup green onion, chopped
- 3 garlic cloves, minced
- 1 onion, chopped
- 1 tbsp olive oil
- 1/4 tsp pepper
- 1 1/2 tsp salt

Directions:

1. Add oil into the instant pot and set the pot on sauté mode.
2. Add onion and sauté for 3 minutes.
3. Add green onion and garlic and sauté for a minute.
4. Add rice, allspice, water, coconut milk, pepper, and salt and stir well.
5. Add beans on top and don't stir.
6. Seal pot with lid and cook on manual high pressure for 6 minutes.
7. Once done then allow to release pressure naturally for 10 minutes then release using the quick-release method. Open the lid.
8. Fluff rice using a fork and serve.

Nutritional Value (Amount per Serving):

Calories 385; Fat 10.2 g; Carbohydrates 64.7 g; Sugar 3.3 g; Protein 9.2 g; Cholesterol 0 mg

Mushroom Brown Rice

Preparation Time: 10 minutes; Cooking Time: 35 minutes; Serve: 4

Ingredients:

- 1 cup of brown rice
- 1 1/2 tbsp chives, chopped
- 2 tbsp butter
- 1 1/4 cup vegetable broth
- 1 lb mushrooms, sliced
- 1/2 tsp dried thyme
- 1 1/2 tsp Worcestershire sauce
- 2 garlic cloves, minced
- 1 onion, diced
- 1 tbsp olive oil
- Pepper
- Salt

Directions:

1. Add oil into the instant pot and set the pot on sauté mode.
2. Add garlic and onion and sauté for 2-3 minutes.
3. Add Worcestershire sauce, thyme, and mushrooms and cook for 4-5 minutes.
4. Add broth and rice and stir well.
5. Seal pot with lid and cook on high pressure for 25 minutes.
6. Once done then release pressure using the quick-release method than open the lid.
7. Add butter and stir until butter is melted.
8. Garnish with chives and serve.

Nutritional Value (Amount per Serving):

Calories 305; Fat 11.3 g; Carbohydrates 43.8 g; Sugar 3.8 g; Protein 9.2 g; Cholesterol 15 mg

Simple & Delicious Parmesan Rice

Preparation Time: 10 minutes; Cooking Time: 23 minutes; Serve: 4

Ingredients:

- 1 cup Jasmine rice
- 1/4 cup parmesan cheese, shredded
- 1 cup vegetable broth
- 1/2 cup sherry
- 2 garlic cloves, minced
- 1/2 small onion, diced
- 3 tbsp butter

Directions:

1. Add butter into the instant pot and set the pot on sauté mode.
2. Add garlic, onion, and rice and stir for 2-3 minutes.
3. Add broth and sherry and stir well.
4. Seal pot with lid and cook on manual high pressure for 20 minutes.
5. Once done then allow to release pressure naturally for 10 minutes then release using the quick-release method. Open the lid.
6. Fluff rice with a fork. Add cheese and stir well.
7. Serve and enjoy.

Nutritional Value (Amount per Serving):

Calories 281; Fat 10.5 g; Carbohydrates 37.9 g; Sugar 0.6 g; Protein 6.8 g; Cholesterol 28 mg

Chicken Cheese Rice

Preparation Time: 10 minutes; Cooking Time: 10 minutes; Serve: 4
Ingredients:

- 1 1/2 lbs chicken breasts, skinless, boneless, and cut into chunks
- 4 oz cream cheese, cut into chunks
- 1 tbsp fresh parsley, chopped
- 1/2 cup cheddar cheese, shredded
- 1 1/2 cups parmesan cheese, shredded
- 1/2 tsp onion powder
- 1 1/2 tsp garlic powder
- 2 cups long-grain rice, uncooked
- 10 oz can chicken soup
- 1 1/2 cup heavy cream
- 2 1/2 cups water
- 1 onion, chopped
- 2 tbsp butter
- 1/2 tsp pepper
- 1 tsp salt

Directions:

1. Add butter into the instant pot and set the pot on sauté mode.
2. Add onion and chicken to the pot and cook for 4-5 minutes.
3. Add chicken soup, heavy cream and water and stir well.
4. Add rice, onion powder, garlic powder, pepper, and salt.
5. Seal pot with lid and cook on manual high pressure for 5 minutes.
6. Once done then release pressure using the quick-release method than open the lid.
7. Stir in cheddar cheese, parmesan cheese, cream cheese, and parsley.
8. Stir well and serve.

Nutritional Value (Amount per Serving):

Calories 1073; Fat 52.2 g; Carbohydrates 80.5 g; Sugar 2.1 g; Protein 66.7 g; Cholesterol 279 mg

Flavorful Fajita Rice

Preparation Time: 10 minutes; Cooking Time: 12 minutes; Serve: 6
Ingredients:

- 2 cups long-grain rice, rinsed
- 4 tbsp sour cream
- 2 cups vegetable broth
- 4 tbsp fajita seasoning
- 1 tomato, diced
- 3 bell peppers, diced
- 1 onion, diced
- 2 chicken breasts, cubed
- 1 tbsp olive oil

Directions:

1. Add oil into the pot and set the pot on sauté mode.
2. Add chicken and cook until lightly brown.
3. Add bell peppers and onion and cook for 3-4 minutes.
4. Add tomatoes and stir well.
5. Add rice, broth, and fajita seasoning and stir well.
6. Seal pot with lid and cook on manual high pressure for 8 minutes.
7. Once done then release pressure using the quick-release method than open the lid.
8. Stir in sour cream and serve.

Nutritional Value (Amount per Serving):

Calories 417; Fat 8.7 g; Carbohydrates 60.8 g; Sugar 4.4 g; Protein 21.2 g; Cholesterol 47 mg

Creamy Pea Risotto

Preparation Time: 10 minutes; Cooking Time: 3 minutes; Serve: 4

Ingredients:

- 1 cup white rice, uncooked
- 3/4 cup asparagus, chopped
- 1 cup peas
- 1/2 tbsp lemon zest
- 1 cup parmesan cheese, shredded
- 1 3/4 cup vegetable broth
- 2 garlic cloves, minced
- 1/2 onion, chopped
- 2 tbsp butter

Directions:

1. Add butter, garlic, onion, rice, and broth into the instant pot and stir well.
2. Seal pot with lid and cook on manual high pressure for 3 minutes.
3. Once done then release pressure using the quick-release method than open the lid.
4. Stir in asparagus, peas, lemon zest, and cheese. Cover with lid and let sit for 5 minutes.
5. Serve and enjoy.

Nutritional Value (Amount per Serving):

Calories 302; Fat 8.4 g; Carbohydrates 15.8 g; Sugar 3.5 g; Protein 10.5 g; Cholesterol 20 mg

Quick & Easy Chicken Rice

Preparation Time: 10 minutes; Cooking Time: 12 minutes; Serve: 4

Ingredients:

- 1 cup jasmine rice, uncooked
- 1/4 cup fresh cilantro, chopped
- 1 cup cheddar cheese, shredded
- 1 cup of water
- 2 tbsp butter
- 1 tsp cumin
- 1 fresh lime juice
- 1 cup corn kernels
- 1 small onion, diced
- 1 1/2 tsp garlic salt
- 14 oz can tomatoes, diced
- 1 lb chicken, skinless, boneless, and cut into cubes

Directions:

1. Add chicken, water, butter, cumin, garlic salt, lime juice, rice, corn, onion, and tomatoes in the instant pot and stir well to combine.
2. Seal pot with lid and cook on poultry mode for 12 minutes.
3. Once done then allow to release pressure naturally for 10 minutes then release using the quick-release method. Open the lid.
4. Fluff rice with a fork. Add cilantro and cheese and stir until cheese is melted.
5. Serve and enjoy.

Nutritional Value (Amount per Serving):

Calories 566; Fat 19.2 g; Carbohydrates 52.3 g; Sugar 6 g; Protein 45.6 g; Cholesterol 132 mg

Garlic Turmeric Rice

Preparation Time: 10 minutes; Cooking Time: 7 minutes; Serve: 4

Ingredients:

- 1 cup jasmine rice, uncooked and rinsed
- 1/4 tsp garlic powder
- 3/4 tsp turmeric
- 1 tbsp olive oil
- 1 cup of water
- 1/2 tsp salt

Directions:

1. Add oil into the instant pot and set the pot on sauté mode.
2. Add turmeric, garlic powder, rice, and salt and stir for 1-2 minutes.
3. Add water and stir everything well.
4. Seal pot with lid and cook on manual high pressure for 6 minutes.
5. Once done then allow to release pressure naturally for 10 minutes then release using the quick-release method. Open the lid.
6. Fluff the rice with a fork and serve.

Nutritional Value (Amount per Serving):

Calories 192; Fat 3.5 g; Carbohydrates 36.4 g; Sugar 0.1 g; Protein 3.1 g; Cholesterol 0 mg

Flavorful Rice Pilaf

Preparation Time: 10 minutes; Cooking Time: 9 minutes; Serve: 4

Ingredients:

- 1/3 cup orzo rice, uncooked
- 1 tbsp fresh parsley, chopped
- 1/2 tsp paprika
- 1/4 tsp onion powder
- 1/2 tsp garlic powder
- 1 1/2 cups vegetable broth
- 1 cup white rice, uncooked and rinsed
- 1/4 cup olive oil
- 1/4 tsp pepper
- 3/4 tsp sea salt

Directions:

1. Add oil into the pot and set the pot on sauté mode.
2. Add orzo and cook for 2-3 minutes. Add rice and cook for 3-4 minutes.
3. Add paprika, onion powder, garlic powder, pepper, broth, and salt and stir well.
4. Sal pot with lid and cook on manual high pressure for 3 minutes.
5. Once done then allow to release pressure naturally for 10 minutes then release using the quick-release method. Open the lid.
6. Stir well and serve.

Nutritional Value (Amount per Serving):

Calories 315; Fat 13.6 g; Carbohydrates 42.2 g; Sugar 0.6 g; Protein 5.9 g; Cholesterol 0 mg

Perfect Jasmine Rice

Preparation Time: 10 minutes; Cooking Time: 5 minutes; Serve: 4

Ingredients:

- 2 cups Jasmine rice, rinsed and drained
- 1 tsp olive oil
- 2 cups of water
- 1 tsp salt

Directions:

1. Add all ingredients into the instant pot and stir well.
2. Seal pot with lid and cook on manual high pressure for 5 minutes.
3. Once done then allow to release pressure naturally for 10 minutes then release using the quick-release method. Open the lid.
4. Fluff rice with a fork and serve.

Nutritional Value (Amount per Serving):
Calories 330; Fat 1.2 g; Carbohydrates 72 g; Sugar 0 g; Protein 6 g; Cholesterol 0 mg

Broccoli Rice

Preparation Time: 10 minutes; Cooking Time: 15 minutes; Serve: 4
Ingredients:
- 2 cups broccoli, chopped
- 1/2 small onion, chopped
- 1 cup cheddar cheese, shredded
- 4 oz cream cheese, cut into cubes
- 2 1/4 cup vegetable broth
- 1 cup rice, uncooked and rinsed

Directions:
1. Add all ingredients to the instant pot and stir well.
2. Seal pot with lid and cook on high pressure for 15 minutes.
3. Once done then release pressure using the quick-release method than open the lid.
4. Stir well and serve.

Nutritional Value (Amount per Serving):
Calories 422; Fat 20.5 g; Carbohydrates 42.4 g; Sugar 1.8 g; Protein 16.6 g; Cholesterol 61 mg

Spanish rice

Preparation Time: 10 minutes; Cooking Time: 12 minutes; Serve: 4
Ingredients:
- 2 cups white rice, uncooked
- 1 cup tomatoes, chopped
- 2 1/2 cups vegetable broth
- 2 garlic cloves, minced
- 1/4 cup green onions, sliced
- 1 1/2 tsp taco seasoning
- 2 tbsp tomato paste
- 1/2 jalapeno pepper, minced
- 1/4 cup cilantro, chopped
- 1 tsp olive oil
- 2 tsp sea salt

Directions:
1. Add oil into the instant pot and set the pot on sauté mode.
2. Add garlic and green onions and sauté for 2 minutes.
3. Add remaining ingredients and stir well.
4. Seal pot with lid and cook on manual high pressure for 10 minutes.
5. Once done then allow to release pressure naturally then open the lid.
6. Fluff the rice with a fork and serve.

Nutritional Value (Amount per Serving):
Calories 530; Fat 10.5 g; Carbohydrates 88.9 g; Sugar 2.9 g; Protein 18.4 g; Cholesterol 21 mg

Onion Pepper Couscous

Preparation Time: 10 minutes; Cooking Time: 8 minutes; Serve: 4
Ingredients:
- 1 cup dry couscous, rinsed and drained
- 1 1/2 cups vegetable broth
- 1/4 cup red pepper, diced
- 1/2 onion, diced
- 1/2 tsp sesame oil
- 2 tbsp vinegar
- 1/4 tsp ground cinnamon
- 1/2 tsp ground coriander
- 1/4 tsp pepper
- Salt

Directions:
1. Add oil into the instant pot and set the pot on sauté mode.

2. Add onion and pepper and sauté for 3-5 minutes.
3. Add remaining ingredients and stir well.
4. Seal pot with lid and cook on high pressure for 3 minutes.
5. Once done then allow to release pressure naturally then open the lid.
6. Fluff with a fork and serve.

Nutritional Value (Amount per Serving):

Calories 192; Fat 1.4 g; Carbohydrates 35.9 g; Sugar 1.3 g; Protein 7.6 g; Cholesterol 0 mg

Lemon Snap Pea Couscous

Preparation Time: 10 minutes; Cooking Time: 6 minutes; Serve: 6

Ingredients:
- 1 cup couscous
- 7 oz snap peas, trimmed
- 1 tbsp fresh lemon juice
- 1/2 tsp dried dill
- 2 cups vegetable broth
- 1 tbsp olive oil
- 1/4 tsp pepper
- 1/2 tsp salt

Directions:
1. Add oil into the pot and set the pot on sauté mode.
2. Add couscous to the pot and stir for a minute. Add broth and stir well.
3. Seal pot with lid and cook on high pressure for 5 minutes.
4. Once done then release pressure using the quick-release method than open the lid.
5. Add snap peas, pepper, and salt. Stir well.
6. Cover the pot again with lid and cook on high pressure for 1 minute.
7. Once done then release pressure using the quick-release method than open the lid.
8. Stir in lemon juice and serve.

Nutritional Value (Amount per Serving):

Calories 169; Fat 3.1 g; Carbohydrates 27.6 g; Sugar 2.2 g; Protein 7.1 g; Cholesterol 0 mg

Pearl Barley

Preparation Time: 10 minutes; Cooking Time: 25 minutes; Serve: 4

Ingredients:
- 1 1/2 cups pearl barley, rinsed and drained
- 3 cups of water
- 3/4 tsp salt

Directions:
1. Add all ingredients to the instant pot and stir well.
2. Seal pot with lid and cook on manual high pressure for 25 minutes.
3. Once done then allow to release pressure naturally then open the lid.
4. Stir and serve.

Nutritional Value (Amount per Serving):

Calories 264; Fat 0.9 g; Carbohydrates 58.3 g; Sugar 0.6 g; Protein 7.4 g; Cholesterol 0 mg

Spanish Quinoa

Preparation Time: 10 minutes; Cooking Time: 10 minutes; Serve: 4

Ingredients:
- 1 cup quinoa, rinsed and drained
- 1 lb ground meat, taco seasoned and cooked
- 1 1/2 cups vegetable broth
- 1 bell pepper, diced
- 1 cup black beans, rinsed and drained
- 1 onion, diced

Directions:
1. Spray instant pot from inside with cooking spray.

2. Add all ingredients into the pot and stir well.
3. Seal pot with lid and cook on manual high pressure for 10 minutes.
4. Once done then release pressure using the quick-release method than open the lid.
5. Serve and enjoy.

Nutritional Value (Amount per Serving):

Calories 537; Fat 13.9 g; Carbohydrates 72.7 g; Sugar 7.9 g; Protein 28.9 g; Cholesterol 30 mg

Buttery Scallions Risotto

Preparation Time: 10 minutes; Cooking Time: 11 minutes; Serve: 4

Ingredients:

- 1 cup Arborio rice
- 2 tbsp butter
- 1/4 cup parsley, chopped
- 4 scallions, chopped
- 2 cups vegetable stock
- 2 tbsp white wine
- 1/2 tsp salt

Directions:

1. Add butter into the pot and set the pot on sauté mode.
2. Add scallions and parsley and sauté for 2 minutes.
3. Add remaining ingredients and stir well.
4. Seal pot with lid and cook on high pressure for 9 minutes.
5. Once done then release pressure using the quick-release method than open the lid.
6. Stir well and serve.

Nutritional Value (Amount per Serving):

Calories 237; Fat 6.1 g; Carbohydrates 38.8 g; Sugar 0.8 g; Protein 3.8 g; Cholesterol 15 mg

Simple Paprika Rice

Preparation Time: 10 minutes; Cooking Time: 7 minutes; Serve: 6

Ingredients:

- 2 cups rice, uncooked
- 2 1/2 tsp paprika
- 2 1/2 cups vegetable broth
- 2 tbsp butter
- 1 cube chicken bouillon
- 1/4 tsp pepper
- 1 tsp salt

Directions:

1. Add all ingredients to the instant pot and stir well.
2. Seal pot with lid and cook on manual high pressure for 7 minutes.
3. Once done then release pressure using the quick-release method than open the lid.
4. Fluff rice with a fork and serve.

Nutritional Value (Amount per Serving):

Calories 280; Fat 5 g; Carbohydrates 50.4 g; Sugar 0.6 g; Protein 6.7 g; Cholesterol 10 mg

Delicious Potato Risotto

Preparation Time: 10 minutes; Cooking Time: 13 minutes; Serve: 4

Ingredients:

- 2 cups rice, uncooked
- 1 potato, peeled and cubed
- 2 tbsp tomato paste
- 4 tbsp white wine
- 1 onion, chopped
- 4 cups vegetable stock
- 1 tbsp olive oil
- 1 tsp salt

Directions:

1. Add olive oil into the instant pot and set the pot on sauté mode.

2. Add onion and sauté for 2 minutes. Add rice and stir for 2-3 minutes.
3. Add wine and stir for 2-3 minutes.
4. Add stock, potatoes, tomato paste, and salt. Stir well.
5. Seal pot with lid and cook on manual high pressure for 5 minutes.
6. Once done then allow to release pressure naturally then open the lid.
7. Serve and enjoy.

Nutritional Value (Amount per Serving):
Calories 436; Fat 4.3 g; Carbohydrates 86.8 g; Sugar 3.4 g; Protein 8.5 g; Cholesterol 0 mg

Jalapeno Brown Rice

Preparation Time: 10 minutes; Cooking Time: 19 minutes; Serve: 3

Ingredients:
- 1 cup brown rice, uncooked
- 1 jalapeno pepper, sliced
- 3 garlic cloves, minced
- 4 tbsp tomato paste
- 1 cup of water
- 1 tbsp olive oil
- 1 onion, chopped
- 1/2 tsp salt

Directions:
1. Add oil into the instant pot and set the pot on sauté mode.
2. Add onion and sauté for 3 minutes. Add garlic and sauté for a minute.
3. Add brown rice, jalapeno, tomato paste, water, and salt. Stir well.
4. Seal pot with lid and cook on manual high pressure for 15 minutes.
5. Once done then allow to release pressure naturally then open the lid.
6. Serve and enjoy.

Nutritional Value (Amount per Serving):
Calories 307; Fat 6.6 g; Carbohydrates 57 g; Sugar 4.3 g; Protein 6.3 g; Cholesterol 0 mg

Chapter 4: Broths & Sauces

Flavorful Spaghetti Sauce

Preparation Time: 10 minutes; Cooking Time: 20 minutes; Serve: 8

Ingredients:

- 28 oz can whole tomatoes
- 1/2 tsp oregano
- 1 tbsp basil
- 1 tbsp onion, minced
- 14 oz tomatoes, diced
- 1 onion, diced
- 6 oz tomato paste
- 6 oz water
- 7.5 oz tomato sauce
- 12 oz spicy sausage
- Salt

Directions:

1. Spray instant pot from inside with cooking spray and set on sauté mode.
2. Add sausage and onions and cook until completely cooked.
3. Add remaining ingredients into the pot and stir to combine.
4. Seal pot with a lid and select soup mode and set timer for 20 minutes.
5. Once done then release pressure using the quick-release method than open the lid.
6. Stir well and serve.

Nutritional Value (Amount per Serving):

Calories 197; Fat 12 g; Carbohydrates 13.4 g; Sugar 7.8 g; Protein 10.6 g; Cholesterol 24 mg

Rich & Tasty Marinara Sauce

Preparation Time: 10 minutes; Cooking Time: 20 minutes; Serve: 6

Ingredients:

- 8 large tomatoes, peeled and diced
- 2 tsp vinegar
- 1 tsp marjoram
- 1 tsp dried oregano
- 1 1/2 tsp dried basil
- 1 tbsp honey
- 1/2 cup red wine
- 1 bay leaf
- 5 garlic cloves, minced
- 1/2 onion, chopped
- 3 tbsp olive oil
- 1/4 tsp pepper
- 1 tsp salt

Directions:

1. Add oil into the instant pot and set the pot on sauté mode.
2. Add garlic and onion to the pot and sauté until onion is softened.
3. Add bay leaf and tomatoes to the pot and sauté for 4-5 minutes.
4. Add remaining ingredients except for vinegar and stir everything well.
5. Seal pot with lid and cook on manual high pressure for 5 minutes.
6. Once done then release pressure using the quick-release method than open the lid.
7. Add vinegar and stir well. Using immersion blender blend until smooth.
8. Pour sauce into the jars and store in the refrigerator for up to three weeks.

Nutritional Value (Amount per Serving):

Calories 140; Fat 7.6 g; Carbohydrates 14.9 g; Sugar 9.9 g; Protein 2.5 g; Cholesterol 0 mg

Italian Beef Bolognese Sauce

Preparation Time: 10 minutes; Cooking Time: 30 minutes; Serve: 8

Ingredients:

- 28 oz can tomatoes, crushed
- 1/3 cup red wine
- 1 lb ground beef
- 1/2 tsp thyme

- 2 tsp sugar
- 3 garlic cloves, minced
- 1 celery stalk, chopped
- 1 large carrot, peeled and chopped
- 1/2 onion, chopped
- 2 tbsp butter
- 1 tsp salt

Directions:
1. Add butter into the instant pot and set the pot on sauté mode.
2. Once butter is melted then add celery, carrot, and onion and sauté for 5 minutes.
3. Add thyme, sugar, garlic, and salt and sauté for a minute.
4. Add meat and sauté until meat is no longer pink.
5. Add red wine and cook for 2-3 minutes.
6. Add tomatoes and stir everything well.
7. Seal pot with a lid and select soup mode and set timer for 15 minutes.
8. Once done then allow to release pressure naturally then open the lid.
9. Stir well and serve on top of spaghetti.

Nutritional Value (Amount per Serving):
Calories 172; Fat 6.4 g; Carbohydrates 8.3 g; Sugar 5.2 g; Protein 18.4 g; Cholesterol 58 mg

Perfect Cherry Tomato Sauce

Preparation Time: 10 minutes; Cooking Time: 20 minutes; Serve: 6
Ingredients:
- 4 cups cherry tomatoes
- 3 garlic clove, minced
- 2 tbsp olive oil
- 1 1/2 tsp Italian seasoning
- 1/2 cup water
- Pepper
- Salt

Directions:
1. Add cherry tomatoes and water into the instant pot.
2. Seal pot with lid and cook on manual high pressure for 5 minutes.
3. Once done then release pressure using the the quick-release method than open the lid.
4. Transfer tomatoes with liquid in a food processor and process until smooth.
5. Add olive oil into the instant pot and set the pot on sauté mode.
6. Add garlic and sauté for a minute.
7. Add blended tomato mixture and Italian seasoning to the pot and cook for 5 minutes or until desired thickness is get. Stirring every 1 minute.
8. Serve and enjoy.

Nutritional Value (Amount per Serving):
Calories 67; Fat 5.3 g; Carbohydrates 5.3 g; Sugar 3.3 g; Protein 1.2 g; Cholesterol 1 mg

Cranberry Orange Sauce

Preparation Time: 10 minutes; Cooking Time: 5 minutes; Serve: 10
Ingredients:
- 1 apple, peeled, cored, and chopped
- 1/2 cup orange juice
- 12 oz cranberries
- 1/2 cup maple syrup

Directions:
1. Add all ingredients into the instant pot and stir well.
2. Seal pot with lid and cook on manual high pressure for 3 minutes.
3. Once done then allow to release pressure naturally for 10 minutes then release using the quick-release method.
4. Open the lid. Lightly mash cranberry with a wooden spoon and cook on sauté mode for 1-2 minutes.

5. Pour sauce into the jar and store in the refrigerator.

Nutritional Value (Amount per Serving):
    Calories 77; Fat 0.1 g; Carbohydrates 18 g; Sugar 14 g; Protein 0.1 g; Cholesterol 0 mg

Meaty Pasta Sauce

Preparation Time: 10 minutes; Cooking Time: 20 minutes; Serve: 6

Ingredients:
- 1 lb ground pork
- 2 tbsp tomato paste
- 1 cup can tomato sauce
- 28 oz can tomatoes, crushed
- 1/2 tsp red pepper, crushed
- 1 tsp fennel seeds
- 1/2 cup red wine
- 2 garlic cloves, chopped
- 1 onion, chopped
- 3 tbsp olive oil
- 1/2 tsp pepper
- 2 tsp kosher salt

Directions:
1. Add olive oil into the instant pot and set the pot on sauté mode.
2. Add meat to the pot and cook until meat is no longer pink.
3. Add garlic and onion and cook for 2 minutes.
4. Add remaining ingredients and stir everything well.
5. Seal pot with lid and cook on manual high pressure for 15 minutes.
6. Once done then allow to release pressure naturally then open the lid.
7. Stir well and serve.

Nutritional Value (Amount per Serving):
    Calories 240; Fat 9.9 g; Carbohydrates 13.6 g; Sugar 8.3 g; Protein 22.2 g; Cholesterol 55 mg

Delicious Cherry Jam

Preparation Time: 10 minutes; Cooking Time: 7 minutes; Serve: 6

Ingredients:
- 1 lb cherries, clean and chopped
- 1 package pectin
- 3/4 cup honey
- 1/2 fresh lemon juice

Directions:
1. Set instant pot on sauté mode.
2. Add honey and cook for 1-2 minutes until just melted. Turn off the instant pot.
3. Add remaining ingredients and stir everything well.
4. Seal pot with lid and cook on manual high pressure for 5 minutes.
5. Once done then allow to release pressure naturally then open the lid.
6. Allow to cool completely then pour the jam in jar and store in the refrigerator.

Nutritional Value (Amount per Serving):
    Calories 219; Fat 0.1 g; Carbohydrates 56.5 g; Sugar 34.9 g; Protein 0.4 g; Cholesterol 0 mg

Homemade BBQ sauce

Preparation Time: 10 minutes; Cooking Time: 10 minutes; Serve: 12

Ingredients:
- 2 cups ketchup
- 1/4 cup Worcestershire sauce
- 1/2 cup brown sugar
- 1/2 cup apple cider vinegar
- 2 tbsp chili powder
- 5 garlic cloves, minced
- 3 tbsp olive oil
- 2 onions, chopped
- 1/4 tsp pepper
- 1 tsp salt

Directions:
1. Add oil into the instant pot and set the pot on sauté mode.

2. Add onion and sauté for 5 minutes.
3. Add ketchup, Worcestershire sauce, brown sugar, vinegar, chili powder, garlic, pepper, and salt. Stir well.
4. Seal pot with lid and cook on manual high pressure for 5 minutes.
5. Once done then allow to release pressure naturally for 5 minutes then release using the quick-release method. Open the lid.
6. Allow to cool completely then pour in jar and store in the refrigerator for a week.

Nutritional Value (Amount per Serving):
Calories 112; Fat 3.9 g; Carbohydrates 19.9 g; Sugar 16.9 g; Protein 1.1 g; Cholesterol 0 mg

Quick Enchilada Sauce

Preparation Time: 10 minutes; Cooking Time: 10 minutes; Serve: 6
Ingredients:
- 14 oz can roasted tomatoes
- 1/2 cup water
- 1 1/2 tsp chili powder
- 1 tsp ground cumin
- 1 chipotle chile in Adobo sauce
- 2 garlic cloves, minced
- 1/2 jalapeno pepper, sliced
- 1/2 bell pepper, chopped
- 1/2 onion, chopped
- 1 tsp salt

Directions:
1. Add all ingredients except tomatoes into the instant pot and stir well.
2. Pour tomatoes on top. Seal pot with lid and cook on manual high pressure for 10 minutes.
3. Once done then allow to release pressure naturally then open the lid.
4. Puree the sauce using an immersion blender.
5. Allow to cool completely then pour in jar and store in the refrigerator for a week.

Nutritional Value (Amount per Serving):
Calories 30; Fat 0.4 g; Carbohydrates 5.9 g; Sugar 2.6 g; Protein 1.1 g; Cholesterol 1 mg

Easy Pear Sauce

Preparation Time: 10 minutes; Cooking Time: 15 minutes; Serve: 6
Ingredients:
- 10 large pears, sliced
- 1 cup of orange juice
- 1/2 tsp nutmeg
- 1 1/2 tsp cinnamon

Directions:
1. Add all ingredients into the instant pot and stir everything well.
2. Seal pot with lid and cook on manual high pressure for 15 minutes.
3. Once done then allow to release pressure naturally then open the lid.
4. Puree the sauce using an immersion blender until get desired consistency.
5. Pour sauce in jar and store in the refrigerator.

Nutritional Value (Amount per Serving):
Calories 222; Fat 0.7 g; Carbohydrates 57.9 g; Sugar 37.5 g; Protein 1.6 g; Cholesterol 0 mg

Strawberry Jam

Preparation Time: 10 minutes; Cooking Time: 1 minute; Serve: 16
Ingredients:
- 1 1/2 lbs fresh strawberries, diced
- 2 tbsp fresh lemon juice
- 3/4 cup sugar
- 3 tsp water
- 2 tsp cornstarch

Directions:

1. Add strawberries, sugar, and lemon juice into the instant pot.
2. Seal pot with lid and cook on high pressure for 1 minute.
3. Once done then allow to release pressure naturally then open the lid.
4. In a small bowl, mix together cornstarch and water and pour into the pot.
5. Set pot on sauté mode and cook for 5 minutes or until jam is thickened.
6. Pour sauce in jar and store in the refrigerator.

Nutritional Value (Amount per Serving):
Calories 51; Fat 0.2 g; Carbohydrates 13 g; Sugar 11.5 g; Protein 0.3 g; Cholesterol 0 mg

Easy & Delicious Applesauce

Preparation Time: 10 minutes; Cooking Time: 5 minutes; Serve: 6
Ingredients:
- 3 lbs apples, peeled, cored, and diced
- 1/4 tsp ground ginger
- 1/2 tsp cinnamon
- 2 tbsp honey
- 1 tbsp fresh lemon juice
- 3/4 cup water

Directions:
1. Add all ingredients except honey into the instant pot and stir well.
2. Seal pot with lid and cook on manual high pressure for 5 minutes.
3. Once done then allow to release pressure naturally then open the lid.
4. Add honey and stir well. Using masher mash apples until get desired consistency.
5. Serve warm and enjoy.

Nutritional Value (Amount per Serving):
Calories 81; Fat 0.2 g; Carbohydrates 21.4 g; Sugar 17.4 g; Protein 0.4 g; Cholesterol 0 mg

Raspberry Jam

Preparation Time: 10 minutes; Cooking Time: 3 minutes; Serve: 6
Ingredients:
- 3 cups fresh raspberries, chopped
- 1 tbsp corn-starch
- 1 tbsp water
- 2 tbsp fresh lemon juice
- 1/2 cup sugar

Directions:
1. Add raspberries, lemon juice, and sugar into the instant pot and stir well.
2. Seal pot with lid and cook on manual high pressure for 3 minutes.
3. Once done then allow to release pressure naturally then open the lid.
4. Mix together water and corn-starch and pour into the pot.
5. Stir everything well. Allow to cool completely.
6. Pour into the jar and store in the refrigerator.

Nutritional Value (Amount per Serving):
Calories 101; Fat 0.4 g; Carbohydrates 25.3 g; Sugar 19.5 g; Protein 0.8 g; Cholesterol 0 mg

Perfect Blueberry Jam

Preparation Time: 10 minutes; Cooking Time: 8 minutes; Serve: 16
Ingredients:
- 3 cups blueberries
- 2 tbsp water
- 2 tbsp corn-starch
- 2 tbsp fresh lemon juice
- 3/4 cup sugar

Directions:
1. Add blueberries, lemon juice, and sugar into the instant pot and stir well.
2. Seal pot with lid and cook on manual high pressure for 3 minutes.

3. Once done then allow to release pressure naturally then open the lid.
4. In a small bowl, whisk together corn-starch and water and pour into the pot.
5. Set pot on sauté mode and cook until thickened, about 5 minutes. Stir constantly.
6. Allow to cool completely. Pour jam in jar and store in the refrigerator.

Nutritional Value (Amount per Serving):
   Calories 55; Fat 0.1 g; Carbohydrates 14.3 g; Sugar 12.1 g; Protein 0.2 g; Cholesterol 0 mg

Vegan Sauce

Preparation Time: 10 minutes; Cooking Time: 5 minutes; Serve: 8
Ingredients:
- 2 cups of water
- 1 tsp turmeric powder
- 1/2 cup nutritional yeast
- 1/2 cup cashews
- 2 garlic cloves, peeled
- 1/2 cup onion, chopped
- 1 cup carrot, chopped
- 2 cups potato, peeled and chopped
- 1 tsp salt

Directions:
1. Add all ingredients into the instant pot and stir well.
2. Seal pot with lid and cook on manual high pressure for 5 minutes.
3. Once done then release pressure using the quick-release method than open the lid.
4. Allow to cool for 15 minutes then using immersion blender puree the sauce until smooth.

Nutritional Value (Amount per Serving):
   Calories 110; Fat 4.6 g; Carbohydrates 13.1 g; Sugar 1.6 g; Protein 6.6 g; Cholesterol 0 mg

Cranberry Applesauce

Preparation Time: 10 minutes; Cooking Time: 4 hours; Serve: 24
Ingredients:
- 1/4 cup maple syrup
- 12 oz fresh cranberries
- 3 lbs apples, peel, core, and dice

Directions:
1. Add all ingredients into the instant pot and stir well.
2. Seal the pot with a lid and select slow cook mode and set a timer for 4 hours.
3. Using immersion blender puree the sauce until smooth.
4. Store in a container and serve.

Nutritional Value (Amount per Serving):
   Calories 31; Fat 0.1 g; Carbohydrates 7.3 g; Sugar 5.4 g; Protein 0.1 g; Cholesterol 0 mg

Orange Strawberry Jam

Preparation Time: 10 minutes; Cooking Time: 1 minute; Serve: 12
Ingredients:
- 2 lbs strawberries, hulled and halved
- 1/2 tsp orange zest
- 2 tbsp orange juice
- 2 tbsp lemon juice
- 1/2 cup sugar

Directions:
1. Add all ingredients into the instant pot and stir everything well.
2. Seal pot with lid and cook on manual high pressure for 1 minute.
3. Once done then allow to release pressure naturally then open the lid.
4. Blend the strawberry mixture using the immersion blender until smooth.
5. Serve and enjoy.

Nutritional Value (Amount per Serving):

Calories 57; Fat 0.3 g; Carbohydrates 14.5 g; Sugar 12.3 g; Protein 0.6 g; Cholesterol 0 mg

Curried Tomato Sauce

Preparation Time: 10 minutes; Cooking Time: 10 minutes; Serve: 8
Ingredients:

- 28 oz can tomatoes, crushed
- 1/2 cup coconut milk
- 1 tbsp thyme
- 1/4 tsp ground cinnamon
- 1/4 tsp red pepper flakes
- 1/2 tsp turmeric
- 1/2 tsp garam masala
- 1 tbsp fresh ginger, minced
- 2 garlic cloves, quartered
- 1/2 onion, peeled and diced
- 1/2 tsp pepper
- 1 tsp sea salt

Directions:

1. Add all ingredients into the instant pot and stir well.
2. Seal pot with lid and cook on manual mode for 10 minutes.
3. Once done then allow to release pressure naturally for 10 minutes then release using the quick-release method. Open the lid.
4. Puree the sauce using immersion blender until smooth.
5. Pour sauce into the container and store in the refrigerator.

Nutritional Value (Amount per Serving):
Calories 64; Fat 3.7 g; Carbohydrates 7.7 g; Sugar 4.2 g; Protein 1.5 g; Cholesterol 0 mg

Carrot Tomato Marinara Sauce

Preparation Time: 10 minutes; Cooking Time: 10 minutes; Serve: 6
Ingredients:

- 14 oz can tomatoes, diced
- 1 1/2 tsp dried oregano
- 2 tsp dried basil
- 1 carrot, diced
- 2 garlic cloves, minced
- 1 onion, chopped
- 2 tbsp olive oil
- 1/4 tsp pepper
- 3/4 tsp sea salt

Directions:

1. Add oil into the instant pot and set the pot on sauté mode.
2. Add carrots, garlic, and onion to the pot and sauté until softened.
3. Stir in oregano, basil, tomatoes, and salt.
4. Seal pot with lid and cook on manual high pressure for 10 minutes.
5. Once done then release pressure using the quick-release method than open the lid.
6. Puree the sauce using immersion blender until smooth.
7. Serve and enjoy.

Nutritional Value (Amount per Serving):
Calories 69; Fat 4.7 g; Carbohydrates 6.7 g; Sugar 3.6 g; Protein 1 g; Cholesterol 0 mg

Chunky Applesauce

Preparation Time: 10 minutes; Cooking Time: 12 minutes; Serve: 16
Ingredients:

- 4 pears, diced
- 4 apples, diced
- 1 1/2 tsp vanilla
- 1 1/2 tbsp ground cinnamon
- 1/3 cup maple syrup
- 3/4 cup water
- Pinch of salt

Directions:

1. Add all ingredients into the instant pot and stir well.

2. Seal pot with lid and cook on high pressure for 12 minutes.
3. Once done then allow to release pressure naturally for 10 minutes then release using the quick-release method. Open the lid.
4. Blend the sauce using immersion blender until get a chunky consistency.
5. Pour sauce in container and store in the refrigerator.

Nutritional Value (Amount per Serving):
   Calories 79; Fat 0.2 g; Carbohydrates 20.6 g; Sugar 14.9 g; Protein 0.4 g; Cholesterol 0 mg

Cranberry Ginger Sauce

Preparation Time: 10 minutes; Cooking Time: 1 minute; Serve: 8
Ingredients:

- 1 lb cranberries, rinsed and drained
- 1 tsp orange zest
- 1 tsp ginger root, grated
- 1 tsp cinnamon
- 1/2 cup sugar
- 1/4 cup orange juice

Directions:
1. Add all ingredients into the instant pot and stir well.
2. Seal pot with lid and cook on high pressure for 1 minute.
3. Once done then allow to release pressure naturally for 5 minutes then release using the quick-release method. Open the lid.
4. Pour sauce in container and store in the refrigerator.

Nutritional Value (Amount per Serving):
   Calories 82; Fat 0 g; Carbohydrates 18.8 g; Sugar 15.2 g; Protein 0.1 g; Cholesterol 0 mg

Turkey Broth

Preparation Time: 10 minutes; Cooking Time: 2 hours; Serve: 20
Ingredients:

- 2 lbs turkey bones
- 1 tsp whole peppercorns
- 2 celery stalks
- 1 bay leaf
- 1/2 onion
- 2 carrots, chopped
- Water

Directions:
1. Add all ingredients into the instant pot. Cover with water 2-inch below the maximum fill line.
2. Seal pot with lid and cook on high pressure for 2 hours.
3. Once done then allow to release pressure naturally then open the lid.
4. Strain the broth in container and store in the refrigerator.

Nutritional Value (Amount per Serving):
   Calories 21; Fat 1 g; Carbohydrates 1 g; Sugar 0.2 g; Protein 1 g; Cholesterol 6 mg

Chicken Broth

Preparation Time: 10 minutes; Cooking Time: 1 hour 20 minutes; Serve: 4
Ingredients:

- 2 lbs chicken carcass
- 8 cups of water
- 1 tsp apple cider vinegar
- 1/4 tsp pepper
- 1/2 tsp sea salt

Directions:
1. Add all ingredients into the instant pot.
2. Seal pot with lid and cook on high pressure for 1 hour 20 minutes.
3. Once done then allow to release pressure naturally then open the lid.

4. Strain the broth in container and store in the refrigerator.

Nutritional Value (Amount per Serving):

Calories 343; Fat 6.9 g; Carbohydrates 0.1 g; Sugar 0 g; Protein 65.7 g; Cholesterol 0.1 mg

Gluten-Free Bone Broth

Preparation Time: 10 minutes; Cooking Time: 1 hour 30 minutes; Serve: 12 cups

Ingredients:
- 1 lb chicken bones
- 1 tsp fish sauce
- 1 tbsp vinegar
- 15 whole black peppercorns
- 2 bay leaves
- 2 cups carrots, chopped
- 2 cups celery, chopped
- 2 cups onion, chopped
- Water

Directions:
1. Add all ingredients into the instant pot and stir well.
2. Add water 1-inch below the maximum fill line.
3. Seal the pot with a lid and cook on soup mode for 1 hour 30 minutes.
4. Once done then allow to release pressure naturally then open the lid.
5. Strain the broth in container and store in the refrigerator.

Nutritional Value (Amount per Serving):

Calories 100; Fat 5.8 g; Carbohydrates 4.4 g; Sugar 2 g; Protein 7.2 g; Cholesterol 32 mg

Hawaiian BBQ Sauce

Preparation Time: 10 minutes; Cooking Time: 15 minutes; Serve: 16

Ingredients:
- 1 3/4 cups ketchup
- 3/4 cup pineapple, diced
- 1/4 tsp red pepper flakes
- 2 onions, minced
- 2 tbsp Dijon mustard
- 2 garlic cloves
- 1/4 cup Worcestershire sauce
- 1/3 cup soy sauce
- 1/3 cup apple cider vinegar
- 6 dates, pitted
- 6 oz can pineapple juice
- 1/4 tsp pepper
- 1 tsp garlic salt

Directions:
1. Add all ingredients except pineapple into the instant pot and stir well.
2. Seal pot with lid and cook on manual high pressure for 15 minutes.
3. Once done then allow to release pressure naturally for 10 minutes then release using the quick-release method. Open the lid.
4. Blend sauce using the immersion blender until smooth.
5. Add pineapple and stir well. Pour sauce into the container and store in the refrigerator.

Nutritional Value (Amount per Serving):

Calories 59; Fat 0.2 g; Carbohydrates 14.1 g; Sugar 11.4 g; Protein 1.3 g; Cholesterol 0 mg

Chia Blackberry jam

Preparation Time: 10 minutes; Cooking Time: 6 hours; Serve: 6

Ingredients:
- 3 cups fresh blackberries
- 4 tbsp sugar
- 3 tbsp fresh lemon juice
- 5 tbsp butter
- 3 tbsp chia seeds

Directions:
1. Add all ingredients into the instant pot and stir well.

2. Seal the pot with a lid and select slow cook mode and set a timer for 6 hours.
3. Once done then release pressure using quick-release method than open the lid.
4. Pour into the container and store in the refrigerator.

Nutritional Value (Amount per Serving):

Calories 216; Fat 14.4 g; Carbohydrates 21.1 g; Sugar 11.7 g; Protein 3.5 g; Cholesterol 25 mg

Spicy Hot Sauce

Preparation Time: 10 minutes; Cooking Time: 2 minutes; Serve: 50
Ingredients:

- 1 lb jalapeno pepper, chopped
- 3 garlic cloves, peeled
- 1 bell pepper, roasted and chopped
- 1/2 cup water
- 1 cup vinegar
- Salt

Directions:
1. Add all ingredients into the instant pot and stir well.
2. Seal pot with lid and cook on manual high pressure for 2 minutes.
3. Once done then allow to release pressure naturally for 10 minutes then release using the quick-release method. Open the lid.
4. Blend the sauce using immersion blender until smooth.
5. Pour sauce into the container and store in the refrigerator.

Nutritional Value (Amount per Serving):

Calories 5; Fat 0.1 g; Carbohydrates 0.8 g; Sugar 0.5 g; Protein 0.2 g; Cholesterol 25 mg

Fish Stock

Preparation Time: 10 minutes; Cooking Time: 45 minutes; Serve: 6
Ingredients:

- 2 salmon heads
- 3 garlic cloves, minced
- 1 tbsp olive oil
- 2 celery stalk, chopped
- 1 carrot, chopped
- 1 lemongrass stalk, chopped

Directions:
1. Add oil into the instant pot and set the pot on sauté mode.
2. Add all ingredients and stir well.
3. Pour eight cups of water into the pot.
4. Seal pot with lid and cook on soup mode for 45 minutes.
5. Once done then allow to release pressure naturally for 10 minutes then release using the quick-release method. Open the lid.
6. Strain stock into the container and store in the refrigerator.

Nutritional Value (Amount per Serving):

Calories 113; Fat 5.9 g; Carbohydrates 4.5 g; Sugar 0.6 g; Protein 11.4 g; Cholesterol 25 mg

Beef Stock

Preparation Time: 10 minutes; Cooking Time: 20 minutes; Serve: 6
Ingredients:

- 1 3/4 lbs beef bones
- 1 celery stalk, chopped
- 3/4 cup apple cider vinegar
- 1 cup sauerkraut
- 1 tsp whole peppercorn
- 1 1/4 cups tomatoes, chopped
- 1 onion, cut into wedges
- 1/2 tsp pepper
- 1 tsp salt

Directions:

1. Add all ingredients into the instant pot.
2. Pour enough water to cover the stock ingredients.
3. Seal pot with lid and cook on manual high pressure for 20 minutes.
4. Once done then release pressure using quick-release method than open the lid.
5. Strain the stock into the container and store.

Nutritional Value (Amount per Serving):
Calories 289; Fat 12 g; Carbohydrates 4.8 g; Sugar 2.4 g; Protein 37 g; Cholesterol 70 mg

Turkey Stock

Preparation Time: 10 minutes; Cooking Time: 60 minutes; Serve: 4
Ingredients:
- 1 lb turkey carcass
- 1 carrot, sliced
- 2 celery stalks, sliced
- 1 onion, diced
- 6 cups of water
- 4 garlic cloves

Directions:
1. Add all ingredients into the instant pot.
2. Seal pot with lid and cook on manual high pressure for 60 minutes.
3. Once done then allow to release pressure naturally for 10 minutes then release using quick-release method. Open the lid.
4. Strain the stock into the container and store.

Nutritional Value (Amount per Serving):
Calories 216; Fat 5.7 g; Carbohydrates 5.3 g; Sugar 2.1 g; Protein 33.9 g; Cholesterol 86 mg

Chapter 5: Soup & Stews

Healthy Chicken Noodle Soup

Preparation Time: 10 minutes; Cooking Time: 10 minutes; Serve: 4

Ingredients:

- 1 chicken breast, skinless, boneless, and chopped
- 2 tbsp cornstarch
- 1 cup milk
- 1 cup pasta
- 4 cups chicken stock
- 1/4 tsp garlic powder
- 1/2 tsp thyme
- 1 tsp parsley
- 1 cup spinach, chopped
- 2 celery stalks, sliced
- 3 carrots, peeled and sliced
- 1/8 tsp pepper
- 1 tsp salt

Directions:

1. Add carrots, stock, garlic powder, thyme, salt, parsley, chicken, spinach, celery, and pepper and stir well.
2. Seal pot with lid and cook on manual high pressure for 4-5 minutes.
3. Once done then release pressure using the quick-release method than open the lid.
4. Set pot on sauté mode. Add pasta and cook for 4-5 minutes or until pasta is dente.
5. In a small bowl, whisk together corn-starch and milk and stir into the soup.
6. Serve and enjoy.

Nutritional Value (Amount per Serving):

Calories 203; Fat 3.3 g; Carbohydrates 30.2 g; Sugar 5.9 g; Protein 13 g; Cholesterol 0 mg

Nutritious Lentil Soup

Preparation Time: 10 minutes; Cooking Time: 18 minutes; Serve: 4

Ingredients:

- 4 cups baby spinach
- 4 cups vegetable broth
- 1 tsp Italian seasoning
- 2 tsp thyme
- 14 oz can tomatoes, diced
- 1 1/2 cups green lentils
- 2 garlic cloves, minced
- 2 celery stalks, chopped
- 1 carrot, peeled and chopped
- 1 onion, chopped
- Pepper
- Salt

Directions:

1. Add all ingredients except spinach into the instant pot and stir well.
2. Seal pot with lid and cook on manual high pressure for 18 minutes.
3. Once done then release pressure using the quick-release method than open the lid.
4. Add spinach and stir until spinach is wilted.
5. Serve and enjoy.

Nutritional Value (Amount per Serving):

Calories 346; Fat 2.7 g; Carbohydrates 55.6 g; Sugar 7.8 g; Protein 25.8 g; Cholesterol 1 mg

Cheesy Broccoli Soup

Preparation Time: 10 minutes; Cooking Time: 19 minutes; Serve: 6

Ingredients:

- 2 cups broccoli florets
- 2 cups cheddar cheese, grated
- 2 cups heavy cream
- 2 cups vegetable stock
- 1/2 tsp nutmeg
- 1 cup carrot, grated
- 3 garlic cloves, minced
- 1/4 cup flour

- 1 onion, chopped
- 1 tbsp butter
- Pepper
- Salt

Directions:

1. Add butter into the instant pot and set the pot on sauté mode.
2. Add onion and sauté for 2 minutes.
3. Add garlic and flour and sauté for 1-2 minutes.
4. Add stock, nutmeg, broccoli, and carrots and stir well.
5. Seal pot with lid and cook on manual high pressure for 15 minutes.
6. Once done then release pressure using the quick-release method than open the lid.
7. Stir in cheese and cream. Season with pepper and salt.
8. Stir well and serve.

Nutritional Value (Amount per Serving):

Calories 356; Fat 29.5 g; Carbohydrates 12 g; Sugar 2.8 g; Protein 12.2 g; Cholesterol 99 mg

Carrot Ginger Soup

Preparation Time: 10 minutes; Cooking Time: 15 minutes; Serve: 4

Ingredients:

- 14 oz coconut milk
- 1 tsp dried thyme
- 3 1/2 cups vegetable broth
- 4 cups carrots, peeled and chopped
- 2 tbsp ginger, chopped
- 2 garlic cloves, minced
- 1 onion, chopped
- 1 tbsp olive oil
- 1/2 lime juice
- 1/4 tsp pepper
- 3/4 tsp salt

Directions:

1. Add oil into the instant pot and set the pot on sauté mode.
2. Add onion and sauté for 4-5 minutes.
3. Add ginger and garlic and sauté for 1-2 minutes.
4. Add carrots, pepper, stock, and salt and stir well.
5. Seal pot with lid and cook on manual high pressure for 5 minutes.
6. Once done then release pressure using the quick-release method than open the lid.
7. Puree the soup using immersion blender until smooth.
8. Stir in lime juice and coconut milk.
9. Serve and enjoy.

Nutritional Value (Amount per Serving):

Calories 362; Fat 28.6 g; Carbohydrates 22.8 g; Sugar 10.7 g; Protein 8.1 g; Cholesterol 0 mg

Cabbage Soup

Preparation Time: 10 minutes; Cooking Time: 16 minutes; Serve: 6

Ingredients:

- 1 lb ground sausage
- 2 tbsp olive oil
- 6 cups cabbage, chopped
- 1/2 cup rice, uncooked
- 1 tbsp Worcestershire sauce
- 32 oz beef broth
- 14 oz spaghetti sauce
- 3 garlic cloves, minced
- 1/2 cup onion, diced

Directions:

1. Add oil into the instant pot and set the pot on sauté mode.
2. Add sausage, onion, and garlic and sauté until meat is no longer pink.
3. Add broth, Worcestershire sauce, spaghetti sauce, and tomatoes and stir well.
4. Add remaining ingredients and stir everything well.

5. Seal pot with lid and cook on manual high pressure for 12 minutes.
6. Once done then release pressure using the quick-release method than open the lid.
7. Stir well and serve.

Nutritional Value (Amount per Serving):

Calories 589; Fat 27.8 g; Carbohydrates 61.4 g; Sugar 3.6 g; Protein 23.9 g; Cholesterol 64 mg

Zucchini Corn Soup

Preparation Time: 10 minutes; Cooking Time: 10 minutes; Serve: 6

Ingredients:

- 1 zucchini, chopped
- 7 oz can corn
- 2 tbsp fresh parsley, chopped
- 32 oz vegetable broth
- 3 garlic cloves, minced
- 3 carrots, diced
- 1 tsp cayenne
- 1 tbsp turmeric
- 3 potatoes, peeled and diced
- 1 cup can peas
- 1 onion, diced
- 1 tsp salt

Directions:

1. Add potatoes, onion, carrots, and zucchini into the instant pot. Top with peas and corn.
2. Add paprika, turmeric, cayenne, pepper, and salt and stir well.
3. Pour broth into the pot then pour water till fill line. Stir.
4. Seal pot with lid and cook on manual high pressure for 10 minutes.
5. Once done then release pressure using the quick-release method than open the lid.
6. Top with parsley and serve.

Nutritional Value (Amount per Serving):

Calories 177; Fat 1.6 g; Carbohydrates 34.4 g; Sugar 6.8 g; Protein 8.1 g; Cholesterol 0 mg

Lentil Sausage Stew

Preparation Time: 10 minutes; Cooking Time: 18 minutes; Serve: 8

Ingredients:

- 1 1/2 cups dry lentils, rinsed
- 5 cups vegetable stock
- 28 oz can tomatoes, diced
- 1/2 tsp red pepper flakes
- 1 1/2 tsp Italian seasoning
- 1 tbsp tomato paste
- 2 garlic cloves, minced
- 2 carrots, peeled and chopped
- 2 celery stalks, chopped
- 1 onion, chopped
- 1 lb Italian sausage
- 2 tbsp olive oil
- 1 tsp salt

Directions:

1. Add oil into the instant pot and set the pot on sauté mode.
2. Add sausage to the pot and break with a spoon and cook until meat is no longer pink.
3. Add carrot, celery, and onion and cook for 3-4 minutes.
4. Stir in red pepper flakes, Italian seasoning, tomato paste, garlic, and salt.
5. Add lentils, stock, and tomatoes and stir to combine.
6. Seal pot with lid and cook on manual high pressure for 10 minutes.
7. Once done then allow to release pressure naturally for 10 minutes then release using the quick-release method. Open the lid.
8. Stir well and serve.

Nutritional Value (Amount per Serving):

Calories 391; Fat 20.2 g; Carbohydrates 30.9 g; Sugar 6.2 g; Protein 21.9 g; Cholesterol 48 mg

Tortellini Tomato Soup

Preparation Time: 10 minutes; Cooking Time: 12 minutes; Serve: 4

Ingredients:

- 28 oz can tomato sauce
- 1/2 onion, diced
- 1/2 package cheese tortellini
- 1/4 cup fresh basil leaves
- 1/2 tbsp garlic
- 1 cup heavy cream
- 1 1/2 tsp pepper

Directions:

1. Spray instant pot from inside with cooking spray and set the pot on sauté mode.
2. Add garlic and onion and cook for 2 minutes.
3. Add tomato sauce and basil leaves and stir well.
4. Seal pot with lid and cook on manual high pressure for 2 minutes.
5. Once done then release pressure using the quick-release method than open the lid.
6. Set pot on sauté mode. Add tortellini and cook for 5-6 minutes.
7. Stir in cream and cook for 2 minutes. Season with pepper.
8. Serve and enjoy.

Nutritional Value (Amount per Serving):

Calories 199; Fat 12.3 g; Carbohydrates 20.2 g; Sugar 9.1 g; Protein 5.1 g; Cholesterol 44 mg

Healthy Split Pea Soup

Preparation Time: 10 minutes; Cooking Time: 17 minutes; Serve: 6

Ingredients:

- 2 cups dry split peas, uncooked
- 1 cup ham, diced
- 1/2 tsp garlic powder
- 2 tbsp olive oil
- 2 celery stalks, chopped
- 2 carrots, sliced
- 1/2 onion, diced
- 40 oz chicken stock
- 1 1/2 tsp salt

Directions:

1. Add oil into the instant pot and set the pot on sauté mode.
2. Add ham and onion to the pot and sauté until onion is softened.
3. Add remaining ingredients and stir well.
4. Seal pot with lid and cook on manual high pressure for 17 minutes.
5. Once done then allow to release pressure naturally for 5 minutes then release using the quick-release method. Open the lid.
6. Stir well and serve.

Nutritional Value (Amount per Serving):

Calories 322; Fat 7.8 g; Carbohydrates 44.3 g; Sugar 7.3 g; Protein 20.7 g; Cholesterol 13 mg

Barley Mushroom Soup

Preparation Time: 10 minutes; Cooking Time: 30 minutes; Serve: 6

Ingredients:

- 1/2 cup pearl barley
- 1 bay leaf
- 1/2 tsp parsley flakes
- 1/2 tsp sage
- 1/4 tsp marjoram
- 2 tbsp olive oil
- 1/2 onion, diced
- 1 carrot, diced
- 2 celery stalks, chopped
- 4 cups vegetable broth
- 8 oz mushrooms, sliced
- 1/4 tsp pepper
- Salt

Directions:

1. Add oil into the instant pot and set the pot on sauté mode.
2. Add onion, carrots, and celery and sauté for 4-5 minutes.
3. Add mushrooms and sauté for 3 minutes.
4. Add barley, herbs, broth, pepper, and salt and stir well.
5. Seal pot with lid and cook on manual high pressure for 20 minutes.
6. Once done then allow to release pressure naturally for 10 minutes then release using the quick-release method. Open the lid.
7. Stir and serve.

Nutritional Value (Amount per Serving):
Calories 142; Fat 5.9 g; Carbohydrates 17 g; Sugar 2.2 g; Protein 6.3 g; Cholesterol 0 mg

Creamy Mushroom Soup

Preparation Time: 10 minutes; Cooking Time: 10 minutes; Serve: 4
Ingredients:
- 4 cups mushrooms, sliced
- 1 tsp dried thyme
- 3 garlic cloves, minced
- 1 cup of water
- 1 jalapeno pepper, chopped
- 3 cups onion, sliced
- 1/2 tsp pepper
- 1 tsp salt

Directions:
1. Add all ingredients into the instant pot and stir well.
2. Seal pot with lid and cook on manual high pressure for 10 minutes.
3. the Once done then allow to release pressure naturally for 10 minutes then release using the quick-release method. Open the lid.
4. Puree the soup using immersion blender until smooth.
5. Stir and serve.

Nutritional Value (Amount per Serving):
Calories 55; Fat 0.4 g; Carbohydrates 11.6 g; Sugar 5 g; Protein 3.4 g; Cholesterol 0 mg

Sweet Potato Soup

Preparation Time: 10 minutes; Cooking Time: 15 minutes; Serve: 6
Ingredients:
- 2 lbs sweet potatoes, peeled and diced
- 1/2 tsp cinnamon
- 1 tsp paprika
- 3 garlic cloves, minced
- 2 cups of water
- 4 cups vegetable broth
- 1/2 onion, chopped
- 1 tbsp olive oil
- Pepper
- Salt

Directions:
1. Add oil into the instant pot and set the pot on sauté mode.
2. Add onion and sweet potato and sauté for 5 minutes.
3. Add remaining ingredients and stir everything well.
4. Seal pot with lid and cook on manual high pressure for 10 minutes.
5. Once done then release pressure using the quick-release method than open the lid.
6. Puree the soup using immersion blender until smooth.
7. Stir well and serve.

Nutritional Value (Amount per Serving):
Calories 231; Fat 3.6 g; Carbohydrates 44.5 g; Sugar 1.7 g; Protein 5.8 g; Cholesterol 0 mg

Healthy Vegetable Soup

Preparation Time: 10 minutes; Cooking Time: 30 minutes; Serve: 12

Ingredients:

- 12 oz frozen peas
- 12 oz frozen corn
- 12 oz frozen green beans
- 12 oz frozen okra
- 4 potatoes, peeled and chopped
- 3 garlic cloves, chopped
- 1/2 onion, chopped
- 4 carrots, chopped
- 2 celery stalks, chopped
- 4 cups chicken broth
- 1/4 tsp pepper
- 1 tsp salt

Directions:

1. Add all ingredients into the instant pot and stir well.
2. Seal pot with lid and cook on soup mode for 30 minutes.
3. Once done then allow to release pressure naturally then open the lid.
4. Stir well and serve.

Nutritional Value (Amount per Serving):

Calories 248; Fat 2.5 g; Carbohydrates 51.4 g; Sugar 9.4 g; Protein 10.6 g; Cholesterol 0 mg

Onion Soup

Preparation Time: 10 minutes; Cooking Time: 3 minutes; Serve: 4

Ingredients:

- 3 onions, sliced
- 3/4 cup gruyere cheese, shredded
- 32 oz chicken broth
- 1/2 tsp thyme
- 2 tbsp Worcestershire sauce
- 3 tbsp butter
- 1 French bread load, sliced
- 3/4 tsp salt

Directions:

1. Add butter into the instant pot and set the pot on sauté mode.
2. Add onion and sauté until onion is caramelized.
3. Add broth, thyme, Worcestershire sauce, and salt and stir well.
4. Seal pot with lid and cook on manual high pressure for 3 minutes.
5. Once done then release pressure using the quick-release method than open the lid.
6. Place bread slices on a pan and sprinkle cheese on top of bread slices. Cook bread slices until cheese are melted.
7. Serve soup with bread slices.

Nutritional Value (Amount per Serving):

Calories 275; Fat 17 g; Carbohydrates 17.7 g; Sugar 6.2 g; Protein 12.6 g; Cholesterol 45 mg

Curried Lentil Stew

Preparation Time: 10 minutes; Cooking Time: 5 minutes; Serve: 6

Ingredients:

- 1 1/2 cups dry green lentils
- 2 cups jasmine rice, cooked
- 1/2 cup fresh cilantro, chopped
- 2 cups spinach, chopped
- 2 bell peppers, diced
- 2 1/2 cups vegetable broth
- 14 oz can coconut milk
- 1 tsp cumin
- 1 tbsp curry powder
- 1 tbsp turmeric
- 1 tbsp ginger root, minced
- 2 garlic cloves, minced
- 2 onion, diced
- 1 tbsp olive oil
- 1/2 tsp salt

Directions:

1. Add oil, broth, milk, lentils, cumin, curry powder, turmeric, ginger, garlic, onions, and salt and stir well.
2. Seal pot with lid and cook on manual high pressure for 5 minutes.

3. Once done then release pressure using the quick-release method than open the lid.
4. Add bell peppers and stir well and let sit for 5 minutes.
5. Add spinach and stir until spinach is wilted.
6. Pour soup to the bowl and top with rice and cilantro.
7. Serve and enjoy.

Nutritional Value (Amount per Serving):
   Calories 592; Fat 18.1 g; Carbohydrates 88.4 g; Sugar 5 g; Protein 21.3 g; Cholesterol 0 mg

Savory Butternut Squash Soup

Preparation Time: 10 minutes; Cooking Time: 30 minutes; Serve: 8
Ingredients:
- 6 cups butternut squash, cut into cubes
- 2 tbsp heavy cream
- 3 cups vegetable broth
- 1/4 tsp cinnamon
- 1 tsp cumin
- 1 tsp chili powder
- 2 garlic cloves
- 1 onion, diced
- 1/4 tsp pepper
- 1 tsp kosher salt

Directions:
1. Add squash, broth, spices, garlic, and onion into the instant pot and stir well.
2. Seal pot with lid and cook on soup mode for 30 minutes.
3. Once done then release pressure using the quick-release method than open the lid.
4. Puree the soup using immersion blender until smooth.
5. Add heavy cream and stir well.
6. Sprinkle chili powder on top of the soup and serve.

Nutritional Value (Amount per Serving):
   Calories 84; Fat 2.1 g; Carbohydrates 14.7 g; Sugar 3.2 g; Protein 3.3 g; Cholesterol 5 mg

Potato Ham Soup

Preparation Time: 10 minutes; Cooking Time: 8 minutes; Serve: 4
Ingredients:
- 5 lbs potatoes, peeled and cubed
- 2 tbsp water
- 2 tbsp corn-starch
- 2 cups cheddar cheese, shredded
- 1/2 cup sour cream
- 1/2 cup milk
- 5 cups chicken broth
- 1/2 tsp pepper
- 1 tsp onion powder
- 1 tsp garlic powder
- 1 lb ham, cubed
- 1/2 tsp salt

Directions:
1. Add potatoes, broth, onion powder, garlic powder, ham, pepper, and salt into the instant pot and stir well.
2. Seal pot with lid and cook on manual high pressure for 8 minutes.
3. Once done then release pressure using the quick-release method than open the lid.
4. Add sour cream and milk and stir well.
5. In a small bowl, whisk together water and corn-starch and pour into the soup and cook on sauté mode until soup is thickened.
6. Add cheese and stir until cheese is melted.
7. Serve and enjoy.

Nutritional Value (Amount per Serving):
   Calories 858; Fat 48.1 g; Carbohydrates 57.5 g; Sugar 3 g; Protein 47.3 g; Cholesterol 164 mg

Northern Bean Soup

Preparation Time: 10 minutes; Cooking Time: 30 minutes; Serve: 4

Ingredients:

- 1 1/2 cups dry great northern bean, soak in water for 2-3 hours and drained
- 2 tbsp olive oil
- 2 garlic cloves, minced
- 1 onion, chopped
- 1 rosemary spring
- 32 oz chicken broth
- 1/4 tsp pepper
- 1 tsp salt

Directions:

1. Add oil into the instant pot and set the pot on sauté mode.
2. Add garlic and onion and cook until softened.
3. Add remaining ingredients and stir well.
4. Seal pot with lid and cook on manual high pressure for 25 minutes.
5. Once done then allow to release pressure naturally then open the lid.
6. Puree the soup using immersion blender until smooth.
7. Stir well and serve.

Nutritional Value (Amount per Serving):

Calories 343; Fat 9.1 g; Carbohydrates 46.8 g; Sugar 3.4 g; Protein 20 g; Cholesterol 0 mg

Squash Apple Soup

Preparation Time: 10 minutes; Cooking Time: 15 minutes; Serve: 8

Ingredients:

- 1 medium butternut squash, peeled and cut into chunks
- 1/2 tsp dried sage
- 1 sweet potato, peeled and cut into chunks
- 2 garlic cloves, chopped
- 1 onion, chopped
- 2 tbsp olive oil
- 7.5 oz can coconut milk
- 1/4 tsp ground ginger
- 1/2 tsp pumpkin pie spice
- 1 apple, cored and cut into chunks
- 1/8 tsp pepper
- 1/2 tsp kosher salt

Directions:

1. Add oil into the instant pot and set the pot on sauté mode.
2. Add garlic and onion and sauté for 3-5 minutes.
3. Add remaining ingredients except for coconut milk and stir well.
4. Seal pot with lid and cook on manual high pressure for 10 minutes.
5. Once done then allow to release pressure naturally then open the lid.
6. Puree the soup using immersion blender until smooth.
7. Stir in coconut milk and serve.

Nutritional Value (Amount per Serving):

Calories 134; Fat 10 g; Carbohydrates 12 g; Sugar 5.7 g; Protein 1.4 g; Cholesterol 0 mg

Delicious Tortilla Chicken Soup

Preparation Time: 10 minutes; Cooking Time: 20 minutes; Serve: 6

Ingredients:

- 1 1/2 lbs chicken breasts, skinless and boneless
- 14 oz can chicken broth
- 20 oz can tomatoes, diced
- 1 tsp cumin
- 1 tsp onion powder
- 1 1/2 tsp garlic powder
- 1 onion, chopped
- 2 chipotle peppers in adobo sauce
- 13.5 oz can coconut milk
- 2 zucchini, chopped
- 1/2 tsp paprika

- 1 tsp dried oregano
- 1 1/2 tsp chili powder
- 1 1/2 tsp salt

Directions:
1. Season chicken with salt and place into the instant pot.
2. Add remaining ingredients except for coconut milk over chicken.
3. Seal pot with lid and cook on manual high pressure for 20 minutes.
4. Once done then allow to release pressure naturally then open the lid.
5. Remove chicken from pot and shred using a fork.
6. Return chicken to the pot with coconut milk and stir well.
7. Serve and enjoy.

Nutritional Value (Amount per Serving):
Calories 412; Fat 23.4 g; Carbohydrates 12.9 g; Sugar 5.8 g; Protein 39.6 g; Cholesterol 103 mg

Hamburger Soup

Preparation Time: 10 minutes; Cooking Time: 25 minutes; Serve: 4
Ingredients:
- 1 lb lean ground beef
- 2 garlic cloves, minced
- 3 cups chicken broth
- 14 oz can tomatoes, diced
- 3/4 cup green beans
- 2 tbsp tomato paste
- 2 celery stalks, sliced
- 2 carrots, peeled and sliced
- 1 onion, chopped
- 2 tsp olive oil
- 1/2 potatoes, diced
- 1/2 tsp pepper
- 2 tsp sea salt

Directions:
1. Add olive oil into the instant pot and set the pot on sauté mode.
2. Add meat and cook until browned.
3. Add remaining ingredients and stir well.
4. Seal pot with lid and cook on soup mode for 25 minutes.
5. Once done then release pressure using the quick-release method than open the lid.
6. Stir and serve.

Nutritional Value (Amount per Serving):
Calories 340; Fat 10.6 g; Carbohydrates 19.4 g; Sugar 8.3 g; Protein 40.9 g; Cholesterol 101 mg

Tasty Taco Soup

Preparation Time: 10 minutes; Cooking Time: 30 minutes; Serve: 6
Ingredients:
- 2 lbs ground beef
- 3 bell peppers, diced
- 1 onion, diced
- 1 1/2 tbsp olive oil
- 7 oz green chilies, diced
- 1/4 tsp onion powder
- 1/4 tsp garlic powder
- 1/4 tsp cinnamon
- 1/2 tsp paprika
- 1 1/2 tsp pepper
- 6 oz coconut milk
- 24 oz chicken broth
- 28 oz tomatoes, diced
- 1/4 tsp cayenne
- 2 tbsp cumin
- 1 1/2 tbsp chili powder
- 2 tsp sea salt

Directions:
1. Add oil into the instant pot and set the pot on sauté mode.

2. Add bell peppers and onion into the pot and cook for 5 minutes.
3. Add meat and cook until meat is no longer pink. Add all spices and stir well.
4. Add broth, green chilies, milk, and tomatoes and stir well.
5. Seal pot with lid and cook on soup mode for 25 minutes.
6. Once done then release pressure using the quick-release method than open the lid.
7. Stir and serve.

Nutritional Value (Amount per Serving):

Calories 568; Fat 23.5 g; Carbohydrates 39.1 g; Sugar 22.4 g; Protein 55 g; Cholesterol 135 mg

Veggie Chicken Soup

Preparation Time: 10 minutes; Cooking Time: 30 minutes; Serve: 6

Ingredients:

- 3 lbs whole chicken
- 5 cups of water
- 2 carrots, chopped
- 1 onion, diced
- 1 tbsp ginger, minced
- 2 garlic cloves, minced
- 1 1/2 cups green beans, cut into 1-inch pieces
- 1/4 tsp pepper
- 1 tbsp sea salt

Directions:

1. Add ginger, garlic, green beans, carrots, and onion into the instant pot.
2. Season chicken with pepper and salt and place on top of veggies in the pot.
3. Pour water into the pot.
4. Seal pot with lid and cook on soup mode for 30 minutes.
5. Once done then allow to release pressure naturally then open the lid.
6. Remove chicken from pot and debone.
7. Shred the chicken using a fork.
8. Return shredded chicken to the pot.
9. Stir and serve.

Nutritional Value (Amount per Serving):

Calories 460; Fat 16.9 g; Carbohydrates 6.7 g; Sugar 2.2 g; Protein 66.6 g; Cholesterol 202 mg

Zucchini Soup

Preparation Time: 10 minutes; Cooking Time: 15 minutes; Serve: 4

Ingredients:

- 3 zucchini, peeled and chopped
- 1/4 cup basil, chopped
- 1 leek, chopped
- 3 cups vegetable broth
- 1 tbsp fresh lemon juice
- 3 tbsp olive oil
- 2 tsp sea salt

Directions:

1. Add 2 tbsp oil into the instant pot and set the pot on sauté mode.
2. Add zucchini and cook for 5 minutes.
3. Add basil and leeks and cook for 2-3 minutes.
4. Stir in lemon juice, broth, and salt.
5. Seal pot with lid and cook on manual high pressure for 8 minutes.
6. Once done then allow to release pressure naturally then open the lid.
7. Puree the soup using immersion blender until smooth.
8. Drizzle with remaining oil and serve.

Nutritional Value (Amount per Serving):

Calories 157; Fat 11.9 g; Carbohydrates 8.9 g; Sugar 4 g; Protein 5.8 g; Cholesterol 0 mg

Curried Cauliflower Soup

Preparation Time: 10 minutes; Cooking Time: 15 minutes; Serve: 4

Ingredients:

- 2 cups cauliflower florets
- 1 carrot, diced
- 1 cup onion, diced
- 1 1/3 tbsp olive oil
- 2 2/3 cups vegetable stock
- 1/8 tsp dried thyme
- 1 1/2 tbsp curry powder
- 1/8 tsp pepper
- 1/8 tsp salt

Directions:

1. Add oil into the instant pot and set the pot on sauté mode.
2. Add carrots, cauliflower, and onion into the pot and sauté for 4-5 minutes.
3. Add spices and stock and stir well.
4. Seal pot with lid and cook on manual high pressure for 10 minutes.
5. Once done then allow to release pressure naturally then open the lid.
6. Stir in milk. Puree the soup using immersion blender until smooth.
7. Serve and enjoy.

Nutritional Value (Amount per Serving):

Calories 82; Fat 5.2 g; Carbohydrates 8.9 g; Sugar 3.7 g; Protein 2 g; Cholesterol 0 mg

Summer Veggie Soup

Preparation Time: 10 minutes; Cooking Time: 10 minutes; Serve: 6

Ingredients:

- 1 summer squash, sliced
- 1 zucchini, sliced
- 2 tomatoes, sliced
- 1 eggplant, sliced
- 2 garlic cloves, smashed
- 1 onion, diced
- 1/4 cup basil, chopped
- 2 bell peppers, sliced
- 1/2 cup green beans, cut into pieces
- 8 cups vegetable broth
- 3/4 cup corn
- Pepper
- Salt

Directions:

1. Add all ingredients into the instant pot and stir well.
2. Seal pot with lid and cook on soup mode for 10 minutes.
3. Once done then release pressure using the quick-release method than open the lid.
4. Serve and enjoy.

Nutritional Value (Amount per Serving):

Calories 128; Fat 2.5 g; Carbohydrates 18.6 g; Sugar 9.2 g; Protein 9.7 g; Cholesterol 0 mg

Vegetable Chicken Stew

Preparation Time: 10 minutes; Cooking Time: 10 minutes; Serve: 8

Ingredients:

- 2 chicken breasts, skinless and boneless
- 1 carrot, diced
- 1 sweet potato, cubed
- 1 onion, diced
- 1/4 tsp red pepper flakes
- 1 tbsp parsley
- 1 3/4 cups celery, diced
- 2 1/2 cups vegetable broth
- 2 tsp sea salt

Directions:

1. Place chicken into the instant pot.

2. Pour remaining ingredients over the chicken.
3. Seal pot with lid and cook on manual mode for 10 minutes.
4. Once done then release pressure using the quick-release method than open the lid.
5. Shred the chicken using the fork and stir well.
6. Serve and enjoy.

Nutritional Value (Amount per Serving):
Calories 113; Fat 3.1 g; Carbohydrates 8.3 g; Sugar 1.6 g; Protein 12.3 g; Cholesterol 31 mg

Thai Sweet Potato Stew

Preparation Time: 10 minutes; Cooking Time: 9 minutes; Serve: 6
Ingredients:

- 2 sweet potatoes, peeled and diced
- 13.5 oz can tomatoes, diced
- 1 bell pepper, diced
- 1 zucchini, diced
- 3 garlic cloves, minced
- 1 tsp ginger, grated
- 3 fresh lime juice
- 14.5 oz coconut milk
- 2 tbsp Thai red curry paste
- 1 tsp turmeric
- 1 1/2 tsp curry powder
- 1/2 onion, diced
- 1 tbsp olive oil
- 1 tsp sea salt

Directions:
1. Add oil into the instant pot and set the pot on sauté mode.
2. Add onion and sauté for 3 minutes,
3. Add ginger and garlic and sauté for a minute.
4. Add remaining ingredients except for lime juice and stir well.
5. Seal pot with lid and cook on manual high pressure for 5 minutes.
6. Once done then release pressure using the quick-release method than open the lid.
7. Stir in lime juice and serve.

Nutritional Value (Amount per Serving):
Calories 297; Fat 20.5 g; Carbohydrates 28.5 g; Sugar 7.1 g; Protein 3.9 g; Cholesterol 0 mg

Chicken Taco Soup

Preparation Time: 10 minutes; Cooking Time: 20 minutes; Serve: 2
Ingredients:

- 1 chicken breast, skinless and boneless
- 2 garlic cloves, chopped
- 1/2 onion, chopped
- 1 potato, peeled and diced
- 2 cups chicken broth
- 3 cups butternut squash, peeled and diced
- 2 oz can green chilies
- 4 oz tomato sauce
- 14 oz cannellini beans, drained
- 1 tsp cumin
- 1 tbsp taco seasoning
- 1/4 cup cheddar cheese, grated
- 1/2 bell pepper, chopped
- Pepper
- Salt

Directions:
1. Add all ingredients except cheese and beans into the instant pot and stir well.
2. Seal pot with lid and cook on manual high pressure for 20 minutes.
3. Once done then release pressure using the quick-release method than open the lid.
4. Remove chicken from pot and shred using a fork.
5. Add 1 cup of soup into the blender and blend until smooth.
6. Stir blended soup into the instant pot along with shredded chicken and beans.
7. Top with cheese and serve.

Nutritional Value (Amount per Serving):

Calories 1214; Fat 20.2 g; Carbohydrates 183.6 g; Sugar 15.6 g; Protein 83.1 g; Cholesterol 79 mg

Tasty Chicken Rice Soup

Preparation Time: 10 minutes; Cooking Time: 9 minutes; Serve: 2

Ingredients:

- 1/2 lb chicken breasts, skinless and boneless
- 1 thyme sprigs
- 2 garlic cloves, chopped
- 1/4 tsp turmeric
- 1 tsp olive oil
- 2 tbsp fresh parsley, chopped
- 1 tbsp fresh lemon juice
- 2 tbsp rice
- 1/4 cup celery, chopped
- 1/2 small onion, chopped
- 1 carrot, diced
- 2 1/2 cup water
- Pepper
- Salt

Directions:

1. Add oil into the instant pot and set the pot on sauté mode.
2. Add garlic, onion, carrot, and celery to the pot and cook for 3 minutes.
3. Stir in water, turmeric, chicken, pepper, and salt.
4. Seal pot with lid and cook on manual high pressure for 6 minutes.
5. Once done then release pressure using the quick-release method than open the lid.
6. Remove chicken from pot and shred using a fork.
7. Return shredded chicken to the pot and stir well.
8. Stir in lemon juice and parsley.
9. Serve and enjoy.

Nutritional Value (Amount per Serving):

Calories 312; Fat 11.1 g; Carbohydrates 16.7 g; Sugar 2.7 g; Protein 34.7 g; Cholesterol 101 mg

Cabbage Pork Soup

Preparation Time: 10 minutes; Cooking Time: 30 minutes; Serve: 2

Ingredients:

- 1/2 lb ground pork
- 1/2 tsp ground ginger
- 1 1/2 cup cabbage, chopped
- 1/2 tbsp soy sauce
- 1 carrot, peeled and shredded
- 1 small onion, chopped
- 2 cup chicken stock
- 1 tbsp olive oil
- Pepper
- Salt

Directions:

1. Add oil into the instant pot and set the pot on sauté mode.
2. Add meat and sauté for 3-4 minutes.
3. Add remaining ingredients and stir well.
4. Seal pot with lid and cook on manual high pressure for 25 minutes.
5. Once done then release pressure using the quick-release method than open the lid.
6. Serve and enjoy.

Nutritional Value (Amount per Serving):

Calories 275; Fat 11.7 g; Carbohydrates 10.7 g; Sugar 5.5 g; Protein 32 g; Cholesterol 83 mg

Healthy Spinach Lentil Soup

Preparation Time: 10 minutes; Cooking Time: 1 hour 15 minutes; Serve: 2

Ingredients:

- 1 cup dried brown lentils, rinsed
- 2 tsp ground cumin
- 1 tsp turmeric
- 1 tsp dried thyme
- 4 cups vegetable stock
- 1 tbsp olive oil
- 1/2 onion, diced
- 2 carrots, peeled and diced
- 1 celery stalk, diced
- 2 garlic cloves, minced
- 8 oz spinach
- 1/4 tsp pepper
- 1 tsp salt

Directions:
1. Add oil into the instant pot and set the pot on sauté mode.
2. Add garlic, onion, carrots, and celery to the pot and cook for 5 minutes.
3. Stir in cumin, thyme, pepper, and salt and stir for a minute. Add lentils and stock and stir well.
4. Seal pot with lid and cook on manual high pressure for 12 minutes.
5. Once done then release pressure using the quick-release method than open the lid.
6. Add spinach and stir until wilted.
7. Serve and enjoy.

Nutritional Value (Amount per Serving):
Calories 191; Fat 8.5 g; Carbohydrates 22.8 g; Sugar 6.8 g; Protein 8.1 g; Cholesterol 0 mg

Mushroom Soup

Preparation Time: 10 minutes; Cooking Time: 11 minutes; Serve: 2
Ingredients:
- 1 cup mushrooms, chopped
- 1/2 tsp chili powder
- 5 cups vegetable stock
- 2 tbsp olive oil
- 1 tsp fresh lemon juice
- 1/4 cup celery, chopped
- 2 garlic cloves, crushed
- 1 onion, chopped
- 2 tsp garam masala
- 1/2 tsp pepper
- 1 tsp sea salt

Directions:
1. Add oil into the instant pot and set the pot on sauté mode.
2. Add garlic and onion and cook for 5 minutes.
3. Add chili powder and garam masala and cook for a minute.
4. Add remaining ingredients and stir well.
5. Seal pot with lid and cook on manual high pressure for 5 minutes.
6. Once done then release pressure using the quick-release method than open the lid.
7. Puree the soup using immersion blender until smooth.
8. Serve and enjoy.

Nutritional Value (Amount per Serving):
Calories 175; Fat 14.6 g; Carbohydrates 10.7 g; Sugar 5 g; Protein 3.2 g; Cholesterol 0 mg

Spinach Soup

Preparation Time: 10 minutes; Cooking Time: 10 minutes; Serve: 2
Ingredients:
- 3 cups spinach, chopped
- 3 cups vegetable broth
- 1 cup cauliflower, chopped
- 1 tsp garlic powder
- 2 tbsp olive oil
- 1/4 cup coconut cream
- 1/2 tsp pepper
- 1/4 tsp sea salt

Directions:
1. Add olive oil into the instant pot and set the pot on sauté mode.

2. Add cauliflower, broth, spinach, garlic powder, pepper, and salt and stir well.
3. Seal pot with lid and cook on manual high pressure for 10 minutes.
4. Once done then allow to release pressure naturally for 10 minutes then release using the quick-release method. Open the lid.
5. Puree the soup using an immersion blender until smooth.
6. Stir in coconut cream and serve.

Nutritional Value (Amount per Serving):
Calories 275; Fat 23.5 g; Carbohydrates 8.7 g; Sugar 3.8 g; Protein 10.5 g; Cholesterol 0 mg

Hearty Beef Stew

Preparation Time: 10 minutes; Cooking Time: 30 minutes; Serve: 2
Ingredients:

- 1 1/4 lb beef, boneless and cut into chunks
- 1/2 tbsp Worcestershire sauce
- 1/4 tbsp soy sauce
- 1/2 tbsp honey
- 1/4 tsp red pepper flakes
- 1 garlic clove, chopped
- 1/2 cup beef broth
- 1/4 cup vinegar

Directions:
1. Add all ingredients into the instant pot and stir well.
2. Seal pot with lid and cook on manual high pressure for 30 minutes.
3. Once done then release pressure using the quick-release method than open the lid.
4. Serve and enjoy.

Nutritional Value (Amount per Serving):
Calories 566; Fat 18.1 g; Carbohydrates 6.4 g; Sugar 5.4 g; Protein 87.5 g; Cholesterol 253 mg

Spinach Chickpea Stew

Preparation Time: 10 minutes; Cooking Time: 10 minutes; Serve: 6
Ingredients:

- 2 cups spinach, chopped
- 28 oz can tomatoes, diced
- 1 cup vegetable broth
- 2 potatoes, diced
- 2 garlic cloves, minced
- 2 celery stalks, diced
- 1 carrot, diced
- 14.5 oz can chickpeas, rinsed and drained
- 1 cup of coconut milk
- 4 tbsp peanut butter
- 1 tbsp curry powder
- 2 onions, sliced
- 1 tsp sea salt

Directions:
1. Add all ingredients into the instant pot and stir to combine.
2. Seal pot with lid and cook on manual high pressure for 10 minutes.
3. Once done then allow to release pressure naturally then open the lid.
4. Stir and serve.

Nutritional Value (Amount per Serving):
Calories 347; Fat 16.2 g; Carbohydrates 43.8 g; Sugar 10 g; Protein 11.2 g; Cholesterol 0 mg

Healthy Eggplant Stew

Preparation Time: 10 minutes; Cooking Time: 26 minutes; Serve: 4
Ingredients:

- 2 eggplants, cut into chunks
- 8 olives
- 1 1/2 tbsp capers
- 1/4 cup fresh basil leaves

- 1 chili pepper, chopped
- 1 onion, chopped
- 3 garlic cloves, minced
- 1 tsp sugar
- 1 tbsp vinegar
- 2 tbsp tomato paste
- 1 1/2 cups tomatoes, chopped
- 1/4 cup olive oil
- 1 tsp salt

Directions:
1. Add oil into the instant pot and set the pot on sauté mode.
2. Add chili pepper and sauté for 30 seconds.
3. Add onion and eggplant and cook for 5 minutes.
4. Add remaining ingredients and stir well.
5. Seal pot with lid and cook on manual high pressure for 20 minutes.
6. Once done then release pressure using the quick-release method than open the lid.
7. Stir and serve.

Nutritional Value (Amount per Serving):
Calories 226; Fat 14.3 g; Carbohydrates 25.4 g; Sugar 13.2 g; Protein 4.3 g; Cholesterol 0 mg

Squash Cauliflower Soup

Preparation Time: 10 minutes; Cooking Time: 19 minutes; Serve: 6
Ingredients:
- 1 cauliflower head, chopped
- 1 butternut squash, peeled and cubed
- 3 garlic cloves, minced
- 1 onion, chopped
- 1 tbsp olive oil
- 2 carrots, peeled and chopped
- 1 apple, peeled and chopped
- 1/2 tsp sage
- 1 cup of water
- 4 cups chicken broth
- 1/4 tsp nutmeg
- 1/4 tsp lemon zest
- 1/2 tsp pepper
- 1/2 tsp salt

Directions:
1. Add oil into the instant pot and set the pot on sauté mode.
2. Add onion and cook for 3 minutes. Add garlic and sauté for a minute.
3. Add cauliflower, carrots, apple, and squash and stir well.
4. Add water, broth, lemon zest, sage, nutmeg, pepper, and salt. Stir.
5. Seal pot with lid and cook on soup mode for 15 minutes.
6. Once done then allow to release pressure naturally then open the lid.
7. Puree the soup using immersion blender until smooth.
8. Serve and enjoy.

Nutritional Value (Amount per Serving):
Calories 106; Fat 3.5 g; Carbohydrates 15.2 g; Sugar 7.7 g; Protein 4.9 g; Cholesterol 0 mg

Corn Soup

Preparation Time: 10 minutes; Cooking Time: 10 minutes; Serve: 4
Ingredients:
- 2 1/2 cups corn kernels
- 2 tsp olive oil
- 1/2 tbsp soy sauce
- 3/4 cup cabbage, minced
- 1 carrot, minced
- 5 cups vegetable broth
- 1 tsp ground cumin
- 1 1/2 tsp ginger, grated
- 2 garlic cloves, minced
- Pepper
- Salt

Directions:
1. Add all ingredients into the instant pot and stir well.

2. Seal pot with lid and cook on manual high pressure for 10 minutes.
3. Once done then allow to release pressure naturally then open the lid.
4. Remove 3 cups of soup from pot and puree using immersion blender until smooth.
5. Return blended soup into the pot and stir well. Season with pepper and salt.
6. Serve and enjoy.

Nutritional Value (Amount per Serving):
Calories 168; Fat 5.4 g; Carbohydrates 22.9 g; Sugar 5.3 g; Protein 9.9 g; Cholesterol 0 mg

Carrot Pea Soup

Preparation Time: 10 minutes; Cooking Time: 20 minutes; Serve: 4

Ingredients
- 1 lb dry split peas, rinsed and drained
- 3 1/2 carrots, peeled and chopped
- 2 onions, chopped
- 5 cups of water
- 1 tbsp lemon juice
- 2 tbsp olive oil
- 1 tsp salt

Directions:
1. Add oil into the instant pot and set the pot on sauté mode.
2. Add onion and carrots and sauté until softened.
3. Add split peas and water and stir well.
4. Seal pot with lid and cook on manual high pressure for 15 minutes.
5. the Once done then allow to release pressure naturally for 10 minutes then release using the quick-release method. Open the lid.
6. Stir in lemon juice and season with salt.
7. Serve and enjoy.

Nutritional Value (Amount per Serving):
Calories 491; Fat 8.4 g; Carbohydrates 78.9 g; Sugar 14.1 g; Protein 28.9 g; Cholesterol 0 mg

Chapter 6: Poultry

Herb Garlic Chicken

Preparation Time: 10 minutes; Cooking Time: 10 minutes; Serve: 4

Ingredients:

- 1 lb chicken breasts, skinless and boneless
- 1 tsp garlic powder
- 1 tsp paprika
- ¾ tsp basil
- ½ tsp thyme
- ½ tsp onion powder
- ½ tsp pepper
- ¾ cup of water
- 1 tsp salt

Directions:

1. In a small bowl, mix together all dry ingredients and rub over chicken.
2. Pour water into the instant pot then place steamer rack into the pot.
3. Place chicken breasts on top of steamer rack.
4. Seal pot with lid and cook on manual high pressure for 10 minutes.
5. Once done then release pressure using the quick-release method than open the lid.
6. Serve and enjoy.

Nutritional Value (Amount per Serving):

Calories 221; Fat 8.5 g; Carbohydrates 1.3 g; Sugar 0.3 g; Protein 33.1 g; Cholesterol 101 mg

Delicious Chicken Burrito Bowl

Preparation Time: 10 minutes; Cooking Time: 10 minutes; Serve: 8

Ingredients:

- 3 chicken breasts, skinless, boneless, and cut into chunks
- 1 cup long-grain rice, uncooked
- 1 cup of salsa
- 14 oz can black beans, rinsed and drained
- 14 oz can corn, rinsed and drained
- 1 cup chicken broth
- ½ tsp cumin
- ½ tsp chili powder
- 1 tsp garlic powder
- 1 packet taco seasoning

Directions:

1. Place chicken into the instant pot.
2. Add ¼ cup broth, spices, and taco seasoning on top of chicken.
3. Pour salsa, beans, and corn to the pot and stir well.
4. Add rice on top of the chicken and do not stir.
5. Pour remaining broth on top. Seal pot with lid and cook on manual high pressure for 10 minutes.
6. Once done then allow to release pressure naturally for 5 minutes then release using quick-release method. Open the lid.
7. Serve into a bowl and top with your favorite topping.

Nutritional Value (Amount per Serving):

Calories 291; Fat 5.2 g; Carbohydrates 39.2 g; Sugar 3.1 g; Protein 22.7 g; Cholesterol 49 mg

Chicken Cheese Spaghetti

Preparation Time: 10 minutes; Cooking Time: 8 minutes; Serve: 5

Ingredients:

- 1 lb chicken breasts, skinless, boneless and cut into chunks
- ½ cup chicken broth
- 8 oz Velveeta cheese
- 8 oz spaghetti noodles, uncooked and broken

- 1 can mushroom soup
- 1 can chicken soup
- 2 cans Rotel
- 1 onion, diced

Directions:
1. Add onion, chicken, and 1 can Rotel into the instant pot and stir well.
2. Add noodles on top of chicken mixture.
3. Pour remaining Rotel, chicken soup, broth, and mushroom soup on top of noodles. Do not stir.
4. Seal pot with lid and cook on manual high pressure for 8 minutes.
5. Once done then release pressure using the quick-release method than open the lid.
6. Add cheese and stir until cheese is melted.
7. Serve and enjoy.

Nutritional Value (Amount per Serving):
Calories 502; Fat 13 g; Carbohydrates 54 g; Sugar 9 g; Protein 40 g; Cholesterol 85 mg

Moist & Tender Chicken

Preparation Time: 10 minutes; Cooking Time: 15 minutes; Serve: 4
Ingredients:
- 4 chicken thighs
- 2 garlic cloves, minced
- 1 tbsp olive oil
- 3 tbsp water
- 2 tbsp soy sauce
- 1 tsp brown sugar
- 3 tbsp honey
- Pepper
- Salt

Directions:
1. Season chicken with pepper and salt and set aside.
2. In a small bowl, mix together honey, brown sugar, soy sauce, and water. Set aside.
3. Add oil into the instant pot and set the pot on sauté mode.
4. Add chicken to the pot and cook on sauté mode until brown.
5. Add garlic and sauté for a minute.
6. Pour honey mixture over chicken.
7. Seal pot with lid and cook on manual high pressure for 10 minutes.
8. Once done then release pressure using the quick-release method than open the lid.
9. Serve and enjoy.

Nutritional Value (Amount per Serving):
Calories 265; Fat 32 g; Carbohydrates 16 g; Sugar 14 g; Protein 29 g; Cholesterol 165 mg

Simple BBQ Chicken

Preparation Time: 10 minutes; Cooking Time: 16 minutes; Serve: 4
Ingredients:
- 1 lb chicken thighs, skinless and boneless
- 1 cup BBQ sauce
- Pepper
- Salt

Directions:
1. Season chicken with pepper and salt and place into the instant pot.
2. Pour half BBQ sauce on top of chicken.
3. Seal pot with lid and cook on manual high pressure for 13 minutes.
4. Once done then allow to release pressure naturally for 5 minutes then release using quick-release method. Open the lid.
5. Set pot on sauté mode. Add remaining BBQ sauce to the pot and cook for 2-3 minutes on sauté mode.

6. Serve and enjoy.

Nutritional Value (Amount per Serving):

Calories 309; Fat 8.6 g; Carbohydrates 22.7 g; Sugar 16.3 g; Protein 32.8 g; Cholesterol 101 mg

Flavourful Chicken Curry

Preparation Time: 10 minutes; Cooking Time: 17 minutes; Serve: 6

Ingredients:

- 2 ½ lbs chicken breasts, skinless and cut into chunks
- 14 oz can coconut milk
- 14 oz can tomatoes, chopped
- 1 tsp garam masala
- 1 tbsp curry powder
- 1 tsp ginger, minced
- 1 tsp garlic, minced
- 6 cloves
- 1 cinnamon stick
- 2 onions, chopped
- 2 tbsp olive oil
- Salt

Directions:

1. Add oil into the instant pot ad set pot on sauté mode.
2. Add cloves, cinnamon, and onion to the pot and sauté for 5 minutes.
3. Add chicken and cook until brown.
4. Add tomatoes, garam masala, curry powder, ginger, garlic, coconut milk, and salt and stir well.
5. Seal pot with lid and cook on manual high pressure for 5 minutes.
6. Once done then allow to release pressure naturally then open the lid.
7. Stir well and serve.

Nutritional Value (Amount per Serving):

Calories 428; Fat 24 g; Carbohydrates 11 g; Sugar 4 g; Protein 41 g; Cholesterol 116 mg

Spicy Chicken Wings

Preparation Time: 10 minutes; Cooking Time: 15 minutes; Serve: 4

Ingredients:

- 2 lbs chicken wings
- ¼ cup hot sauce
- 1 cup of water
- For seasonings:
- ½ tsp garlic powder
- 1 tsp paprika
- ½ tsp pepper
- 1 tsp salt

Directions:

1. Spray a baking tray with cooking spray and set aside.
2. In a small bowl, mix together all seasoning ingredients.
3. Add chicken wings into the large bowl. Sprinkle seasoning over chicken and toss until chicken is well coated.
4. Pour 1 cup of water into the instant pot then place steamer rack in the pot.
5. Place chicken on top of steamer rack.
6. Seal pot with lid and cook on manual high pressure for 10 minutes.
7. Once done then release pressure using the quick-release method than open the lid.
8. Transfer chicken wings into the large bowl. Pour hot sauce over the chicken wings and toss well.
9. Arrange chicken wings on a prepared baking tray and broil for 5 minutes.
10. Serve and enjoy.

Nutritional Value (Amount per Serving):

Calories 451; Fat 18 g; Carbohydrates 2.6 g; Sugar 0 g; Protein 64 g; Cholesterol 170 mg

BBQ Honey Chicken Wings

Preparation Time: 10 minutes; Cooking Time: 10 minutes; Serve: 6

Ingredients:

- 2 lbs chicken wings
- 1/2 tsp cayenne
- 1 tbsp garlic, minced
- 2 tbsp Worcestershire sauce
- 1/3 cup brown sugar
- 1/2 cup honey
- 1/2 cup water
- 1 cup BBQ sauce

Directions:

1. Add all ingredients except chicken wings into the instant pot and stir well.
2. Add chicken wings and stir to coat.
3. Seal pot with lid and cook on manual high pressure for 10 minutes.
4. Once done then release pressure using the quick-release method than open the lid.
5. Serve and enjoy.

Nutritional Value (Amount per Serving):

Calories 474; Fat 11.4 g; Carbohydrates 47.8 g; Sugar 42.9 g; Protein 43.9 g; Cholesterol 135 mg

Honey Mustard Chicken

Preparation Time: 10 minutes; Cooking Time: 13 minutes; Serve: 6

Ingredients:

- 6 chicken drumsticks
- 2 garlic cloves, minced
- 1 tsp Worcestershire sauce
- 1 tbsp vinegar
- 1 jalapeno pepper, chopped
- 1/4 cup water
- 3/4 cup orange juice
- 3/4 cup honey mustard

Directions:

1. Add all ingredients into the instant pot and stir well.
2. Seal pot with lid and cook on manual high pressure for 13 minutes.
3. Once done then release pressure using the quick-release method than open the lid.
4. Serve and enjoy.

Nutritional Value (Amount per Serving):

Calories 155; Fat 2.7 g; Carbohydrates 15.9 g; Sugar 8.9 g; Protein 13 g; Cholesterol 40 mg

Teriyaki Chicken Drumsticks

Preparation Time: 10 minutes; Cooking Time: 20 minutes; Serve: 4

Ingredients:

- 8 chicken drumsticks
- 1 tbsp sesame seeds
- 1 tsp ginger, grated
- 2 garlic cloves, minced
- 2 tbsp honey
- 3 tbsp rice wine
- 1/4 cup soy sauce

Directions:

1. Add soy sauce, wine, honey, garlic, and ginger into the instant pot and stir well and cook on sauté mode for 2 minutes.
2. Add chicken and coat well with the sauce.
3. Seal pot with lid and cook on manual high pressure for 20 minutes.
4. Once done then release pressure using the quick-release method than open the lid.
5. Sprinkle sesame seeds over the chicken drumsticks and serve.

Nutritional Value (Amount per Serving):

Calories 231; Fat 6.4 g; Carbohydrates 16.5 g; Sugar 11.9 g; Protein 26.9 g; Cholesterol 81 mg

Mexican Salsa Chicken

Preparation Time: 10 minutes; Cooking Time: 15 minutes; Serve: 4

Ingredients:
- 4 chicken breasts, skinless, boneless, and cut in half
- 1 bell pepper, sliced
- 1 onion, sliced
- 2 tbsp taco seasoning
- 1/4 cup water
- 14 oz salsa

Directions:
1. Add all ingredients into the instant pot and stir well.
2. Seal pot with lid and cook on poultry mode for 15 minutes.
3. Once done then release pressure using the quick-release method than open the lid.
4. Stir well and serve.

Nutritional Value (Amount per Serving):

Calories 406; Fat 15.8 g; Carbohydrates 17.7 g; Sugar 5.7 g; Protein 47.8 g; Cholesterol 139 mg

Artichoke Chicken

Preparation Time: 10 minutes; Cooking Time: 25 minutes; Serve: 4

Ingredients:
- 4 chicken breasts, skinless and boneless
- 1/4 cup water
- 3 tbsp corn-starch
- 14 oz can artichoke hearts, drained
- 1/4 tsp dried thyme
- 14 oz chicken broth
- 4 tbsp butter
- 1/2 tsp paprika
- 1/2 tsp pepper
- 1 tsp salt

Directions:
1. Add butter into the instant pot and set the pot on sauté mode.
2. Season chicken with paprika, pepper, and salt and place into the instant pot and cook until brown from both the sides.
3. Remove chicken from pot and place on a plate.
4. Add thyme, broth, and chicken to the pot.
5. Seal pot with lid and cook on manual high pressure for 5 minutes.
6. Once done then release pressure using the quick-release method than open the lid.
7. Set pot on sauté mode. In a small bowl, whisk together corn-starch and water and pour to the pot and stir until the sauce thickened.
8. Add artichokes and stir well.
9. Serve and enjoy.

Nutritional Value (Amount per Serving):

Calories 437; Fat 22.5 g; Carbohydrates 11.2 g; Sugar 1.2 g; Protein 44.4 g; Cholesterol 155 mg

Creamy Peanut Butter Chicken

Preparation Time: 10 minutes; Cooking Time: 20 minutes; Serve: 4

Ingredients:
- 2 lbs chicken breasts, skinless, boneless and cut into chunks
- 1 1/2 tsp ginger powder
- 1 1/2 tsp garlic powder
- 2 tbsp honey
- 1 tbsp sriracha sauce
- 1 tbsp vinegar
- 4 tbsp soy sauce
- 4 tbsp peanut butter
- 1 cup chicken broth

- 1 tbsp sesame oil
- 1 tbsp olive oil
- 2 tbsp peanuts, roasted chopped
- Pepper
- Salt

Directions:
1. Add oil into the instant pot and set the pot on sauté mode.
2. Add chicken, ginger powder, garlic powder, honey, sriracha sauce, vinegar, soy sauce, peanut butter, broth, pepper, and salt and stir well.
3. Seal pot with lid and cook on manual mode for 9 minutes.
4. Once done then release pressure using the quick-release method than open the lid.
5. Stir everything well and cook on sauté mode until sauce thickens.
6. Garnish with peanuts and serve.

Nutritional Value (Amount per Serving):
Calories 668; Fat 34.4 g; Carbohydrates 15.3 g; Sugar 11 g; Protein 73.3 g; Cholesterol 202 mg

BBQ Pulled Chicken

Preparation Time: 10 minutes; Cooking Time: 24 minutes; Serve: 4
Ingredients:
- 2 1/2 lbs chicken breasts, skinless and boneless
- 1/2 tsp allspice
- 1 tsp chipotle powder
- 2 tsp garlic powder
- 2 tsp Dijon mustard
- 1 1/2 tsp molasses
- 1 tbsp onion powder
- 1 tbsp liquid smoke
- 4 tbsp Dietz sweet
- 2 tbsp soy sauce
- 1/4 cup apple cider vinegar
- 7 oz tomato paste
- 3/4 cup chicken broth
- 2 tsp salt

Directions:
1. Place chicken into the instant pot.
2. Whisk together remaining ingredients and pour over chicken.
3. Seal pot with lid and cook on poultry mode for 24 minutes.
4. Once done then release pressure using the quick-release method than open the lid.
5. Remove chicken from pot and shred using a fork.
6. Return shredded chicken to the pot and stir well.
7. Serve and enjoy.

Nutritional Value (Amount per Serving):
Calories 614; Fat 21.7 g; Carbohydrates 14.9 g; Sugar 2.5 g; Protein 86.1 g; Cholesterol 252 mg

Buffalo Chicken Breasts

Preparation Time: 5 minutes; Cooking Time: 20 minutes; Serve: 4
Ingredients:
- 1 lb chicken breasts, skinless and boneless
- 1/4 cup buffalo sauce
- 3/4 cup water

Directions:
1. Place chicken into the instant pot then pour water and buffalo sauce over the chicken.
2. Seal pot with lid and cook on manual high pressure for 20 minutes.
3. Once done then release pressure using the quick-release method than open the lid.
4. Remove chicken from pot and shred using the fork.
5. Return shredded chicken to the pot and stir well.

6. Serve and enjoy.

Nutritional Value (Amount per Serving):
Calories 219; Fat 8.4 g; Carbohydrates 0.5 g; Sugar 0 g; Protein 32.8 g; Cholesterol 101 mg

Enchilada Chicken

Preparation Time: 5 minutes; Cooking Time: 15 minutes; Serve: 8

Ingredients:
- 2 1/2 lbs chicken breasts, skinless and boneless
- 10 oz can red enchilada sauce
- 1 1/2 tsp dried oregano
- 1 1/2 tsp cumin
- 1/2 cup chicken broth

Directions:
1. Add all ingredients into the instant pot and stir well.
2. Seal pot with lid and cook on manual high pressure for 15 minutes.
3. Once done then release pressure using the quick-release method than open the lid.
4. Remove chicken from pot and shred using a fork.
5. Return shredded chicken to the pot and stir well.
6. Serve and enjoy.

Nutritional Value (Amount per Serving):
Calories 288; Fat 11.6 g; Carbohydrates 2.1 g; Sugar 0.6 g; Protein 41.4 g; Cholesterol 126 mg

Moist & Tender Turkey Breast

Preparation Time: 5 minutes; Cooking Time: 35 minutes; Serve: 6

Ingredients:
- 5 lbs turkey breasts, bone-in
- 2 cups chicken broth
- 1 tsp garlic powder
- 1 tsp dried sage
- 2 tsp dried thyme
- 1/2 tsp pepper
- 2 tsp salt

Directions:
1. Season turkey breast with garlic powder, sage, thyme, pepper, and salt.
2. Pour broth into the instant pot then place the trivet in the pot.
3. Place turkey breasts on top of the trivet.
4. Seal pot with lid and cook on manual high pressure for 35 minutes.
5. Once done then allow to release pressure naturally for 10 minutes then release using quick-release method. Open the lid.
6. Slice and serve.

Nutritional Value (Amount per Serving):
Calories 409; Fat 6.8 g; Carbohydrates 17 g; Sugar 13.6 g; Protein 66.3 g; Cholesterol 163 mg

Cafe Rio Chicken

Preparation Time: 5 minutes; Cooking Time: 12 minutes; Serve: 6

Ingredients:
- 2 lbs chicken breasts, skinless and boneless
- 1/2 cup water
- 3 tbsp ranch dressing mix
- 1/2 tbsp ground cumin
- 1/2 tbsp chili powder
- 1/2 tbsp garlic, minced
- 2/3 cup Italian dressing

Directions:
1. Place chicken into the instant pot.

2. In a small bowl, mix together Italian dressing, ranch dressing mix, water, cumin, chili powder, and garlic and pour over chicken.
3. Seal pot with lid and cook on manual high pressure for 12 minutes.
4. Once done then allow to release pressure naturally then open the lid.
5. Remove chicken from pot and shred using a fork.
6. Return shredded chicken to the pot and stir well.
7. Serve and enjoy.

Nutritional Value (Amount per Serving):
Calories 371; Fat 18.9 g; Carbohydrates 3.9 g; Sugar 2.4 g; Protein 44.2 g; Cholesterol 152 mg

Marinara Chicken

Preparation Time: 5 minutes; Cooking Time: 12 minutes; Serve: 3
Ingredients:

- 3 chicken breasts, skinless and boneless
- 1 tbsp Italian seasoning
- 1 cup parmesan cheese, shredded
- 1 tbsp olive oil
- 1 cup pasta sauce
- Pepper
- Salt

Directions:
1. Add oil into the instant pot and set the pot on sauté mode.
2. Season chicken with Italian seasoning, pepper, and salt.
3. Add chicken to the pot and cook until brown.
4. Pour pasta sauce over chicken.
5. Seal pot with lid and cook on manual mode for 12 minutes.
6. Once done then release pressure using the quick-release method than open the lid.
7. Top with cheese and serve.

Nutritional Value (Amount per Serving):
Calories 423; Fat 20.7 g; Carbohydrates 12.3 g; Sugar 7.8 g; Protein 45 g; Cholesterol 136 mg

Chicken Adobo

Preparation Time: 5 minutes; Cooking Time: 12 minutes; Serve: 6
Ingredients:

- 2 lbs chicken thighs, skinless and boneless
- 1 bay leaf
- 2 tbsp palm sugar
- 1/3 cup coconut aminos
- 1/3 cup apple cider vinegar
- 1 onion, diced
- 2 tbsp olive oil
- Pepper
- Salt

Directions:
1. Add oil into the instant pot and set the pot on sauté mode.
2. Season chicken with pepper and salt. Add chicken to the pot and cook until brown.
3. Add remaining ingredients over chicken.
4. Seal pot with lid and cook on manual mode for 12 minutes.
5. Once done then release pressure using the quick-release method than open the lid.
6. Serve and enjoy.

Nutritional Value (Amount per Serving):
Calories 356; Fat 15.9 g; Carbohydrates 5.9 g; Sugar 2.1 g; Protein 44 g; Cholesterol 135 mg

Tasty BBQ Ranch Chicken

Preparation Time: 5 minutes; Cooking Time: 4 minutes; Serve: 8

Ingredients:
- 1 1/2 lbs chicken thighs, skinless and boneless
- 12 oz BBQ sauce
- 1 tsp vinegar
- 1/4 cup heavy cream
- 1/4 cup mayonnaise
- 2 1/2 tbsp ranch seasoning mix
- 1 lb chicken breasts, skinless and boneless

Directions:
1. Place chicken into the instant pot and sprinkle ranch seasoning mix over chicken.
2. Whisk together vinegar, heavy cream, and mayonnaise and pour over chicken.
3. Pour BBQ sauce over chicken.
4. Seal pot with lid and cook on manual high pressure for 4 minutes.
5. Once done then allow to release pressure naturally for 5 minutes then release using quick-release method. Open the lid.
6. Remove chicken from pot and shred using a fork.
7. Return shredded chicken to the pot and stir well.
8. Serve and enjoy.

Nutritional Value (Amount per Serving):
Calories 273; Fat 10.3 g; Carbohydrates 17.3 g; Sugar 11.6 g; Protein 24.8 g; Cholesterol 83 mg

Indian Chicken Tikka Masala

Preparation Time: 10 minutes; Cooking Time: 20 minutes; Serve: 6
Ingredients:
- 2 lbs chicken breast, skinless and boneless
- 3/4 tsp turmeric
- 1 1/2 tsp garam masala
- 1 tsp coriander
- 1 tsp cumin
- 2 tbsp butter
- 1 tsp ginger, grated
- 2 garlic cloves, minced
- 1/2 cup coconut milk
- 14 oz can tomatoes, diced
- 1/4 tsp cayenne pepper
- 1/2 bell pepper, chopped
- 1 small onion, chopped
- 1 1/2 tsp sea salt

Directions:
1. Add butter into the instant pot and set the pot on sauté mode.
2. Add bell peppers and onion to the pot and cook for 3 minutes.
3. Add ginger, garlic, spices, and salt and cook for 2-3 minutes.
4. Add coconut milk and tomatoes and stir well.
5. Add chicken to the pot. Seal pot with lid and cook on manual high pressure for 15 minutes.
6. Once done then release pressure using the quick-release method than open the lid.
7. Remove chicken from pot and shred using a fork.
8. Puree the sauce using an immersion blender. Return shredded chicken to the pot and stir well.
9. Serve and enjoy.

Nutritional Value (Amount per Serving):
Calories 279; Fat 12.6 g; Carbohydrates 2.7 g; Sugar 4 g; Protein 33.6 g; Cholesterol 107 mg

Bacon Pineapple Chicken

Preparation Time: 10 minutes; Cooking Time: 35 minutes; Serve: 8
Ingredients:

- 3 lbs chicken breast
- 2 garlic cloves, minced
- 1 onion, diced
- 1 1/2 cups pineapple, diced
- 3 bacon slices
- 1/2 tbsp ginger, grated
- 3 tsp fish sauce
- 2 tbsp coconut aminos
- 1 tsp sea salt

Directions:
1. Place chicken into the instant pot and season with salt.
2. Arrange bacon on top of chicken.
3. Add pineapple, ginger, 1 1/2 tsp fish sauce, coconut aminos, and onion on top of chicken.
4. Seal pot with lid and cook on manual high pressure for 25 minutes.
5. Once done then release pressure using the quick-release method than open the lid.
6. Transfer pot mixture into the large bowl.
7. Set the instant pot on sauté mode.
8. Add garlic and remaining fish sauce and simmer for 10 minutes.
9. Meanwhile, shred chicken using a fork.
10. Pour sauce over chicken and serve.

Nutritional Value (Amount per Serving):
Calories 260; Fat 7.3 g; Carbohydrates 6.8 g; Sugar 3.7 g; Protein 39.2 g; Cholesterol 117 mg

Flavorful Chicken Cacciatore

Preparation Time: 5 minutes; Cooking Time: 12 minutes; Serve: 6
Ingredients:
- 2 lbs chicken breast
- 3/4 tsp dried oregano
- 1/4 cup red wine vinegar
- 14.5 oz can tomatoes
- 3 garlic cloves, minced
- 1 onion, diced
- 3/4 cup chicken broth
- 3/4 cup artichoke hearts, diced
- 7.5 oz mushrooms, sliced
- 1 bell pepper, diced
- 3 tbsp tomato paste
- 1/2 tsp dried thyme
- 3/4 tsp dried rosemary
- 1/2 tsp paprika
- 2 tbsp olive oil
- 1 tsp salt

Directions:
1. Add oil into the instant pot and set the pot on sauté mode.
2. Season chicken with pepper and salt.
3. Place chicken into the pot and cook for 2 minutes on each side.
4. Remove chicken from pot and place on a plate.
5. Add garlic and onion and sauté for 2 minutes.
6. In a small bowl, whisk together all dry spices, thyme, rosemary, paprika, oregano, and salt.
7. Add vinegar, tomato paste, tomatoes, and spices into the pot and stir well.
8. Return chicken to the pot with bell pepper, artichoke hearts, and mushrooms.
9. Pour broth into the pot.
10. Seal pot with lid and cook on manual high pressure for 8 minutes.
11. Once done then release pressure using quick-release method than open the lid.
12. Serve and enjoy.

Nutritional Value (Amount per Serving):
Calories 273; Fat 8.9 g; Carbohydrates 12.1 g; Sugar 6 g; Protein 35.8 g; Cholesterol 97 mg

Sweet Potato Chicken Curry

Preparation Time: 10 minutes; Cooking Time: 20 minutes; Serve: 4

Ingredients:
- 1 sweet potato, cubed
- 1 lb chicken breast, cubed
- 2 garlic cloves, minced
- 1/2 onion, diced
- 2 tsp coconut oil
- 14.5 oz coconut milk
- 1/2 tsp cayenne
- 1/2 tsp ground turmeric
- 1 tsp cumin
- 2 1/2 tbsp curry powder
- 2/3 cup chicken broth
- 1 3/4 cups green beans, trimmed
- 1 red pepper, diced
- 1/2 tsp sea salt

Directions:
1. Add oil into the instant pot and set the pot on sauté mode.
2. Add garlic and onion and sauté until translucent.
3. Add remaining ingredients except for coconut milk and stir well.
4. Seal pot with lid and cook on manual mode for 12 minutes.
5. Once done then allow to release pressure naturally then open the lid.
6. Stir in coconut milk and serve.

Nutritional Value (Amount per Serving):
Calories 466; Fat 30.8 g; Carbohydrates 22 g; Sugar 8.3 g; Protein 29.9 g; Cholesterol 73 mg

Chicken Chili

Preparation Time: 5 minutes; Cooking Time: 35 minutes; Serve: 8
Ingredients:
- 2 1/2 lbs chicken breasts, skinless and boneless
- 13.5 oz tomatoes, diced
- 2 sweet potatoes, peeled and diced
- 2 garlic cloves, minced
- 2 celery stalks, diced
- 1 onion, diced
- 1/2 tsp white pepper
- 1/4 cup buffalo sauce
- 1 cup chicken broth
- 1 tbsp olive oil

Directions:
1. Add oil into the instant pot and set the pot on sauté mode.
2. Add celery and onion into the pot and sauté until translucent.
3. Add garlic and sauté for a minute.
4. Add sweet potatoes, buffalo sauce, chicken broth, tomatoes, and white pepper. Stir everything well.
5. Add chicken. Seal pot with lid and cook on manual high pressure for 15 minutes.
6. Once done then release pressure using quick-release method than open the lid.
7. Remove chicken from pot and place on a dish.
8. Mash sweet potatoes using a masher and shred the chicken using a fork.
9. Return shredded chicken to the pot and stir well.
10. Serve and enjoy.

Nutritional Value (Amount per Serving):
Calories 350; Fat 12.6 g; Carbohydrates 14.2 g; Sugar 2.2 g; Protein 42.9 g; Cholesterol 126 mg

Chicken Meatballs

Preparation Time: 10 minutes; Cooking Time: 20 minutes; Serve: 6
Ingredients:
- 1 3/4 lbs ground chicken
- 5 tbsp hot sauce
- 2 green onions, sliced
- 2 garlic cloves, minced
- 2 tbsp ghee
- 4 tbsp butter

- 3/4 cup almond flour
- 1 tsp sea salt

Directions:

1. Combine together ground chicken, green onions, garlic, almond flour, and salt.
2. Make small balls from the meat mixture and set aside.
3. Add ghee into the instant pot and set the pot on sauté mode.
4. Place meatballs into the pot and cook until brown.
5. Meanwhile, mix together butter and hot sauce in oven-safe bowl and microwave until butter is melted.
6. Pour butter mixture over meatballs.
7. Seal pot with lid and cook on poultry mode for 20 minutes.
8. Once done then release pressure using the quick-release method than open the lid.
9. Serve and enjoy.

Nutritional Value (Amount per Serving):

Calories 445; Fat 28.4 g; Carbohydrates 3.9 g; Sugar 0.3 g; Protein 41.6 g; Cholesterol 149 mg

Easy Adobo Chicken

Preparation Time: 10 minutes; Cooking Time: 25 minutes; Serve: 6

Ingredients:

- 2 lbs chicken breasts, skinless and boneless
- 13.5 oz can tomatoes
- 1 tbsp adobo seasoning
- 1/2 tbsp turmeric
- 1/2 cup water
- 7.5 oz can green chilies, diced

Directions:

1. Place chicken into the instant pot and season with seasoning.
2. Add tomatoes, turmeric, water, and green chilies over chicken.
3. Seal pot with lid and cook on manual mode for 25 minutes.
4. Once done then allow to release pressure naturally then open the lid.
5. Shred the chicken using a fork and serve.

Nutritional Value (Amount per Serving):

Calories 310; Fat 11.4 g; Carbohydrates 5.3 g; Sugar 2.2 g; Protein 44.6 g; Cholesterol 135

Yummy Orange Chicken

Preparation Time: 10 minutes; Cooking Time: 10 minutes; Serve: 6

Ingredients:

- 1 1/2 lbs chicken breasts, boneless and cut into cubes
- 1/4 tsp garlic powder
- 1/2 cup coconut aminos
- 1/4 cup apple cider vinegar
- 1 cup of orange juice
- 1 tbsp arrowroot powder
- 1 tbsp water
- 1/4 tsp ground ginger

Directions:

1. Add all ingredients except arrowroot powder and water into the instant pot and stir well.
2. Seal pot with lid and cook on manual high pressure for 6 minutes.
3. Once done then release pressure using the quick-release method than open the lid.
4. Remove chicken from pot and place on a dish.
5. In a small bowl, whisk together arrowroot powder and water and pour into the pot and cook until thickened on sauté mode.
6. Return chicken into the pot and stir well.
7. Serve and enjoy.

Nutritional Value (Amount per Serving):
Calories 263; Fat 8.5 g; Carbohydrates 9.9 g; Sugar 3.5 g; Protein 33.1 g; Cholesterol 101 mg

Thai Chicken

Preparation Time: 10 minutes; Cooking Time: 11 minutes; Serve: 4
Ingredients:
- 2 lbs chicken breasts, boneless and quarter
- 2 garlic cloves, minced
- 1 tbsp cumin
- 1 tbsp coconut aminos
- 1/2 cup chicken broth
- 1 1/4 cup onion, diced
- 1 1/2 cups bell pepper, diced
- 3 tbsp fresh lime juice
- 2/3 cup almond butter
- 2 tbsp arrowroot
- 1/4 tsp red pepper flakes
- 1/8 tsp pepper
- 1/8 tsp salt

Directions:
1. Add chicken, pepper flakes, garlic, cumin, coconut aminos, broth, onion, pepper, and salt into the instant pot and stir well.
2. Seal pot with lid and cook on manual mode for 10 minutes.
3. Once done then release pressure using the quick-release method than open the lid.
4. In a bowl, whisk together arrowroot powder, lime juice, and almond butter.
5. Add arrowroot mixture and bell pepper to the pot and stir well.
6. Seal pot with lid and cook on the manual high pressure for 1 minute.
7. Once done then release pressure using the quick-release method than open the lid.
8. Stir and serve.

Nutritional Value (Amount per Serving):
Calories 501; Fat 19 g; Carbohydrates 11.7 g; Sugar 4.4 g; Protein 68.3 g; Cholesterol 202 mg

Curried Chicken

Preparation Time: 10 minutes; Cooking Time: 20 minutes; Serve: 6
Ingredients:
- 4 lbs chicken breasts
- 3 tbsp fresh lemon juice
- 13.5 oz coconut milk
- 1 tsp turmeric
- 1 1/2 tbsp curry powder
- 1/2 tsp salt

Directions:
1. In a bowl, mix together coconut milk, spices, and lemon juice.
2. Add chicken and coconut milk to the pot.
3. Seal pot with lid and cook on poultry mode for 15 minutes.
4. Once done then release pressure using the quick-release method than open the lid.
5. Shred the chicken using a fork and serve.

Nutritional Value (Amount per Serving):
Calories 730; Fat 37.9 g; Carbohydrates 4.9 g; Sugar 2.3 g; Protein 89.2 g; Cholesterol 269 mg

Olive Chicken

Preparation Time: 10 minutes; Cooking Time: 15 minutes; Serve: 4
Ingredients:
- 4 chicken breasts, skinless and boneless
- 1/2 cup butter
- 1/2 tsp cumin
- 1/4 tsp pepper
- 1/2 cup onion, sliced
- 7.5 oz can olive, pitted
- 1 cup chicken broth

- 1 fresh lemon juice
- 1 tsp sea salt

Directions:
1. Season chicken with pepper and salt.
2. Add butter into the instant pot and set the pot on sauté mode.
3. Place chicken into the pot and sauté until browned.
4. Add remaining ingredients and stir well.
5. Seal pot with lid and cook on manual mode for 10 minutes.
6. Once done then release pressure using the quick-release method than open the lid.
7. Serve and enjoy.

Nutritional Value (Amount per Serving):
Calories 575; Fat 42.5 g; Carbohydrates 5.5 g; Sugar 1.1 g; Protein 42.3 g; Cholesterol 186 mg

Sweet Mango Chicken

Preparation Time: 10 minutes; Cooking Time: 10 minutes; Serve: 4
Ingredients:
- 3 chicken breasts, skinless and boneless
- 13.5 oz pineapple mango salsa
- 1 tsp red chili flakes
- 1 cup pineapple, cubed
- 1 mango, peel and cubed
- Pepper
- Salt

Directions:
1. Set instant pot on sauté mode.
2. Season chicken with pepper and salt and place into the pot and cook on sauté mode until browned.
3. Add remaining ingredients and stir well.
4. Seal pot with lid and cook on manual high pressure for 10 minutes.
5. Once done then release pressure using the quick-release method than open the lid.
6. Serve and enjoy.

Nutritional Value (Amount per Serving):
Calories 320; Fat 8.2 g; Carbohydrates 21.2 g; Sugar 25.4 g; Protein 31.3 g; Cholesterol 93 mg

Herb Chicken

Preparation Time: 10 minutes; Cooking Time: 5 minutes; Serve: 2
Ingredients:
- 2 chicken breasts, skinless and boneless
- 1/2 tsp ground ginger
- 1/4 tsp ground coriander
- 1/4 tsp paprika
- 2 tbsp olive oil
- 1 cup chicken stock
- 1/2 tsp ground garlic
- 1 tsp dried mixed herbs
- Pepper
- Salt

Directions:
1. In a large bowl, mix garlic, ginger, coriander, paprika, mixed herbs, pepper, salt, 2 tbsp stock, and 1 tbsp oil.
2. Add chicken to a bowl and coat well with spice mixture.
3. Set pot on sauté mode and add remaining oil to the pot.
4. Add chicken to the pot and cook until browned.
5. Remove chicken from pot and place on a plate.
6. Add the remaining stock into the pot and stir well.

7. Place trivet in the pot.
8. Place chicken on top of the trivet.
9. Seal pot with lid and cook on manual mode for 5 minutes.
10. Once done then allow to release pressure naturally for 10 minutes then release using quick-release method. Open the lid.
11. Serve and enjoy.

Nutritional Value (Amount per Serving):
Calories 395; Fat 24.7 g; Carbohydrates 1.3 g; Sugar 0.4 g; Protein 41 g; Cholesterol 125 mg

Creamy Pesto Chicken

Preparation Time: 10 minutes; Cooking Time: 8 minutes; Serve: 2

Ingredients:
- 2 chicken breasts, skinless and boneless
- 3/4 tbsp basil pesto
- 1 tbsp corn-starch
- 1/4 cup roasted red peppers
- 5 tbsp heavy cream
- 1 tsp Italian seasoning
- 1/4 tsp garlic, minced
- 1/2 cup chicken stock
- 1/4 tsp pepper
- 1/4 tsp salt

Directions:
1. Add stock and chicken into the instant pot.
2. Sprinkle Italian seasoning, garlic, pepper, and salt over the chicken.
3. Seal pot with lid and cook on manual high pressure for 8 minutes.
4. Once done then allow to release pressure naturally for 10 minutes then release using quick-release method. Open the lid.
5. Remove chicken from pot and place on a dish.
6. Set pot on sauté mode. Add red peppers, pesto, heavy cream, and corn-starch to the pot. Stir well and cook for 3-4 minutes.
7. Return chicken to the pot and stir well and serve.

Nutritional Value (Amount per Serving):
Calories 162; Fat 14.8 g; Carbohydrates 6.9 g; Sugar 1.4 g; Protein 41.8 g; Cholesterol 178 mg

Lemon Butter chicken

Preparation Time: 10 minutes; Cooking Time: 15 minutes; Serve: 2

Ingredients:
- 4 chicken thighs, bone-in
- 1/2 tsp oregano
- 1 lemon juice
- 2 garlic cloves, diced
- 1 small onion, diced
- 1 cup chicken broth
- 1 tsp parsley flakes
- 1 tsp lemon pepper seasoning
- 2 tbsp butter, melted
- 1/4 tsp pepper
- 1/2 tsp salt

Directions:
1. Add all ingredients into the instant pot and stir well.
2. Seal pot with lid and cook on manual high pressure for 15 minutes.
3. Once done then allow to release pressure naturally for 10 minutes then release using quick-release method. Open the lid.
4. Serve and enjoy.

Nutritional Value (Amount per Serving):
Calories 679; Fat 33.2 g; Carbohydrates 6 g; Sugar 2.2 g; Protein 84.4 g; Cholesterol 280 mg

Instant Pot Turkey Breast

Preparation Time: 10 minutes; Cooking Time: 30 minutes; Serve: 8
Ingredients:

- 6 lbs turkey breast
- 1 1/2 cups chicken broth
- 1 onion, quartered
- 1/2 cup celery, chopped
- 1 1/4 tsp thyme
- Pepper
- Salt

Directions:

1. Add broth, onion, celery, and thyme to the instant pot and stir well.
2. Season turkey breast with pepper and salt.
3. Place trivet into the pot then place turkey breast on top of the trivet.
4. Seal pot with lid and cook on manual high pressure for 30 minutes.
5. Once done then allow to release pressure naturally then open the lid.
6. Slice and serve.

Nutritional Value (Amount per Serving):

Calories 368; Fat 5.9 g; Carbohydrates 16.1 g; Sugar 12.7 g; Protein 59.2 g; Cholesterol 146 mg

Ranch Chicken

Preparation Time: 10 minutes; Cooking Time: 15 minutes; Serve: 4
Ingredients:

- 2 lbs chicken breast, boneless
- 5 bacon slices, cooked and chopped
- 1 cup cheddar cheese, shredded
- 1/2 cup water
- 7.5 oz cream cheese
- 1 packet ranch seasoning

Directions:

1. Add cream cheese and water into the instant pot.
2. Season chicken with ranch seasoning place into the pot.
3. Seal pot with lid and cook on manual high pressure for 15 minutes.
4. Once done then release pressure using the quick-release method than open the lid.
5. Remove chicken from pot and shred using a fork.
6. Return shredded chicken to the pot along with bacon and cheese and stir well.
7. Serve and enjoy.

Nutritional Value (Amount per Serving):

Calories 765; Fat 43.5 g; Carbohydrates 2.1 g; Sugar 0.3 g; Protein 67.9 g; Cholesterol 259 mg

Orange BBQ Chicken

Preparation Time: 10 minutes; Cooking Time: 10 minutes; Serve: 6
Ingredients:

- 4 chicken breasts, boneless and cut into chunks
- 2 tbsp soy sauce
- 1 cup BBQ sauce
- 2 tsp corn-starch
- 1 cup orange marmalade

Directions:

1. Add chicken, soy sauce, and BBQ sauce into the instant pot and stir well.
2. Seal pot with lid and cook on manual high pressure for 4 minutes.
3. Once done then release pressure using quick-release method than open the lid.
4. In a small bowl, whisk corn-starch with 1 tbsp water and pour into the pot. Stir well.
5. Add marmalade and stir well and cook on sauté mode for 5 minutes.
6. Stir and serve.

Nutritional Value (Amount per Serving):
Calories 377; Fat 7 g; Carbohydrates 51.7 g; Sugar 43 g; Protein 27.5 g; Cholesterol 83 mg

Mustard Chicken

Preparation Time: 10 minutes; Cooking Time: 15 minutes; Serve: 4

Ingredients:

- 2 lb chicken thighs, boneless and skinless
- 3 tbsp Dijon mustard
- 2 lb potatoes, diced
- 3/4 cup chicken stock
- 3 tbsp lemon juice
- 1 1/2 tbsp Italian seasoning
- 2 tbsp olive oil
- Pepper
- Salt

Directions:

1. Add oil into the instant pot and set the pot on sauté mode.
2. Season chicken with pepper and salt and place into the instant pot.
3. In a small bowl, mix together lemon juice, stock, and Dijon mustard and pour into the pot.
4. Add potatoes and Italian seasoning and stir well.
5. Seal pot with lid and cook on manual high pressure for 15 minutes.
6. Once done then release pressure using quick-release method than open the lid.
7. Serve and enjoy.

Nutritional Value (Amount per Serving):
Calories 676; Fat 26.3 g; Carbohydrates 37.2 g; Sugar 3.5 g; Protein 70.2 g; Cholesterol 206 mg

Chapter 7: Beef, Pork & Lamb

Delicious Beef Tips

Preparation Time: 10 minutes; Cooking Time: 30 minutes; Serve: 4
Ingredients:

- 2 lbs sirloin beef tips
- 10 oz can mushroom soup
- 1/2 cup red wine
- 1 cup beef broth
- 1/4 cup onions, diced
- 1/2 tsp pepper
- 3 tbsp flour
- 2 tbsp olive oil
- 1/2 tsp garlic salt

Directions:

1. Season meat with pepper and garlic salt and coat with flour.
2. Add oil into the instant pot and set the pot on sauté mode.
3. Add meat to the pot and sauté until browned.
4. Add onion and sauté for a minute.
5. Add broth, wine, and mushroom soup and stir well.
6. Seal pot with lid and cook on manual mode for 25 minutes.
7. Once done then allow to release pressure naturally for 10 minutes then release using the quick-release method. Open the lid.
8. Stir and serve.

Nutritional Value (Amount per Serving):
Calories 268; Fat 11.6 g; Carbohydrates 12.3 g; Sugar 2.3 g; Protein 23.9 g; Cholesterol 2 mg

Shredded Mexican Beef

Preparation Time: 10 minutes; Cooking Time: 35 minutes; Serve: 12
Ingredients:

- 2 lbs sirloin beef tips
- 10 oz can mushroom soup
- 1/2 cup red wine
- 1 cup beef broth
- 1/4 cup onions, diced
- 1/2 tsp pepper
- 3 tbsp flour
- 2 tbsp olive oil
- 1/2 tsp garlic salt

Directions:

1. Add oil into the instant pot and set the pot on sauté mode.
2. Add onion to the pot and sauté until onion is softened.
3. Add remaining ingredients to the pot and stir everything well.
4. Seal pot with lid and cook on manual high pressure for 35 minutes.
5. Once done then allow to release pressure naturally then open the lid.
6. Remove meat from pot and shred using a fork.
7. Return shredded meat to the pot and stir well.
8. Serve and enjoy.

Nutritional Value (Amount per Serving):
Calories 98; Fat 5 g; Carbohydrates 3.8 g; Sugar 0.5 g; Protein 8.1 g; Cholesterol 1 mg

Korean Beef

Preparation Time: 10 minutes; Cooking Time: 45 minutes; Serve: 6
Ingredients:

- 4 lbs bottom roast, cut into chunks
- 1 apple, peeled and chopped
- 1 tbsp ginger, grated
- 4 garlic cloves, minced

- 1/2 cup soy sauce
- 1 cup beef broth
- 2 tbsp olive oil
- 1 large orange juice
- Pepper
- Salt

Directions:
1. Season meat with pepper and salt.
2. Add oil into the instant pot and set the pot on sauté mode.
3. Add the meat into the pot and cook until browned.
4. Add soy sauce and broth to the pot and stir well.
5. Add remaining ingredients and stir well.
6. Seal pot with lid and cook on manual high pressure for 45 minutes.
7. Once done then release pressure using the quick-release method than open the lid.
8. Shred the meat using a fork.
9. Stir well and serve.

Nutritional Value (Amount per Serving):
Calories 530; Fat 21.2 g; Carbohydrates 12.5 g; Sugar 7.9 g; Protein 69.6 g; Cholesterol 201 mg

Italian Beef

Preparation Time: 10 minutesl; Cooking Time: 55 minutes; Serve: 12
Ingredients:
- 3 1/2 lbs beef chuck, boneless
- 1/2 tsp red pepper, crushed
- 1 tbsp Italian seasoning
- 2 tbsp brown sugar
- 1 cup beef broth
- 1/2 cup Worcestershire sauce
- 1/4 cup pepperoncini juices
- 18 pepperoncini peppers
- 1 onion, sliced
- 4 garlic cloves, minced
- 4 tbsp butter

Directions:
1. Add butter into the instant pot and set the pot on sauté mode.
2. Add garlic and onion and sauté until onion is softened.
3. Add remaining ingredients and stir everything well.
4. Seal pot with lid and cook on manual high pressure for 50 minutes.
5. Once done then release pressure using the quick-release method than open the lid.
6. Remove meat from pot and shred using the fork.
7. Return shredded meat to the pot and stir well.
8. Serve and enjoy.

Nutritional Value (Amount per Serving):
Calories 324; Fat 12.6 g; Carbohydrates 9.7 g; Sugar 5.5 g; Protein 41.2 g; Cholesterol 129 mg

Beef Stroganoff

Preparation Time: 10 minutes; Cooking Time: 24 minutes; Serve: 6
Ingredients:
- 2 lbs stew meat
- 1/2 cup sour cream
- 8 oz mushrooms, sliced
- 1 1/2 tbsp Worcestershire sauce
- 1/2 tsp dried thyme
- 1 tsp parsley flakes
- 1 tsp onion powder
- 1 1/4 cup beef broth
- 1/2 cup onion, chopped
- 2 tbsp olive oil
- 1/2 tsp garlic powder
- 1/2 tsp paprika
- 1/3 cup flour
- 1 tsp pepper

- 2 tsp salt

Directions:
1. Add flour, garlic powder, and paprika into the large zip-lock bag.
2. Add meat to the bag. Seal bag and shake until well coated.
3. Add oil into the instant pot and set the pot on sauté mode.
4. Add onion and meat to the pot and sauté until browned.
5. Add remaining ingredients except for sour cream and stir well.
6. Seal pot with lid and cook on manual high pressure for 20 minutes.
7. Once done then release pressure using the quick-release method than open the lid.
8. Stir in sour cream and serve.

Nutritional Value (Amount per Serving):
Calories 513; Fat 29 g; Carbohydrates 10.1 g; Sugar 2.2 g; Protein 50.8 g; Cholesterol 169 mg

Asian Pot Roast

Preparation Time: 10 minutes; Cooking Time: 70 minutes; Serve: 6
Ingredients:
- 3 lbs chuck roast, trimmed
- 2 bell peppers, chopped
- 2 tbsp corn-starch
- 1 beef bouillon cube
- 2/3 cup water
- 1/4 cup soy sauce
- 15 oz mushrooms, sliced
- 2 tbsp honey
- 1/4 cup soy sauce
- 2 tbsp ginger, minced
- 1 onion, diced
- 3 garlic cloves, minced
- 2 tbsp olive oil
- Pepper
- Salt

Directions:
1. Add oil into the instant pot and set the pot on sauté mode.
2. Add ginger, garlic, onion, pepper, and salt and cook for 5 minutes.
3. Add water, meat, bouillon cube, honey, mushrooms, and soy sauce and stir well.
4. Seal pot with lid and cook on manual high pressure for 60 minutes.
5. Once done then allow to release pressure naturally for 10 minutes then release using the quick-release method. Open the lid.
6. Remove meat from the pot.
7. Add bell pepper and corn-starch and stir well and cook on sauté mode until sauce thickens.
8. Return meat to the pot and stir well.
9. Serve and enjoy.

Nutritional Value (Amount per Serving):
Calories 612; Fat 24 g; Carbohydrates 18 g; Sugar 10.1 g; Protein 78.8 g; Cholesterol 229 mg

Italian Ribs

Preparation Time: 10 minutes; Cooking Time: 40 minutes; Serve: 4
Ingredients:
- 3 lbs beef short ribs
- 1 1/4 cup pasta sauce
- 1/2 cup olives
- 1/2 cup dry white wine
- 1 1/4 cup leeks, chopped
- 1 tsp Italian seasoning
- 2 tbsp olive oil
- 1/4 tsp pepper
- 3/4 tsp salt

Directions:
1. Add oil into the instant pot and set the pot on sauté mode.

2. Add ribs to the pot and cook until browned.
3. Remove ribs from pot and season with Italian seasoning, pepper, and salt.
4. Add leeks to the pot and cook until softened.
5. Add wine and stir everything well. Return ribs to pot with pasta sauce and olives.
6. Seal pot with lid and cook on manual high pressure for 30 minutes.
7. Once done then allow to release pressure naturally for 10 minutes then release using the quick-release method. Open the lid.
8. Stir and serve.

Nutritional Value (Amount per Serving):
   Calories 890; Fat 42 g; Carbohydrates 16.8 g; Sugar 8.3 g; Protein 100.2 g; Cholesterol 312 mg

Shredded Thai Beef

Preparation Time: 10 minutes; Cooking Time: 45 minutes; Serve: 8
Ingredients:
- 3 lbs chuck roast
- 1/2 cup chili sauce
- 1/2 cup orange juice
- 1 tsp garlic powder
- 1 tsp curry powder
- 2 tbsp olive oil
- Pepper
- Salt

Directions:
1. Add oil into the instant pot and set the pot on sauté mode.
2. Add meat to the pot and sauté until meat is browned.
3. Add remaining ingredients and stir well.
4. Seal pot with lid and cook on manual high pressure for 45 minutes.
5. Once done then release pressure using the quick-release method than open the lid.
6. Shred the meat using a fork and stir well.
7. Serve and enjoy.

Nutritional Value (Amount per Serving):
   Calories 408; Fat 17.7 g; Carbohydrates 2.3 g; Sugar 1.6 g; Protein 56.4 g; Cholesterol 172 mg

Mexican Barbecue

Preparation Time: 10 minutes; Cooking Time: 40 minutes; Serve: 6
Ingredients:
- 3 lbs beef stew meat
- 1 bay leaf
- 1/8 tsp ground cloves
- 1 tbsp dried oregano
- 2 tsp chipotle powder
- 1 tbsp ground cumin
- 1/2 cup beef broth
- 2 tbsp apple cider vinegar
- 1/2 small onion, diced
- 2 garlic cloves
- 1 tbsp olive oil
- 1/2 tsp pepper
- 3/4 tsp salt

Directions:
1. Add oil into the instant pot and set the pot on sauté mode.
2. Add meat to the pot and sauté until browned.
3. Add remaining ingredients and stir well.
4. Seal pot with lid and cook on manual high pressure for 30 minutes.
5. Once done then allow to release pressure naturally then open the lid.
6. Shred the meat using a fork and stir well.
7. Serve and enjoy.

Nutritional Value (Amount per Serving):

Calories 470; Fat 17.6 g; Carbohydrates 2.3 g; Sugar 0.7 g; Protein 71.2 g; Cholesterol 208 mg

Korean Beef Tacos

Preparation Time: 10 minutes; Cooking Time: 45 minutes; Serve: 6
Ingredients:

- 2 lbs top sirloin, cut into chunks
- 1 tsp sesame oil
- 1/2 cup brown sugar
- 1/2 cup soy sauce
- 2 garlic cloves
- 1 tbsp ginger, grated
- 14 oz can pears, drained

Directions:
1. Add all ingredients into the instant pot and stir well.
2. Seal pot with lid and cook on manual high pressure for 45 minutes.
3. Once done then release pressure using the quick-release method than open the lid.
4. Shred the meat using a fork and stir well.
5. Serve and enjoy.

Nutritional Value (Amount per Serving):

Calories 362; Fat 10.4 g; Carbohydrates 17.3 g; Sugar 13.4 g; Protein 47.9 g; Cholesterol 135 mg

Delicious Italian Beef

Preparation Time: 10 minutes; Cooking Time: 50 minutes; Serve: 6
Ingredients:

- 2 3/4 lbs beef roast
- 1 onion, sliced
- 1 1/2 tbsp Italian seasoning
- 2 tbsp olive oil
- 1 cup celery, chopped
- 1 cup beef stock
- 3/4 cup red wine
- 4 garlic cloves, sliced

Directions:
1. Add half oil into the instant pot and set the pot on sauté mode.
2. Add meat into and sear from all the sides.
3. Transfer seared meat to a plate.
4. Add remaining oil, celery, and onions to the pot and cook for 3 minutes.
5. Add seasoning and garlic and cook for a minute.
6. Return meat to the pot.
7. Add stock and red wine and stir well.
8. Seal pot with lid and cook on manual high pressure for 40 minutes.
9. Once done then allow to release pressure naturally then open the lid.
10. Serve and enjoy.

Nutritional Value (Amount per Serving):

Calories 477; Fat 18.8 g; Carbohydrates 4.1 g; Sugar 1.6 g; Protein 64 g; Cholesterol 188 mg

Flavorful Barbacoa

Preparation Time: 10 minutes; Cooking Time: 1 hour 10 minutes; Serve: 8
Ingredients:

- 2 3/4 lbs beef chuck roast, cut into chunks
- 2 tbsp cumin
- 4 garlic cloves, minced
- 1 green chili, diced
- 3 chipotles peppers, minced
- 1 1/4 cup chicken stock
- 2 bay leaves

- 6 tbsp honey
- 1/4 cup fresh lime juice
- 1 tbsp oregano
- 2 tbsp olive oil
- 1/4 tsp pepper
- 1 tsp salt

Directions:
1. Add oil in the instant pot and set the pot on sauté mode.
2. Add meat in the pot and sear until browned.
3. Add remaining ingredients and stir well.
4. Seal pot with lid and cook on manual high pressure for 1 hour.
5. Once done then release pressure using the quick-release method than open the lid.
6. Shred the meat using a fork and serve.

Nutritional Value (Amount per Serving):
Calories 656; Fat 47.4 g; Carbohydrates 14.9 g; Sugar 13.2 g; Protein 41.4 g; Cholesterol 161 mg

Asian Beef

Preparation Time: 10 minutes; Cooking Time: 40 minutes; Serve: 8
Ingredients:
- 2 3/4 lbs beef chuck roast, boneless and cut into cubes
- 1/4 tsp onion powder
- 2 garlic cloves, minced
- 1/4 cup beef stock
- 1/3 cup brown sugar
- 7 tbsp soy sauce
- 1/4 tsp pepper
- 2 tbsp gochujang sauce
- 1 tbsp fresh ginger, grated
- 1 tbsp rice vinegar
- 2 tbsp sesame oil

Directions:
1. In a bowl, whisk together all ingredients except meat.
2. Place meat into the instant pot.
3. Pour bowl mixture over meat.
4. Seal pot with lid and cook on meat mode for 40 minutes.
5. Once done then allow to release pressure naturally for 10 minutes then release using the quick-release method. Open the lid.
6. Stir and serve.

Nutritional Value (Amount per Serving):
Calories 632; Fat 17.8 g; Carbohydrates 7.8 g; Sugar 6.2 g; Protein 16.1 g; Cholesterol 161 mg

Tasty Steak Bites

Preparation Time: 10 minutes; Cooking Time: 20 minutes; Serve: 6
Ingredients:
- 2 3/4 lbs round steak, cut into bites
- 2 garlic cloves, minced
- 1/2 onion, diced
- 1 cup chicken stock
- 1/4 cup butter
- 1/4 tsp pepper
- 1/2 tsp salt

Directions:
1. Add all ingredients in the instant pot and stir well.
2. Seal pot with lid and cook on manual high pressure for 20 minutes.
3. Once done then release pressure using the quick-release method than open the lid.
4. Stir and serve.

Nutritional Value (Amount per Serving):

Calories 524; Fat 27.8 g; Carbohydrates 1.4 g; Sugar 0.5 g; Protein 63.1 g; Cholesterol 197 mg

Smoky Beef

Preparation Time: 10 minutes; Cooking Time: 15 minutes; Serve: 4
Ingredients:
- 1 1/2 lbs flank steak, cut into strips
- 3 garlic cloves, minced
- 1/2 cup chicken stock
- 1/2 cup tomato sauce
- 2 bell peppers, sliced
- 1/4 tsp oregano
- 1 1/2 tsp paprika
- 1 chipotle pepper in adobo sauce
- 1 small onion, sliced
- 2 tbsp olive oil
- Pepper
- Salt

Directions:
1. Season meat with pepper and salt.
2. Add oil into the instant pot and set the pot on sauté mode.
3. Add meat and sauté until brown.
4. Add remaining ingredients and stir to combine.
5. Seal pot with lid and cook on manual high pressure for 15 minutes.
6. Once done then allow to release pressure naturally then open the lid.
7. Shred the meat using a fork and serve.

Nutritional Value (Amount per Serving):
Calories 431; Fat 21.6 g; Carbohydrates 9.1 g; Sugar 5.2 g; Protein 48.9 g; Cholesterol 94 mg

Flank Steak

Preparation Time: 10 minutes; Cooking Time: 20 minutes; Serve: 2
Ingredients:
- 1 lb flank steak
- 1/4 cup olive oil
- 1/2 tbsp Worcestershire sauce
- 1 1/2 tbsp vinegar
- 2 tbsp onion soup mix

Directions:
1. Place flank steak in instant pot and cook on sauté mode until browned.
2. Add remaining ingredients and stir well.
3. Seal pot with a lid and select manual high pressure for 25 minutes.
4. Once done then allow to release pressure naturally then open the lid.
5. Stir and serve.

Nutritional Value (Amount per Serving):
Calories 776; Fat 44.2 g; Carbohydrates 26.2 g; Sugar 2.6 g; Protein 66 g; Cholesterol 125 mg

Moist & Tender Ribs

Preparation Time: 10 minutes; Cooking Time: 35 minutes; Serve: 4
Ingredients:
- 2 lbs country-style spareribs, boneless
- 14 oz can chicken stock
- 1 tbsp liquid smoke
- 1 tbsp sea salt

Directions:
1. Season spareribs with sea salt and set aside.
2. Add liquid smoke and broth into the instant pot.
3. Place spareribs into the pot.
4. Seal pot with lid and cook on meat mode for 35 minutes.
5. Once done then release pressure using the quick-release method than open the lid.

6. Serve and enjoy.

Nutritional Value (Amount per Serving):

Calories 516; Fat 33.2 g; Carbohydrates 3.5 g; Sugar 1.6 g; Protein 46.5 g; Cholesterol 133 mg

Spicy Beef Curry

Preparation Time: 10 minutes; Cooking Time: 20 minutes; Serve: 4

Ingredients:

- 1 lb beef chuck roast, cut into pieces
- 2 tomatoes, quarters
- 1 1/2 tsp garam masala
- 1/4 tsp ground coriander
- 1/2 tsp cayenne pepper
- 1/4 cup fresh cilantro, chopped
- 2 garlic cloves, chopped
- 1 small onion, quarters
- 1 tsp ground cumin
- 1 tsp salt

Directions:

1. Add tomatoes, cilantro, garlic, and onion into the blender and blend until smooth.
2. Add cumin, cayenne, garam masala, coriander, and salt and blend well.
3. Place beef into the instant pot then pour blended mixture over the beef.
4. Seal pot with lid and cook on manual high pressure for 20 minutes.
5. Once done then allow to release pressure naturally then open the lid.
6. Stir and serve.

Nutritional Value (Amount per Serving):

Calories 435; Fat 31.9 g; Carbohydrates 4.9 g; Sugar 2.4 g; Protein 30.6 g; Cholesterol 117 mg

Pork Tenderloin

Preparation Time: 10 minutes; Cooking Time: 7 minutes; Serve: 6

Ingredients:

- 2 pork tenderloin
- 1/4 tsp nutmeg
- 1 tbsp brown sugar
- 1 tbsp cinnamon
- 1 cup chicken stock
- 1/4 cup honey
- 2 cups apples, diced

Directions:

1. Mix together all dry ingredients and rub over pork tenderloin.
2. Add stock, honey, apples, and tenderloins in the pot.
3. Seal pot with lid and cook on manual mode for 7 minutes.
4. Once done then release pressure using the quick-release method than open the lid.
5. Slice and serve.

Nutritional Value (Amount per Serving):

Calories 251; Fat 4.2 g; Carbohydrates 24.4 g; Sugar 21 g; Protein 29.5 g; Cholesterol 81 mg

Tasty Beef Chili

Preparation Time: 10 minutes; Cooking Time: 35 minute; Serve: 8

Ingredients:

- 1 lb ground beef
- 1/2 tbsp chili powder
- 1 tbsp ground cumin
- 1 jalapeno pepper, chopped
- 1 tsp garlic powder
- 5 oz tomato paste
- 1/2 onion, chopped
- 3 tomatillos, chopped
- 1 lb ground pork
- Salt

Directions for Cooking:

1. Set instant pot on sauté mode.
2. Add beef and pork into the pot and cook on sauté mode until browned.
3. Add remaining ingredients and stir well.
4. Seal pot with lid and cook on manual high pressure for 35 minutes.
5. Once done then allow to release pressure naturally then open the lid.
6. Stir and serve.

Nutritional Value (Amount per Serving):
Calories 214; Fat 6 g; Carbohydrates 5.7 g; Sugar 2.7 g; Protein 33.3 g; Cholesterol 92 mg

Chipotle Chili

Preparation Time: 10 minutes; Cooking Time: 35 minutes; Serve: 4
Ingredients:
- 1 lb ground beef
- 2 tbsp flour
- 1 can black beans
- 1 cup beef broth
- 1 tsp garlic, minced
- 13.5 oz can red kidney beans, rinsed and drained
- 1/2 bell pepper, diced
- 1 tsp chili powder
- 1 cup of water
- 1/2 chipotle pepper, minced
- 1/2 onion, diced
- Salt

Directions:
1. Brown onion and ground beef until meat is no longer pink.
2. Add spices and garlic and cook for a minute.
3. Add remaining ingredients except for flour and stir well.
4. Seal pot with lid and cook on stew mode for 35 minutes.
5. Once done then release pressure using the quick-release method than open the lid.
6. Whisk together flour and 3 tbsp water and stir in instant pot.
7. Set pot on sauté mode and cook until the sauce thickened.
8. Stir and serve.

Nutritional Value (Amount per Serving):
Calories 496; Fat 8.7 g; Carbohydrates 51.9 g; Sugar 4.7 g; Protein 52.1 g; Cholesterol 101 mg

Veggie Beef Roast

Preparation Time: 10 minutes; Cooking Time: 30 minutes; Serve: 4
Ingredients:
- 2 lbs beef chunks, boneless
- 2 cups hot water
- 2 tbsp onion soup mix, dried
- 1 1/2 onion, diced
- 2 carrots, chunk
- 6 cups potato, peel and cut into chunk

Directions:
1. Add beef chunks in instant pot.
2. In a bowl mix together hot water and onion soup mix.
3. Once it dissolves then pour over the beef chunks.
4. Add carrots chunk, onion chunks, and potato chunks to the pot and stir well.
5. Seal pot with lid and cook on meat/ stew mode.
6. Once done then release pressure using the quick-release method than open the lid.
7. Serve and enjoy.

Nutritional Value (Amount per Serving):
Calories 416; Fat 8.3 g; Carbohydrates 43.2 g; Sugar 5 g; Protein 40.9 g; Cholesterol 101 mg

Meatballs

Preparation Time: 10 minutes; Cooking Time: 5 minutes; Serve: 8

Ingredients:

- 1 lb ground beef
- 1/2 tsp garlic salt
- 1 3/4 cups pasta sauce
- 1 egg, beaten
- 2 carrots, shredded
- 2 cups of water
- 2 bread slices, crumbled
- 1 small onion, minced
- Pepper
- Salt

Directions:

1. In a bowl, mix together ground beef, egg, carrots, crumbled bread, onion, garlic salt, pepper, and salt.
2. Make small balls from meat mixture and set aside.
3. Pour 2 cups of water and 2 cups of pasta sauce into the instant pot stir well.
4. Add meatballs to the instant pot.
5. Seal pot with lid and cook on manual high pressure for 5 minutes.
6. Once done then allow to release pressure naturally then open the lid.
7. Serve and enjoy.

Nutritional Value (Amount per Serving):

Calories 177; Fat 5.6 g; Carbohydrates 11.2 g; Sugar 6.1 g; Protein 19.3 g; Cholesterol 72 mg

Mongolian Beef

Preparation Time: 10 minutes; Cooking Time: 25 minutes; Serve: 4

Ingredients:

- 1 1/2 lbs flank steak, sliced
- 1/4 cup arrowroot powder
- 1 carrot, grated
- 1/2 cup honey
- 3/4 cup water
- 1/2 cup coconut aminos
- 1/2 tsp ginger powder
- 2 tbsp olive oil

Directions:

1. Coat flank steak with arrowroot powder and set aside.
2. Add all other ingredients into the instant pot and cook on sauté mode for 1 minute.
3. Add sliced beef and stir well.
4. Seal pot with lid and cook on manual high pressure for 25 minutes.
5. Once done then release pressure using the quick-release method than open the lid.
6. Stir and serve.

Nutritional Value (Amount per Serving):

Calories 591; Fat 21.2 g; Carbohydrates 50.6 g; Sugar 35.6 g; Protein 47.6 g; Cholesterol 94 mg

Flavors Taco Meat

Preparation Time: 10 minutes; Cooking Time: 15 minutes; Serve: 6

Ingredients:

- 1 1/4 lbs beef minced
- 1/2 tsp smoked paprika
- 1/4 tsp garlic powder
- 1/4 tsp onion powder
- 1 tsp dried basil
- 1 1/2 tsp paprika
- 2 tomatoes, chopped
- 2 garlic cloves, minced
- 1 bell pepper, chopped
- 1 onion, chopped
- 1 tsp oregano
- 1/2 tbsp oil
- 1/2 tsp ground cumin
- 1/4 tsp black pepper
- 1 tsp salt

Directions:
1. Add oil into the instant pot and set the pot on sauté mode.
2. Add meat and sauté for 3 minutes.
3. Add remaining ingredients into the pot and stir well.
4. Seal pot with lid and cook on manual high pressure for 15 minutes.
5. Once done then release pressure using the quick-release method than open the lid.
6. Serve and enjoy.

Nutritional Value (Amount per Serving):
Calories 186; Fat 4.4 g; Carbohydrates 5.7 g; Sugar 5.2 g; Protein 1 g; Cholesterol 0 mg

Leg of Lamb

Preparation Time: 10 minutes; Cooking Time: 35 minutes; Serve: 8
Ingredients:
- 3 lbs leg of lamb, boneless
- 2 tbsp fresh rosemary, chopped
- 3 garlic cloves, crushed
- 2 cups of water
- 2 tbsp olive oil
- Pepper
- Salt

Directions:
1. Season lamb with pepper and salt.
2. Add oil into the instant pot and set the pot on sauté mode.
3. Add lamb to the pot and cook until browned. Remove lamb from the pot.
4. Add rosemary and garlic to the pot.
5. Pour water into the pot then place the rack into the pot.
6. Place lamb on top of the rack. Seal pot with lid and cook on meat/stew mode for 35 minutes.
7. Once done then allow to release pressure naturally for 10 minutes then release using the quick-release method. Open the lid.
8. Slice and serve.

Nutritional Value (Amount per Serving):
Calories 351; Fat 16.1 g; Carbohydrates 0.9 g; Sugar 0 g; Protein 47.9 g; Cholesterol 153 mg

Flavors Lamb Shanks

Preparation Time: 10 minutes; Cooking Time: 38 minutes; Serve: 6
Ingredients:
- 1 1/2 lbs lamb shanks, chopped
- 2 tsp rosemary powder
- 1 tbsp garlic powder
- 2 tbsp butter
- 2 tbsp fresh lemon juice
- 1 cup chicken stock
- Pepper
- Salt

Directions:
1. Rub lamb shanks with rosemary, garlic, pepper, and salt.
2. Add butter into the instant pot and set the pot on sauté mode.
3. Add shanks to the pot and cook until browned.
4. Add lemon and stock. Seal pot with lid and cook on manual high pressure for 30 minutes.
5. Once done then release pressure using the quick-release method than open the lid.
6. Set pot on sauté mode and cook for 3 minutes until sauce thickened.
7. Serve and enjoy.

Nutritional Value (Amount per Serving):

Calories 354; Fat 16.7 g; Carbohydrates 10.6 g; Sugar 0.6 g; Protein 37.2 g; Cholesterol 112 mg

Perfect Dinner Lamb

Preparation Time: 10 minutes; Cooking Time: 1 hour 30 minutes; Serve: 6
Ingredients:

- 4 lbs lamb shoulder, bone-in
- 1 tsp dried oregano
- 1 tsp garlic, minced
- 5 anchovies fillets, chopped
- 2 cups chicken stock
- 2 tsp olive oil
- Salt

Directions:
1. Add oil into the instant pot and set the pot on sauté mode.
2. Add lamb into the pot and cook until browned from both the sides. Remove lamb from the pot and set aside.
3. Add stock to the pot and stir well.
4. Add garlic and anchovies and stir.
5. Return meat to the pot and season with oregano and salt.
6. Seal pot with lid and cook on manual high pressure for 90 minutes.
7. Once done then allow to release pressure naturally for 10 minutes then release using the quick-release method. Open the lid.
8. Slice and serve.

Nutritional Value (Amount per Serving):
Calories 601; Fat 24.8 g; Carbohydrates 0.6 g; Sugar 0.3 g; Protein 88.5 g; Cholesterol 285 mg

Flavorful Taco Mince

Preparation Time: 10 minutes; Cooking Time: 18 minutes; Serve: 6
Ingredients:

- 1 1/2 lbs ground lamb
- 1/4 tsp paprika
- 1/2 tsp garlic powder
- 1/2 tsp onion powder
- 1/2 tsp ground cumin
- 1/2 tsp dried basil
- 1 tsp oregano
- 1/2 tbsp olive oil
- 2 tomatoes, chopped
- 2 garlic cloves, chopped
- 1 bell pepper, chopped
- 1 onion, chopped
- 1 tsp salt

Directions:
1. Add oil into the instant pot and set the pot on sauté mode.
2. Add meat, bell pepper, garlic, and onion to the pot and sauté for 2-3 minutes.
3. Add tomato and seasonings and stir well.
4. Seal pot with lid and cook on manual high pressure for 15 minutes.
5. Once done then release pressure using the quick-release method than open the lid.
6. Stir well and serve.

Nutritional Value (Amount per Serving):
Calories 265; Fat 12.5 g; Carbohydrates 5.8 g; Sugar 3 g; Protein 31.1 g; Cholesterol 99 mg

Delicious Lamb Curry

Preparation Time: 10 minutes; Cooking Time: 30 minutes; Serve: 4
Ingredients:

- 2 lbs lamb, diced
- 1 bay leaf

- 1 cinnamon stick
- 1 red chili, chopped
- 1 cup beef stock
- 14 oz can tomatoes, diced
- 1/2 cup split red lentils, rinsed
- 1 tsp ginger, grated
- 1 tsp cardamom powder
- 1/2 tbsp turmeric
- 1/2 tbsp ground coriander
- 1 tbsp ground cumin
- 2 garlic cloves, minced
- 2 onion, diced
- 2 tbsp olive oil
- 1/2 tsp salt

Directions:
1. Add oil into the pot and set the pot on sauté mode.
2. Add meat to the pot and cook until browned. Remove meat from the pot.
3. Add onion to the pot and sauté for 5 minutes.
4. Add ginger, garlic, all spices, and salt and stir well.
5. Add lentils and meat and stir well.
6. Add remaining ingredients and stir everything well.
7. Seal pot with lid and cook on manual high pressure for 20 minutes.
8. Once done then allow to release pressure naturally for 10 minutes then release using the quick-release method. Open the lid.
9. Stir well and serve.

Nutritional Value (Amount per Serving):
Calories 630; Fat 24.6 g; Carbohydrates 27.7 g; Sugar 6.4 g; Protein 72.6 g; Cholesterol 204 mg

Eastern Lamb Stew

Preparation Time: 10 minutes; Cooking Time: 60 minutes; Serve: 4
Ingredients:
- 1 1/2 lbs lamb stew meat, cut into cubes
- 1/4 cup raisins
- 15 oz can chickpeas, rinsed and drained
- 1 1/4 cup beef broth
- 2 tbsp brown sugar
- 1/4 cup apple cider vinegar
- 2 tbsp tomato paste
- 1/2 tsp chili flakes
- 1 tsp cumin
- 1 tsp coriander
- 1 tsp turmeric
- 1 tsp cinnamon
- 4 garlic cloves, chopped
- 1 onion, diced
- 2 tbsp olive oil
- 1 tsp salt

Directions:
1. Add oil into the instant pot and set the pot on sauté mode.
2. Add onion and sauté for 3-4 minutes.
3. Add lamb, all spices, garlic, and salt and cook for 5 minutes.
4. Add vinegar, raisins, chickpeas, stock, brown sugar, and tomato paste and stir to combine.
5. Seal pot with lid and cook on manual high pressure for 50 minutes.
6. Once done then allow to release pressure naturally then open the lid.
7. Stir well and serve.

Nutritional Value (Amount per Serving):
Calories 590; Fat 21.4 g; Carbohydrates 42.2 g; Sugar 12.2 g; Protein 55.8 g; Cholesterol 153 mg

Irish Lamb Stew

Preparation Time: 10 minutes; Cooking Time: 60 minutes; Serve: 6
Ingredients:

- 1 lb ground lamb
- 3 cups of water
- 1 bay leaf
- 1 tbsp Worcestershire sauce
- 8 potatoes, peeled and chopped
- 4 carrots, chopped
- 1 tbsp olive oil
- 1 small onion, chopped

Directions:

1. Add oil into the instant pot and set the pot on sauté mode.
2. Add onion and sauté until softened.
3. Add remaining ingredients and stir everything well.
4. Seal pot with lid and cook on manual high pressure for 25 minutes.
5. Once done then allow to release pressure naturally then open the lid.
6. Stir and serve.

Nutritional Value (Amount per Serving):

Calories 381; Fat 8.2 g; Carbohydrates 50.3 g; Sugar 6.3 g; Protein 26.5 g; Cholesterol 68 mg

Soy Honey Pork Tenderloin

Preparation Time: 10 minutes; Cooking Time: 25 minutes; Serve: 6

Ingredients:

- 1 1/2 lbs pork tenderloin
- 2 tsp corn-starch
- 1 tbsp sesame oil
- 3 garlic cloves, minced
- 1 tbsp ginger, minced
- 1/4 cup honey
- 1/3 cup water
- 1/3 cup soy sauce

Directions:

1. Whisk together soy sauce, oil, garlic, ginger, honey, and water and pout into the instant pot.
2. Place pork tenderloin into the pot.
3. Seal pot with lid and cook on manual high pressure for 7 minutes.
4. Once done then allow to release pressure naturally for 10 minutes then release using the quick-release method. Open the lid.
5. Remove pork from pot and set the pot on sauté mode.
6. Whisk cornstarch with 2 tsp water and pour into the pot. Stir and cook until the sauce thickened.
7. Pour sauce over pork tenderloin and serve.

Nutritional Value (Amount per Serving):

Calories 79; Fat 2.3 g; Carbohydrates 14.7 g; Sugar 11.9 g; Protein 1.1 g; Cholesterol 0 mg

Creamy Pork Chops

Preparation Time: 10 minutes; Cooking Time: 20 minutes; Serve: 4

Ingredients:

- 4 pork chops
- 1/3 cup sour cream
- 1 tsp corn starch
- 1 tsp Worcestershire sauce
- 1 cup beef stock
- 2 onions, sliced
- 1 tbsp butter
- Pepper
- Salt

Directions:

1. Add butter into the pot and set the pot on sauté mode.
2. Add onion to the pot and sauté until softened.
3. Season pork chops with pepper and salt. Place pork chops into the pot and cook until browned.
4. Add Worcestershire sauce and stock and stir well.

5. Seal pot with lid and cook on manual high pressure for 8 minutes.
6. Once done then allow to release pressure naturally for 5 minutes then release using the quick-release method. Open the lid.
7. Remove pork chops from pot and place on a plate.
8. Whisk corn starch with 1 tbsp water and pour into the pot and cook on sauté mode until sauce thickens.
9. Turn off the pot. Add sour cream and stir well.
10. Pour sauce over pork chops and serve.

Nutritional Value (Amount per Serving):
Calories 353; Fat 27 g; Carbohydrates 6.9 g; Sugar 2.6 g; Protein 19.9 g; Cholesterol 85 mg

Juicy & Tender Pork Chops

Preparation Time: 10 minutes; Cooking Time: 7 minutes; Serve: 2
Ingredients:
- 2 pork chops, boneless and 1-inch thick
- 1 tsp liquid smoke
- 1/2 tbsp Worcestershire sauce
- 1 cup beef broth
- 1 tbsp butter
- 1/2 tsp onion powder
- 1/2 tsp paprika
- 2 tbsp brown sugar
- 1/2 tsp pepper
- 1 tsp salt

Directions:
1. Mix together brown sugar and spices and rub over pork chops.
2. Add butter into the instant pot and set the pot on sauté mode.
3. Add pork chops to the pot and cook until browned. Remove pork chops from pot and set aside.
4. Pour broth into the pot and stir well.
5. Add liquid smoke and Worcestershire sauce to the pot and stir. Place pork chops into the pot.
6. Seal pot with lid and cook on manual high pressure for 7 minutes.
7. Once done then allow to release pressure naturally for 10 minutes then release using the quick-release method. Open the lid.
8. Serve and enjoy.

Nutritional Value (Amount per Serving):
Calories 369; Fat 26.4 g; Carbohydrates 11.2 g; Sugar 10.1 g; Protein 20.7 g; Cholesterol 84 mg

Filipino Pork Adobo

Preparation Time: 10 minutes; Cooking Time: 35 minutes; Serve: 4
Ingredients:
- 3 lbs pork butt, cut into cubes
- 1/4 cup soy sauce
- 1/4 cup vinegar
- 1 bay leaf
- 1/2 tsp whole peppercorns
- 4 garlic cloves, crushed
- 1 onion, sliced
- 1 tbsp olive oil
- 1/4 cup water
- Pepper
- Salt

Directions:
1. Add oil into the instant pot and set the pot on sauté mode.
2. Add meat to the pot and cook until browned. Season with pepper and salt.
3. Add bay leaf, peppercorns, garlic, and onion.

4. In a bowl, whisk together vinegar, water, and soy sauce and pour over meat.
5. Seal pot with lid and cook on high pressure for 10 minutes.
6. Once done then release pressure using the quick-release method than open the lid.
7. Set pot on sauté mode and cook for 15 minutes or until the sauce thickened.
8. Serve and enjoy.

Nutritional Value (Amount per Serving):
Calories 715; Fat 26.3 g; Carbohydrates 5.2 g; Sugar 1.5 g; Protein 107.4 g; Cholesterol 313 mg

Korean Pork Chops

Preparation Time: 10 minutes; Cooking Time: 30 minutes; Serve: 6
Ingredients:
- 6 pork chops
- 2 tbsp corn starch
- 3 tsp sriracha sauce
- 2 tsp ginger, minced
- 3 tsp sesame oil
- 6 garlic cloves, minced
- 6 tbsp honey
- 3/4 cup soy sauce
- 1 tbsp olive oil
- Pepper
- Salt

Directions:
1. Add olive oil into the instant pot and set the pot on sauté mode.
2. Season pork chops with pepper and salt.
3. Add pork chops to the pot and cook until browned.
4. In a bowl, whisk together soy sauce, sriracha sauce, sesame oil, ginger, garlic, and honey.
5. Pour soy sauce mixture over pork chops.
6. Seal pot with lid and cook on manual high pressure for 12 minutes.
7. Once done then allow to release pressure naturally for 10 minutes then release using the quick-release method. Open the lid.
8. Remove pork chops from pot and place on a plate.
9. Whisk together corn-starch and 1 tbsp water pour into the pot and cook on sauté mode for 2 minutes or until the sauce thickened.
10. Pour sauce over pork chops and serve.

Nutritional Value (Amount per Serving):
Calories 410; Fat 26.2 g; Carbohydrates 23.8 g; Sugar 18 g; Protein 20.3 g; Cholesterol 70 mg

Simple Lamb Curry

Preparation Time: 10 minutes; Cooking Time: 35 minutes; Serve: 4
Ingredients:
- 1 1/2 lbs lamb chunks
- 1 1/2 tsp ginger garlic paste
- 1 1/4 cups can tomatoes, chopped
- 1/4 tsp fennel powder
- 1/2 tsp coriander powder
- 2 bay leaves
- 2 onion, chopped
- 1 tbsp olive oil
- 1 tsp garam masala
- 1 tsp chili powder
- 1/2 tsp cumin powder
- Salt

Directions:
1. Add oil into the instant pot and set the pot on sauté mode.
2. Add bay leaves and onion to the pot and sauté until softened.
3. Add ginger-garlic paste, meat, and all spices and stir well.
4. Add remaining ingredients and stir well.
5. Seal pot with lid and cook on manual high pressure for 5 minutes.

6. Once done then allow to release pressure naturally then open the lid.
7. Stir and serve.

Nutritional Value (Amount per Serving):

Calories 425; Fat 207 g; Carbohydrates 10.7 g; Sugar 4.9 g; Protein 47 g; Cholesterol 148 mg

Herb Seasoned Lamb

Preparation Time: 10 minutes; Cooking Time: 15 minutes; Serve: 4

Ingredients:

- 2 lbs lamb, boneless and cut into chunks
- 1 tsp rosemary, chopped
- 2 carrots, chopped
- 1 large onion, chopped
- 1 cup red wine
- 2 garlic cloves, sliced
- 1 tbsp olive oil
- 2 tbsp tomato paste
- 1/2 cup chicken stock
- 1/2 tsp oregano, chopped
- 2 tsp thyme, chopped
- Pepper
- Salt

Directions:

1. Season meat with pepper and salt.
2. Add oil into the instant pot and set the pot on sauté mode.
3. Add meat to the pot and sauté until browned.
4. Add garlic and sauté for 30 seconds.
5. Add wine and stir well.
6. Add remaining ingredients and stir well.
7. Seal pot with lid and cook on manual high pressure for 15 minutes.
8. Once done then allow to release pressure naturally then open the lid.
9. Serve and enjoy.

Nutritional Value (Amount per Serving):

Calories 541; Fat 20.4 g; Carbohydrates 10.9 g; Sugar 4.7 g; Protein 65 g; Cholesterol 204 mg

Flavourful Lamb Korma

Preparation Time: 10 minutes; Cooking Time: 20 minutes; Serve: 4

Ingredients:

- 1 lb lamb leg, cut into pieces
- 1/2 tsp fresh lime juice
- 2 tbsp cilantro, chopped
- 1/4 tsp cardamom powder
- 1 tsp paprika
- 1/2 tsp cayenne pepper
- 1/2 tsp turmeric
- 1 1/2 tsp garam masala
- 3/4 cup water
- 1/2 cup coconut milk
- 2 tbsp tomato paste
- 2 tbsp ginger garlic paste
- 1 onion, chopped
- 1 tbsp olive oil
- 1 tsp salt

Directions:

1. Add oil into the instant pot and set the pot on sauté mode.
2. Add ginger-garlic paste and cook for a minute.
3. Add 1/4 cup water, tomato paste, and all spices. Stir well.
4. Add coconut milk, remaining water and meat. Stir well.
5. Seal pot with lid and cook on manual high pressure for 15 minutes.
6. Once done then allow to release pressure naturally then open the lid.
7. Stir in lime juice.
8. Garnish with cilantro and serve.

Nutritional Value (Amount per Serving):

Calories 423; Fat 35.98 g; Carbohydrates 6.9 g; Sugar 3.3 g; Protein 20.6 g; Cholesterol 80 mg

Tasty & Spicy Lamb

Preparation Time: 10 minutes; Cooking Time: 35 minutes; Serve: 4
Ingredients:

- 1 lb lamb, cut into pieces
- 2 tbsp lemon juice
- 1/2 cup fresh cilantro, chopped
- 2 onions, chopped
- 2 cups chicken stock
- 1 cup of coconut milk
- 3 tbsp butter
- 1 cup grape tomatoes, chopped
- 1/2 tbsp cumin powder
- 1 1/2 tsp turmeric
- 2 tsp garam masala
- 2 1/2 tbsp chili powder
- 2 tbsp apple cider
- 1 tsp salt

Directions:

1. Set instant pot on sauté mode.
2. Season meat with pepper and salt and place into the pot.
3. Cook meat for 5 minutes.
4. Add remaining ingredients and stir well.
5. Seal pot with lid and cook on manual high pressure for 15 minutes.
6. Once done then allow to release pressure naturally for 10 minutes then release using the quick-release method. Open the lid.
7. Stir and serve.

Nutritional Value (Amount per Serving):
Calories 487; Fat 32.8 g; Carbohydrates 15.2 g; Sugar 7.3 g; Protein 35.5 g; Cholesterol 125 mg

Lamb Stew

Preparation Time: 10 minutes; Cooking Time: 30 minutes; Serve: 3
Ingredients:

- 1 lb lamb loin, cut into pieces
- 2 cups chicken stock
- 1 chili pepper, chopped
- 1 cup cabbage, shredded
- 1 zucchini, sliced
- 1/2 tsp dried thyme
- 1 tsp oregano
- ½ tsp chili powder
- 3 tbsp olive oil
- 2 garlic cloves, crushed
- 1 tsp salt

Directions:

1. Add oil into the instant pot and set the pot on sauté mode.
2. Add garlic and meat and sauté for a minute.
3. Season with thyme, oregano, chili powder, and salt.
4. Stir everything well and cook for 5 minutes.
5. Add zucchini and cook for 3-4 minutes.
6. Add cabbage, chili pepper, and stock. Stir well.
7. Seal pot with lid and cook on manual high pressure for 12 minutes.
8. Once done then allow to release pressure naturally for 10 minutes then release using the quick-release method. Open the lid.
9. Stir and serve.

Nutritional Value (Amount per Serving):
Calories 455; Fat 29.4 g; Carbohydrates 5.5 g; Sugar 2.5 g; Protein 42 g; Cholesterol 132 mg

Lamb Shanks

Preparation Time: 10 minutes; Cooking Time: 35 minutes; Serve: 4

Ingredients:

- 4 lamb shanks
- 3 garlic cloves
- 1 small onion, chopped
- 1/4 cup apple cider vinegar
- 3 tbsp olive oil
- 3 cups chicken broth
- 7 oz mushrooms, sliced
- 1/2 tsp dried rosemary
- 1 tomato, chopped
- 1/4 cup leeks, chopped
- 2 celery stalks, chopped
- 2 tsp sea salt

Directions:

1. Add all ingredients into the instant pot and stir well.
2. Seal pot with lid and cook on manual high pressure for 25 minutes.
3. Once done then allow to release pressure naturally for 10 minutes then release using the quick-release method. Open the lid.
4. Serve and enjoy.

Nutritional Value (Amount per Serving):

Calories 309; Fat 18 g; Carbohydrates 6.6 g; Sugar 2.9 g; Protein 29.7 g; Cholesterol 77 mg

Asian Lamb Curry

Preparation Time: 10 minutes; Cooking Time: 30 minutes; Serve: 4

Ingredients:

- 1 1/2 lbs lamb chunks
- 2 tsp ginger garlic paste
- 1 1/2 cups can tomatoes, chopped
- 1/2 tsp fennel powder
- 1/2 tsp coriander powder
- 1/2 tsp garam masala
- 1 tsp chili powder
- 2 bay leaves
- 2 onion, chopped
- 1 tbsp oil
- 3/4 tsp cumin powder
- Salt

Directions:

1. Add oil into the instant pot and set the pot on sauté mode.
2. Add bay leaves and onion to the pot and cook for 5 minutes.
3. Add ginger-garlic paste, meat, and all spices and stir well.
4. Add remaining ingredients and stir well to combine.
5. Seal pot with lid and cook on manual high pressure for 5 minutes.
6. Once done then allow to release pressure naturally for 10 minutes then release using the quick-release method. Open the lid.
7. Stir and serve.

Nutritional Value (Amount per Serving):

Calories 433; Fat 20.8 g; Carbohydrates 12.3 g; Sugar 5.4 g; Protein 47.4 g; Cholesterol 148 mg

Indian Lamb Curry

Preparation Time: 10 minutes; Cooking Time: 20 minutes; Serve: 6

Ingredients:

- 2 lbs lamb meat, bone-in
- 2 1/2 tbsp green curry paste
- 1/2 cup coconut cream
- 1/4 cup cilantro, chopped
- 1/2 tbsp lime juice
- 6 oz green beans, chopped
- 1/2 tbsp soy sauce
- 1/2 tbsp fish sauce
- 2 garlic cloves, crushed
- 1/2 cup chicken broth
- 4.5 oz coconut milk
- 1 small onion, minced

- 1 tbsp olive oil
- Pepper
- Salt

Directions:
1. Season meat with pepper and salt.
2. Add oil into the instant pot and set the pot on sauté mode.
3. Add garlic and onion to the pot and sauté for 3-4 minutes.
4. Add curry paste and coconut cream and cook for 4-5 minutes.
5. Add meat, fish sauce, soy sauce, broth, and coconut milk. Stir well.
6. Seal pot with lid and cook on manual high pressure for 8 minutes.
7. Once done then release pressure using the quick-release method than open the lid.
8. Add lime juice and green beans and cook on sauté mode for 4 minutes.
9. Garnish with cilantro and serve.

Nutritional Value (Amount per Serving):
Calories 413; Fat 28.6 g; Carbohydrates 7 g; Sugar 1.8 g; Protein 29.9 g; Cholesterol 107 mg

Rogan Josh

Preparation Time: 10 minutes; Cooking Time: 35 minutes; Serve: 4
Ingredients:
- 1 lb leg of lamb, cut into cubes
- 2 garlic cloves, minced
- 1/4 tsp ground cinnamon
- 1 small onion, diced
- 1 tbsp tomato paste
- 1/2 cup yogurt
- 1/4 cup water
- 1/2 tsp turmeric
- 1 tsp paprika
- 2 tsp garam masala
- 1/4 cup cilantro, chopped
- 1/2 tsp cayenne pepper
- 2 tsp ginger, minced
- 1 tsp salt

Directions:
1. Add all ingredients into the bowl and stir well.
2. Place bowl in the refrigerator for 2 hours.
3. Add marinated meat with marinade into the instant pot.
4. Seal pot with lid and cook on manual high pressure for 20 minutes.
5. Once done then allow to release pressure naturally for 10 minutes then release using the quick-release method. Open the lid.
6. Serve and enjoy.

Nutritional Value (Amount per Serving):
Calories 620; Fat 42.9 g; Carbohydrates 10.5 g; Sugar 2.7 g; Protein 44.8 g; Cholesterol 161 mg

Cheesy Lamb Chops

Preparation Time: 10 minutes; Cooking Time: 18 minutes; Serve: 3
Ingredients:
- 3 lamb chops
- 1/2 tsp garlic powder
- 1 tbsp olive oil
- 3/4 cup parmesan cheese
- 1/4 tsp dried basil, crushed
- 1 cup of water
- 1/4 tsp dried oregano, crushed
- Pepper
- Salt

Directions:
1. Season lamb chops with pepper, garlic powder, and salt.
2. Place lamb chops into the instant pot and cook for 4 minutes on each side.
3. Remove lamb chops from pot and place on a plate.

4. Pour water to the pot then place a trivet in the pot.
5. Place lamb chops on the trivet.
6. Seal pot with lid and cook on manual high pressure for 10 minutes.
7. Once done then release pressure using the quick-release method than open the lid.
8. Serve and enjoy.

Nutritional Value (Amount per Serving):

Calories 530; Fat 19.3 g; Carbohydrates 10.5 g; Sugar 2.7 g; Protein 44.8 g; Cholesterol 161 mg

Garlicky Lamb

Preparation Time: 10 minutes; Cooking Time: 17 minutes; Serve: 6

Ingredients:
- 2 lbs lamb steak, cut into strips
- 1 tbsp olive oil
- 2 1/2 scallions, chopped
- 3 tbsp water
- 2 tbsp arrowroot
- 1/2 cup soy sauce, low-sodium
- 1/2 cup water
- 4 garlic cloves, minced

Directions:
1. Add oil into the instant pot and set the pot on sauté mode.
2. Add meat to the pot and cook for 5 minutes.
3. Add the ginger and garlic and cook for 1-2 minutes.
4. Add remaining ingredients and stir well.
5. Seal pot with lid and cook on manual high for 12 minutes.
6. Once done then release pressure using the quick-release method than open the lid.
7. Serve and enjoy.

Nutritional Value (Amount per Serving):

Calories 319; Fat 13.5 g; Carbohydrates 3.1 g; Sugar 0.5 g; Protein 44.1 g; Cholesterol 136 mg

Teriyaki Pork

Preparation Time: 10 minutes; Cooking Time: 40 minutes; Serve: 4

Ingredients:
- 2 lb pork loin
- 1/2 tsp onion powder
- 1 tsp ground ginger
- 2 tbsp brown sugar
- 1/2 cup water
- 1/4 cup soy sauce
- 1 cup chicken stock
- 1 1/2 tbsp honey
- 2 garlic cloves, crushed

Directions:
1. In a small bowl, mix together all ingredients except meat and stock.
2. Pour the stock into the instant pot.
3. Place meat into the pot then pour bowl mixture over the pork.
4. Seal pot with lid and cook on manual high pressure for 45 minutes.
5. Once done then allow to release pressure naturally then open the lid.
6. Serve and enjoy.

Nutritional Value (Amount per Serving):

Calories 606; Fat 31.8 g; Carbohydrates 13.4 g; Sugar 11.4 g; Protein 63.3 g; Cholesterol 181 mg

Easy & Tasty Ribs

Preparation Time: 10 minutes; Cooking Time: 40 minutes; Serve: 4

Ingredients:

- 2 3/4 lbs country-style pork ribs
- Dry Rub:
- 1 tsp garlic powder
- 1 tbsp brown sugar
- 1 tsp cumin
- 1 tsp pepper
- 1 cup chicken stock
- 1 tsp cayenne pepper
- 1 tsp paprika
- 1 tsp onion powder
- 1 tsp salt

Directions:

1. In a small bowl, mix together all rub ingredients and rub over meat.
2. Pour the stock into the instant pot then place ribs into the pot.
3. Seal pot with lid and cook on high pressure for 45 minutes.
4. Once done then allow to release pressure naturally then open the lid.
5. Stir and serve.

Nutritional Value (Amount per Serving):

Calories 601; Fat 36.3 g; Carbohydrates 4.5 g; Sugar 2.9 g; Protein 61.3 g; Cholesterol 235 mg

Shredded Pork

Preparation Time: 10 minutes; Cooking Time: 30 minutes; Serve: 4

Ingredients:

- 2 lbs pork shoulder
- 1/2 tsp oregano
- 1 onion, chopped
- 2 lime juice
- 1/2 cup of water
- 2 cups chicken broth
- 1 tbsp olive oil
- 2 garlic cloves, minced
- 1/2 tsp cumin

Directions:

1. Add oil into the instant pot and set the pot on sauté mode.
2. Add meat to the pot and sauté until browned.
3. Add remaining ingredients to the pot and stir well.
4. Seal pot with lid and cook on manual high pressure for 30 minutes.
5. Once done then allow to release pressure naturally then open the lid.
6. Shred the meat using a fork and serve.

Nutritional Value (Amount per Serving):

Calories 732; Fat 52.8 g; Carbohydrates 5.6 g; Sugar 1.9 g; Protein 55.8 g; Cholesterol 204 mg

Pork Curry

Preparation Time: 10 minutes; Cooking Time: 37 minutes; Serve: 8

Ingredients:

- 4 lbs pork shoulder, boneless and cut into chunks
- 2 garlic cloves, minced
- 1 onion, chopped
- 3 cups chicken broth
- 2 cups of coconut milk
- 1/2 tsp turmeric
- 2 tbsp olive oil
- 1/2 tbsp ground cumin
- 1 1/2 tbsp curry paste
- 2 tbsp fresh ginger, grated
- Pepper
- Salt

Directions:

1. Add oil into the pot and set the pot on sauté mode.
2. Season meat with pepper and salt. Add meat to the pot and cook until browned.

3. Add remaining ingredients and stir everything well.
4. Seal pot with lid and cook on soup/stew mode for 30 minutes.
5. Once done then release pressure using the quick-release method than open the lid.
6. Stir well and serve.

Nutritional Value (Amount per Serving):
Calories 877; Fat 68.6 g; Carbohydrates 7.2 g; Sugar 2.9 g; Protein 56.5 g; Cholesterol 204 mg

Meatloaf

Preparation Time: 10 minutes; Cooking Time: 45 minutes; Serve: 6
Ingredients:
- 2 1/4 lbs ground beef
- 1 tsp thyme
- 1 1/2 cups water
- 2 eggs, lightly beaten
- 3 tbsp olive oil
- 1/2 tsp garlic salt
- 1 tsp rosemary
- 1/4 tsp sage
- 1 tsp parsley
- 1 tsp oregano

Directions:
1. Pour water into the instant pot and place trivet in the pot.
2. Spray loaf pan with cooking spray.
3. Add all ingredients into the bowl and mix until combined.
4. Pour meat mixture into the loaf pan and place the pan on top of the trivet.
5. Seal pot with lid and cook on manual high pressure for 30 minutes.
6. Once done then allow to release pressure naturally for 10 minutes then release using the quick-release method. Open the lid.
7. Serve and enjoy.

Nutritional Value (Amount per Serving):
Calories 400; Fat 19.1 g; Carbohydrates 0.7 g; Sugar 0.2 g; Protein 53.6 g; Cholesterol 207 mg

Cajun Beef

Preparation Time: 10 minutes; Cooking Time: 12 minutes; Serve: 4
Ingredients:
- 1 lb ground beef
- 1 cup beef broth
- 10 oz Mexican cheese
- 1 tbsp olive oil
- 2 tbsp tomato paste
- 1 1/2 tbsp Cajun seasoning

Directions:
1. Add oil into the instant pot and set the pot on sauté mode.
2. Add meat to the pot and sauté until browned.
3. Add Cajun seasoning, broth, and tomato paste. Stir well.
4. Seal pot with lid and cook on manual high pressure for 7 minutes.
5. Release pressure using the quick-release method than open the lid.
6. Add cheese and stir well.
7. Cover the pot again and cook on manual high pressure for 5 minutes.
8. Once done then release pressure using the quick-release method than open the lid.
9. Stir and serve.

Nutritional Value (Amount per Serving):
Calories 510; Fat 33.7 g; Carbohydrates 4.3 g; Sugar 1.1 g; Protein 51.2 g; Cholesterol 165 mg

Cheesy Beef

Preparation Time: 10 minutes; Cooking Time: 22 minutes; Serve: 4
Ingredients:

- 1 lb ground beef
- 13.5 oz can tomatoes, diced
- 1/2 cup mozzarella cheese, shredded
- 1/2 cup tomato puree
- 1 tsp basil
- 1 tsp oregano
- 1 tbsp olive oil
- 1/2 onion, diced
- 1 carrot, sliced

Directions:

1. Add oil into the instant pot and set the pot on sauté mode.
2. Add onion to the pot and sauté for 2-3 minutes.
3. Add meat and cook until browned.
4. Add tomatoes, oregano, basil, and tomato puree. Stir well.
5. Seal pot with lid and cook on manual high pressure for 15 minutes.
6. Once done then release pressure using the quick-release method than open the lid.
7. Set pot on sauté mode. Add cheese and cook for 5 minutes.
8. Serve and enjoy.

Nutritional Value (Amount per Serving):
Calories 296; Fat 11.3 g; Carbohydrates 10.9 g; Sugar 6.1 g; Protein 37.1 g; Cholesterol 103 mg

Corned Beef

Preparation Time: 10 minutes; Cooking Time: 35 minutes; Serve: 8
Ingredients:

- 2 1/4 lbs corned beef, chopped
- 1 onion, chopped
- 2 celery stalks, chopped
- 1/2 tsp cumin
- 1 tsp garlic powder
- 3 cups chicken broth
- 1 tbsp butter
- 2 bacon slices, diced
- 2 1/2 lbs cabbage, chopped
- 1 carrot, sliced
- 1/2 tsp salt

Directions:

1. Add butter into the instant pot and set the pot on sauté mode.
2. Add bacon to the pot and cook until bacon is crispy.
3. Add meat and cook until browned. Add remaining ingredients and stir well.
4. Seal pot with lid and cook on manual high pressure for 35 minutes.
5. Once done then release pressure using the quick-release method than open the lid.
6. Stir and serve.

Nutritional Value (Amount per Serving):
Calories 316; Fat 20.1 g; Carbohydrates 11.1 g; Sugar 5.9 g; Protein 22.8 g; Cholesterol 89 mg

Pork Posole

Preparation Time: 10 minutes; Cooking Time: 30 minutes; Serve: 8
Ingredients:

- 1 lb pork shoulder, cut into cubes
- 1 tsp dried oregano
- 3 tsp chili sauce
- 24 oz posole
- 1 cup of water
- 2 tsp chili powder
- 1 tsp ground cumin
- 2 garlic cloves
- 1 tsp salt

Directions:
1. Add all ingredients into the instant pot and stir well.
2. Seal pot with lid and cook on manual high pressure for 30 minutes.
3. Once done then allow to release pressure naturally then open the lid.
4. Stir and serve.

Nutritional Value (Amount per Serving):
Calories 620; Fat 30.3 g; Carbohydrates 24.9 g; Sugar 3.1 g; Protein 49.4 g; Cholesterol 156 mg

Sauerkraut Pork

Preparation Time: 10 minutes; Cooking Time: 40 minutes; Serve: 8
Ingredients:
- 2 lbs pork loin
- 3 garlic cloves, minced
- 14 oz sauerkraut, drained
- 1 tbsp olive oil
- 1 onion, sliced
- 1 apple, sliced
- 1 cup chicken stock
- Pepper
- Salt

Directions:
1. Season pork loin with pepper and salt.
2. Add oil into the instant pot and set the pot on sauté mode.
3. Sear meat until lightly browned.
4. Add stock, garlic, onions, and apples to the pot. Pour sauerkraut on top.
5. Seal pot with lid and cook on high pressure for 40 minutes.
6. Once done then allow to release pressure naturally for 10 minutes then release using the quick-release method. Open the lid.
7. Serve and enjoy.

Nutritional Value (Amount per Serving):
Calories 322; Fat 17.8 g; Carbohydrates 7.7 g; Sugar 4.5 g; Protein 31.8 g; Cholesterol 91 mg

Pork Adobo

Preparation Time: 10 minutes; Cooking Time: 35 minutes; Serve: 4
Ingredients:
- 3 lbs pork butt, cut into cubes
- 1/4 cup water
- 3 tbsp soy sauce
- 1 onion, sliced
- 1 tbsp olive oil
- 1/4 cup vinegar
- 1 bay leaf
- 1 tsp peppercorns
- 3 garlic cloves, crushed
- Pepper
- Salt

Directions:
1. Add oil in the instant pot and set the pot on sauté mode.
2. Add meat and cook until browned. Season with pepper and salt.
3. Add onions, bay leaf, peppercorns, and garlic.
4. Mix together vinegar, water, and soy sauce and pour over meat.
5. Seal pot with lid and cook on high pressure for 10 minutes.
6. Once done then release pressure using the quick-release method than open the lid.
7. Set pot on sauté mode and cook for 15-20 minutes.
8. Serve and enjoy.

Nutritional Value (Amount per Serving):

Calories 712; Fat 26.3 g; Carbohydrates 4.8 g; Sugar 1.5 g; Protein 107.2 g; Cholesterol 313 mg

Easy Pork Chops

Preparation Time: 10 minutes; Cooking Time: 15 minutes; Serve: 4
Ingredients:

- 4 pork loin chops, bone-in
- 1 cup chicken stock
- 1 tbsp olive oil
- 1/4 tsp pepper
- 1/2 tsp salt

Directions:

1. Season pork chops with pepper and salt.
2. Add oil in the instant pot and set the pot on sauté mode.
3. Add pork chops to the pot and sear until lightly browned. Transfer pork chops to a plate.
4. Add broth to the pot then place the trivet in the pot.
5. Place pork chops on top of the trivet.
6. Seal pot with lid and cook on meat mode for 5 minutes.
7. Once done then allow to release pressure naturally for 10 minutes then release using the quick-release method. Open the lid.
8. Serve and enjoy.

Nutritional Value (Amount per Serving):
Calories 289; Fat 23.5 g; Carbohydrates 0.3 g; Sugar 0.2 g; Protein 18.2 g; Cholesterol 69 mg

Garlicky Pork Roast

Preparation Time: 10 minutes; Cooking Time: 35 minutes; Serve: 2
Ingredients:

- 1 lb pork roast
- 1 tbsp basil
- 1 1/2 tbsp soy sauce
- 2 tbsp grated parmesan cheese
- 2 tbsp honey
- 3 garlic cloves, minced
- 1/2 cup chicken stock
- 1/2 tbsp corn-starch
- 1/2 tbsp olive oil
- Salt

Directions:

1. Add all ingredients into the instant pot and stir well.
2. Seal pot with lid and cook on meat mode for 35 minutes.
3. Once done then allow to release pressure naturally then open the lid.
4. Stir and serve.

Nutritional Value (Amount per Serving):
Calories 578; Fat 47.1 g; Carbohydrates 0.5 g; Sugar 0.4 g; Protein 36.3 g; Cholesterol 138 mg

Orange pulled pork

Preparation Time: 10 minutes; Cooking Time: 30 minutes; Serve: 8
Ingredients:

- 2 lbs pork shoulder roast, cut into chunks
- 1/4 cup fresh lime juice
- 1 cup of orange juice
- 1 bay leaf
- 3/4 tsp ground cumin
- 2 tbsp olive oil
- 1/4 tsp pepper
- 1 tsp salt

Directions:

1. Add oil into the instant pot and set the pot on sauté mode.

2. Season meat with pepper and salt and place into the pot and cook until browned.
3. Add cumin, bay leaf, lime juice, orange juice, and salt and stir well.
4. Seal pot with lid and cook on manual high pressure for 25 minutes.
5. Once done then allow to release pressure naturally then open the lid. Discard bay leaf from pot.
6. Shred the meat using a fork and serve.

Nutritional Value (Amount per Serving):

Calories 337; Fat 26.7 g; Carbohydrates 3.7 g; Sugar 2.6 g; Protein 19.4 g; Cholesterol 80 mg

Pork with Cabbage

Preparation Time: 10 minutes; Cooking Time: 10 minutes; Serve: 4
Ingredients:

- 1 1/4 lbs pork loin, boneless and cut into cubes
- 1/2 tsp pepper
- 1/4 tsp fennel seeds
- 1 tbsp vinegar
- 1 cup chicken stock
- 1 tsp dried dill weed
- 1/2 small cabbage, cored and cut into wedges
- 1 onion, cut into wedges
- 2 tsp olive oil

Directions:
1. Add oil into the instant pot and set the pot on sauté mode.
2. Add onion and sauté for 2 minutes.
3. Add meat and cook for 3 minutes.
4. Add cabbage and stir well.
5. In a small bowl, mix dill weed, pepper, and fennel seeds and sprinkle over cabbage.
6. Pour vinegar and stock to the pot.
7. Seal pot with lid and cook on manual high pressure for 5 minutes.
8. Once done then allow to release pressure naturally then open the lid.
9. Serve and enjoy.

Nutritional Value (Amount per Serving):

Calories 382; Fat 22.3 g; Carbohydrates 3.8 g; Sugar 1.7 g; Protein 39.4 g; Cholesterol 113 mg

Salsa Pork

Preparation Time: 10 minutes; Cooking Time: 15 minutes; Serve: 4
Ingredients:

- 2 lbs pork shoulder, boneless and cut into chunks
- 3 tbsp fresh cilantro, chopped
- 1/2 cup chicken stock
- 1/2 tsp ground cumin
- 1 1/2 tbsp honey
- 14.5 oz can tomatoes, drained and diced
- 14 oz salsa
- 1/2 tsp dried oregano
- Pepper
- Salt

Directions:
1. Season meat with pepper and salt.
2. Add meat, stock, oregano, cumin, honey, tomatoes, and salsa to the pot.
3. Seal pot with lid and cook on manual high pressure for 15 minutes.
4. Once done then allow to release pressure naturally then open the lid.
5. Shred the meat using a fork.
6. Garnish with cilantro and serve.

Nutritional Value (Amount per Serving):

Calories 738; Fat 48.8 g; Carbohydrates 18.3 g; Sugar 13.1 g; Protein 55.5 g; Cholesterol 204 mg

Pork Fajitas

Preparation Time: 10 minutes; Cooking Time: 20 minutes; Serve: 6

Ingredients:

- 1 3/4 lbs pork loin sirloin chops, cut into strips
- 1 onion, sliced
- 2 bell pepper, cut into strips
- 1 1/2 tbsp Italian seasoning
- 1/2 cup chicken stock
- 2 tbsp fresh lime juice
- 13.5 oz salsa

Directions:

1. Add all ingredients into the instant pot and stir well.
2. Seal pot with lid and cook on manual high pressure for 1 minute.
3. Once done then allow to release pressure naturally for 10 minutes then release using the quick-release method. Open the lid.
4. Stir and serve.

Nutritional Value (Amount per Serving):

Calories 369; Fat 19.7 g; Carbohydrates 9.2 g; Sugar 5.1 g; Protein 37.8 g; Cholesterol 108 mg

Chapter 8: Fish & Seafood

Rosemary Salmon

Preparation Time: 10 minutes; Cooking Time: 5 minutes; Serve: 4
Ingredients:

- 1 lb salmon
- 1 tsp mustard powder
- 3 sprigs rosemary
- 1 cup chicken broth
- Pepper
- Salt

Directions:
1. Pour broth into the instant pot then place rack in the pot.
2. Place salmon on the rack and sprinkle with mustard powder, rosemary, pepper, and salt.
3. Seal pot with lid and cook on manual high pressure for 5 minutes.
4. Once done then allow to release pressure naturally then open the lid.

Nutritional Value (Amount per Serving):
Calories 164; Fat 7.6 g; Carbohydrates 0.5 g; Sugar 0.2 g; Protein 23.4 g; Cholesterol 50 mg

Crab Legs

Preparation Time: 10 minutes; Cooking Time: 4 minutes; Serve: 2
Ingredients:

- 1 ½ lbs crab legs
- 3 garlic cloves, minced
- 2 tbsp butter, melted
- 1 cup chicken stock
- Salt

Directions:
1. Pour the stock into the pot then place the trivet in the pot.
2. Place crab legs on top of trivet and season with salt.
3. Seal pot with lid and cook on manual high pressure for 4 minutes.
4. Once done then release pressure using the quick-release method than open the lid.
5. Mix together garlic and butter and pour over crab legs.
6. Serve and enjoy.

Nutritional Value (Amount per Serving):
Calories 457; Fat 17 g; Carbohydrates 2 g; Sugar 0.5 g; Protein 66 g; Cholesterol 220 mg

Lemon Garlic Mussels

Preparation Time: 10 minutes; Cooking Time: 7 minutes; Serve: 4
Ingredients:

- 1 lb mussels, clean
- ¾ cup sour cream
- 1 ½ tbsp lemon juice
- 2 garlic cloves, minced
- ½ small onion, chopped
- ½ cup beef broth
- ½ tsp dried rosemary
- ½ tbsp olive oil
- Pepper

Directions:
1. Add oil into the instant pot and set the pot on sauté mode.
2. Add onion and cook for 4-5 minutes.
3. Add rosemary and garlic and cook for a minute.
4. Add pepper, broth, and lemon juice and stir well.
5. Add mussels in the steamer basket and place into the pot.
6. Seal pot with lid and cook on manual low pressure for 1 minute.
7. Once done then release pressure using the quick-release method than open the lid.

8. Transfer mussels to the bowl and top with cream and serve.

Nutritional Value (Amount per Serving):
Calories 217; Fat 13 g; Carbohydrates 7 g; Sugar 0.7 g; Protein 15 g; Cholesterol 51 mg

Zesty Salmon

Preparation Time: 10 minutes; Cooking Time: 7 minutes; Serve: 2

Ingredients:
- 2 salmon fillets
- 1 tbsp orange juice
- ½ tbsp olive oil
- ½ cup white wine
- 1 tsp orange zest
- 1 tsp ginger, minced
- Pepper

Directions:
1. Add all ingredients into the instant pot and stir well.
2. Seal pot with lid and cook on manual high pressure for 7 minutes.
3. Once done then allow to release pressure naturally then open the lid.
4. Serve and enjoy.

Nutritional Value (Amount per Serving):
Calories 322; Fat 14 g; Carbohydrates 3g; Sugar 1 g; Protein 34 g; Cholesterol 78 mg

Delicious Basa Fillets

Preparation Time: 10 minutes; Cooking Time: 6 minutes; Serve: 2

Ingredients:
- 2 basa fillets
- ½ tsp turmeric
- 2 tbsp chili paste
- ½ tsp coriander seeds
- ½ tsp fennel seeds
- ¼ tsp cumin seeds
- 4 garlic cloves, minced
- ¼ cup coriander
- 2 ½ tsp fresh lime juice
- ½ cup yogurt
- 1 tbsp ghee

Directions:
1. Roast all spices and ground them.
2. Mix together yogurt, ghee, lime juice, garlic, and spice mixture in a large bowl.
3. Add fish fillets to the bowl and coat well with marinade.
4. Pour 1 cup water into the instant pot then place the trivet in the pot.
5. Place fish fillets on top of the trivet.
6. Seal pot with lid and cook on manual low pressure for 6 minutes.
7. Once done then allow to release pressure naturally then open the lid.
8. Serve and enjoy.

Nutritional Value (Amount per Serving):
Calories 209; Fat 9 g; Carbohydrates 7 g; Sugar 4 g; Protein 22 g; Cholesterol 20 mg

Indian Fried Prawns

Preparation Time: 10 minutes; Cooking Time: 6 minutes; Serve: 4

Ingredients:
- 1 lb prawns
- 1 tsp red chili, chopped
- 1 ¼ tsp chili powder
- 1 tsp turmeric
- ½ cup fresh coriander, chopped
- 1 tsp lemon juice
- 1 small onion, chopped
- 5 curry leaves
- 1 tsp mustard seeds
- 2 tbsp coconut oil
- 1 tsp salt

Directions:
1. Add oil into the instant pot and set the pot on sauté mode.
2. Add spices and prawns and cook for 2 minutes.
3. Add remaining ingredients except for coriander and stir well.
4. Seal pot with lid and cook on manual high pressure for 4 minutes.
5. Once done then release pressure using the quick-release method than open the lid.
6. Garnish with coriander and serve.

Nutritional Value (Amount per Serving):
Calories 212; Fat 9 g; Carbohydrates 4 g; Sugar 1 g; Protein 26 g; Cholesterol 239 mg

Spicy Salmon

Preparation Time: 10 minutes; Cooking Time: 10 minutes; Serve: 6
Ingredients:
- 2 lbs salmon fillets
- 4 garlic cloves
- 3 fresh thyme sprigs
- 1 small onion, diced
- 2 tsp red pepper flakes
- 1 lemon
- 1 tsp garlic powder
- 2 tsp paprika
- 2 tbsp olive oil
- Pepper
- Salt

Directions:
1. In a small bowl, mix together oil, red pepper flakes, garlic powder, pepper, and salt.
2. Stuff onion, thyme, lemon, and garlic in the cavity of fish fillets.
3. Coat fish fillets with oil mixture and place into the instant pot.
4. Cook on sauté for 3 minutes.
5. Seal pot with lid and cook on manual high pressure for 7 minutes.
6. Once done then allow to release pressure naturally then open the lid.
7. Serve and enjoy.

Nutritional Value (Amount per Serving):
Calories 253; Fat 14 g; Carbohydrates 2.8 g; Sugar 0.8 g; Protein 29 g; Cholesterol 67 mg

Basil Salmon

Preparation Time: 10 minutes; Cooking Time: 10 minute; Serve: 2
Ingredients:
- 2 salmon fillets
- ¼ cup Dijon mustard
- 1 bay leaf
- 1 cup of water
- ¼ cup fresh basil leaves, chopped

Directions:
1. Coat salmon fillets with mustard and top with basil leaves.
2. Pour water into the instant pot then place the trivet in the pot.
3. Place salmon fillets on top of the trivet.
4. Seal pot with lid and cook on manual high pressure for 5 minutes.
5. Once done then allow to release pressure naturally then open the lid.
6. Serve and enjoy.

Nutritional Value (Amount per Serving):
Calories 257; Fat 12 g; Carbohydrates 1.8 g; Sugar 0.3 g; Protein 36 g; Cholesterol 78 mg

Lemon Pepper Cod

Preparation Time: 10 minutes; Cooking Time: 10 minutes; Serve: 4
Ingredients:

- 4 cod steaks
- 2 tbsp vinegar
- 1 tbsp soy sauce
- 2 tbsp lemon pepper seasoning
- ½ cup sherry

Directions:
1. Add all ingredients into the large bowl and coat well and place in the refrigerator for 20 minutes.
2. Place marinated fish fillets into the instant pot.
3. Seal pot with lid and cook on manual high pressure for 6 minutes.
4. Once done then allow to release pressure naturally then open the lid.
5. Serve and enjoy.

Nutritional Value (Amount per Serving):
Calories 142; Fat 5.9 g; Carbohydrates 8.4 g; Sugar 2.6 g; Protein 13 g; Cholesterol 0 mg

Easy Salmon Stew

Preparation Time: 10 minutes; Cooking Time: 6 minutes; Serve: 6
Ingredients:
- 2 lbs salmon fillets, cubed
- 1 large onion, chopped
- 2 cups fish broth
- 2 tbsp butter
- Pepper
- Salt

Directions:
1. Add all ingredients into the instant pot and stir well.
2. Seal pot with lid and cook on manual high pressure for 6 minutes.
3. Once done then allow to release pressure naturally then open the lid.
4. Stir and serve.

Nutritional Value (Amount per Serving):
Calories 244; Fat 13 g; Carbohydrates 2.4 g; Sugar 1.1 g; Protein 29 g; Cholesterol 77 mg

Sweet & Sour Fish

Preparation Time: 10 minutes; Cooking Time: 9 minutes; Serve: 6
Ingredients:
- 1 ¾ lbs fish fillets, cut into chunks
- 2 tbsp vinegar
- 1 ½ tbsp soy sauce
- 1 tbsp sugar
- 1 tbsp olive oil
- Pepper
- Salt

Directions:
1. Add oil into the instant pot and set the pot on sauté mode.
2. Add all ingredients into the pot sauté for 3 minutes.
3. Seal pot with lid and cook on manual high pressure for 6 minutes.
4. Once done then allow to release pressure naturally then open the lid.
5. Stir well and serve.

Nutritional Value (Amount per Serving):
Calories 338; Fat 18 g; Carbohydrates 24.8 g; Sugar 2.1 g; Protein 19 g; Cholesterol 45 mg

Spicy Shrimp Noodles

Preparation Time: 10 minutes; Cooking Time: 4 minutes; Serve: 4
Ingredients:
- ½ lb shrimp, precooked
- ½ lb spaghetti noodles
- ½ tsp lime juice
- ½ tsp sriracha sauce
- ½ tbsp honey
- 4 tbsp sweet chili sauce

- ½ tbsp mayonnaise
- ½ cup parsley, chopped
- 1 ½ cups water

Directions:
1. Add noodles and water into the instant pot.
2. Seal pot with lid and cook on high pressure for 4 minutes.
3. Once done then release pressure using the quick-release method than open the lid.
4. Add remaining ingredients and stir everything well.
5. Serve and enjoy.

Nutritional Value (Amount per Serving):
Calories 249; Fat 2.9 g; Carbohydrates 35 g; Sugar 2.3 g; Protein 19.6 g; Cholesterol 161 mg

Nutritious Salmon

Preparation Time: 10 minutes; Cooking Time: 2 minutes; Serve: 3
Ingredients:
- 1 lb salmon fillet, cut into pieces
- 1 tsp ground cumin
- 1 tsp chili powder
- 2 garlic cloves, minced
- Pepper
- Salt

Directions:
1. Pour 1 ½ cups of water into the instant pot then place the trivet in the pot.
2. In a small bowl, mix together all ingredients except salmon.
3. Rub salmon with spice mixture and place on top of the trivet.
4. Seal pot with lid and cook on steam mode for 2 minutes.
5. Once done then release pressure using the quick-release method than open the lid.
6. Serve and enjoy.

Nutritional Value (Amount per Serving):
Calories 211; Fat 9.7 g; Carbohydrates 1.7 g; Sugar 0 g; Protein 29.7 g; Cholesterol 67 mg

Vegetable Fish Curry

Preparation Time: 10 minutes; Cooking Time: 60 minutes; Serve: 6
Ingredients:
- 1 ½ lbs fish fillets
- 2 cups of water
- 2 cans of coconut milk
- 1 tbsp fish sauce
- 2 tbsp green curry paste
- 1 zucchini, chopped
- 1 bell pepper, sliced
- 1 carrot, peeled and sliced

Directions:
1. Add all ingredients into the instant pot and stir well.
2. Seal pot with lid and cook on soup mode for 60 minutes.
3. Once done then release pressure using the quick-release method than open the lid.
4. Stir well and serve.

Nutritional Value (Amount per Serving):
Calories 295; Fat 15 g; Carbohydrates 24.4 g; Sugar 2.2 g; Protein 17.5 g; Cholesterol 39 mg

Tuna Pasta

Preparation Time: 10 minutes; Cooking Time: 10 minutes; Serve: 6
Ingredients:
- 15 oz pasta
- 2 .5 oz can tuna
- 2 tbsp capers
- 2 cups tomato sauce
- 2 anchovies
- 2 garlic cloves, minced
- 1 tbsp olive oil
- 1 ½ tsp salt

Directions:
1. Add oil into the instant pot and set the pot on sauté mode.
2. Add garlic and anchovies and sauté for 2-3 minutes.
3. Add pasta, tuna, tomato sauce, and salt and stir well.
4. Pour enough water to cover the pasta.
5. Seal pot with lid and cook on manual mode for 4 minutes.
6. Once done then allow to release pressure naturally then open the lid.
7. Cook on sauté mode 2-3 minutes.
8. Serve and enjoy.

Nutritional Value (Amount per Serving):
Calories 269; Fat 5.2 g; Carbohydrates 43.7 g; Sugar 3.5 g; Protein 12.4 g; Cholesterol 59 mg

Cajun Seafood Gumbo

Preparation Time: 10 minutes; Cooking Time: 20 minutes; Serve: 8
Ingredients:
- 2 lbs shrimp, deveined
- 29 oz tomatoes, diced
- 2 celery ribs, diced
- 2 bell peppers, diced
- 2 onions, diced
- 2 1/2 tbsp Cajun seasoning
- 1 1/2 cups bone broth
- 25 oz sea bass fillets, cut into chunks
- 2 bay leaves
- 1/4 cup tomato paste
- 3 tbsp olive oil
- Pepper
- Sea salt

Directions:
1. Season fish filets with half cajun seasoning, pepper, and salt.
2. Add oil into the instant pot and set the pot on sauté mode.
3. Place fish fillets into the pot and cook for 4 minutes.
4. Add onion, celery, pepper, and remaining Cajun seasoning and cook for 2 minutes.
5. Add broth, bay leaves, tomato paste, and tomatoes and stir well.
6. Seal pot with lid and cook on manual high pressure for 5 minutes.
7. Once done then release pressure using the quick-release method than open the lid.
8. Set pot on sauté mode. Add shrimp and cook for 3 minutes.
9. Stir and serve.

Nutritional Value (Amount per Serving):
Calories 353; Fat 9.9 g; Carbohydrates 12.6 g; Sugar 6.4 g; Protein 52.5 g; Cholesterol 286 mg

Lemon Pepper Salmon

Preparation Time: 10 minutes; Cooking Time: 10 minutes; Serve: 4
Ingredients:
- 1 lb salmon fillet
- 1 lemon, sliced
- 1 basil sprigs
- 1 dill sprigs
- 1 parsley sprigs
- 1 tarragon sprigs
- 3 tsp ghee
- 3/4 cup water
- 1 carrot, cut sliced
- 1 bell pepper, sliced
- 1 zucchini, sliced
- 1/4 tsp pepper
- 1/4 tsp salt

Directions:
1. Pour water and herbs into the instant pot then place the trivet in the pot.
2. Place salmon on top of the trivet.

3. Drizzle salmon with ghee and season with pepper and salt.
4. Arrange lemon slices on top of salmon.
5. Seal pot with lid and cook on steam mode for 3 minutes.
6. Once done then release pressure using the quick-release method than open the lid.
7. Transfer salmon on a plate. Discard water and herbs from the instant pot.
8. Add vegetables into the pot and sauté for 2 minutes.
9. Serve salmon with veggies and enjoy.

Nutritional Value (Amount per Serving):
Calories 205; Fat 10.4 g; Carbohydrates 6.1 g; Sugar 3.1 g; Protein 23.3 g; Cholesterol 58 mg

Lemon Garlic Salmon

Preparation Time: 10 minutes; Cooking Time: 8 minutes; Serve: 2
Ingredients:

- 2 salmon fillets
- 2 tbsp lemon juice
- 2 tbsp honey
- 2 tbsp olive oil
- 2 tbsp fresh parsley, minced
- 2 garlic cloves, minced
- Pepper
- Salt

Directions:
1. In a small bowl, mix together garlic, lemon juice, honey, and oil.
2. Place each salmon on foil piece and brush with garlic mixture.
3. Sprinkle with parsley, pepper, and salt. Wrap foil around the salmon fillet.
4. Pour 1 1/2 cups of water into the instant pot then place the trivet in the pot.
5. Place salmon packets on top of the trivet.
6. Seal pot with lid and cook on manual high pressure for 8 minutes.
7. Once done then release pressure using the quick-release method than open the lid.
8. Serve and enjoy.

Nutritional Value (Amount per Serving):
Calories 429; Fat 25.2 g; Carbohydrates 18.9 g; Sugar 17.6 g; Protein 35 g; Cholesterol 18.9 mg

Dill Salmon

Preparation Time: 10 minutes; Cooking Time: 3 minutes; Serve: 2
Ingredients:

- 2 salmon fillets
- 1/2 tbsp fresh rosemary, chopped
- 1/2 tbsp parsley, chopped
- 1 tsp dill
- 1 tbsp basil, chopped
- 2 tbsp lemon juice
- 1 cup of water
- 1 lemon, sliced
- 1 tsp garlic, minced
- 2 tbsp olive oil
- Pepper
- Salt

Directions:
1. In a small bowl, mix together olive oil, fresh herbs, garlic, and salt.
2. Place salmon filets on foil and season with pepper and salt.
3. Pour oil mixture over salmon and coat well.
4. Pour lemon juice over salmon and arrange lemon slices on top of salmon. Cover salmon with foil.
5. Pour 1 cup of water into the instant pot then place a trivet in the pot.
6. Place salmon packet on top of the trivet.
7. Seal pot with lid and cook on manual high pressure for 3 minutes.
8. Once done then release pressure using the quick-release method than open the lid.

9. Serve and enjoy.

Nutritional Value (Amount per Serving):

Calories 367; Fat 25.3 g; Carbohydrates 2.1 g; Sugar 0.4 g; Protein 35 g; Cholesterol 78 mg

Lemon Haddock

Preparation Time: 10 minutes; Cooking Time: 8 minutes; Serve: 2

Ingredients:

- 4 haddock fillets
- 1 tbsp ginger, chopped
- 2 tbsp olive oil
- 2 fresh lemon juice
- 1 cup white wine
- 3 green onions, chopped
- Pepper
- Salt

Directions:

1. Rub fish fillets with oil and season with pepper and salt.
2. Add all ingredients except fish fillets in the instant pot and stir well.
3. Place a steamer basket in the pot.
4. Place fish in a steamer basket.
5. Seal pot with lid and cook on manual high pressure for 8 minutes.
6. Once done then release pressure using the quick-release method than open the lid.
7. Serve and enjoy.

Nutritional Value (Amount per Serving):

Calories 57; Fat 1.7 g; Carbohydrates 0.7 g; Sugar 0.2 g; Protein 7.3 g; Cholesterol 22 mg

Quick Coconut Shrimp Curry

Preparation Time: 10 minutes; Cooking Time: 1 minute; Serve: 2

Ingredients:

- 1 lb frozen shrimp
- 1/2 tsp curry powder
- 1/2 cup water
- 2 tbsp fresh cilantro, chopped
- 2 tbsp coconut milk
- 1 tbsp garam masala
- 1/8 tsp cayenne
- 1/2 tsp salt

Directions:

1. Add all ingredients into the instant pot except coconut milk and cilantro.
2. Stir well and seal the pot with a lid and cook on manual high pressure for 1 minute.
3. Once done then release pressure using the quick-release method than open the lid.
4. Stir in coconut milk. Garnish with cilantro and serve.

Nutritional Value (Amount per Serving):

Calories 278; Fat 7.8 g; Carbohydrates 3.3 g; Sugar 0.5 g; Protein 46.8 g; Cholesterol 341 mg

Yummy Fish Tacos

Preparation Time: 10 minutes; Cooking Time: 8 minutes; Serve: 2

Ingredients:

- 2 tilapia fillets
- 1/4 cup fresh cilantro, chopped
- 2 tbsp lime juice
- 1 1/2 tbsp paprika
- 1 tsp olive oil
- Pinch of salt

Directions:

1. Place fish fillets in the middle of parchment paper piece.
2. Drizzle fish fillet with oil and lime juice and season with paprika and salt.
3. Sprinkle cilantro on top of fish fillet.
4. Fold parchment paper around the fish fillet.
5. Pour 1 1/2 cups of water into the instant pot then place a trivet in the pot.

6. Place fish packet on top of the trivet.
7. Seal pot with lid and cook on manual high pressure for 8 minutes.
8. Once done then release pressure using the quick-release method than open the lid.
9. Serve and enjoy.

Nutritional Value (Amount per Serving):
Calories 139; Fat 4.1 g; Carbohydrates 6.7 g; Sugar 1.3 g; Protein 22 g; Cholesterol 55 mg

Delicious Scallops

Preparation Time: 10 minutes; Cooking Time: 2 minutes; Serve: 2

Ingredients:
- 1 lb scallops, thawed
- 2 1/2 tbsp maple syrup
- 1/2 cup coconut aminos
- 1/4 tsp ground ginger
- 1/4 tsp garlic powder
- 1 tbsp olive oil
- 1/2 tsp sea salt

Directions:
1. Add oil into the instant pot and set the pot on sauté mode.
2. Add scallops to the pot and sear for 1 minute on each side.
3. In a small bowl, whisk together all remaining ingredients and pour over scallops.
4. Seal pot with lid and cook on steam mode for 2 minutes.
5. Once done then release pressure using the quick-release method than open the lid.
6. Serve and enjoy.

Nutritional Value (Amount per Serving):
Calories 327; Fat 8.8 g; Carbohydrates 34.5 g; Sugar 15 g; Protein 38.1 g; Cholesterol 75 mg

Healthy Shrimp Rice

Preparation Time: 10 minutes; Cooking Time: 3 minutes; Serve: 2

Ingredients:
- 1 egg, lightly beaten
- 1/4 tsp ground ginger
- 1/8 tsp cayenne pepper
- 2 cups of water
- 1 small onion, chopped
- 1 1/2 tbsp soy sauce
- 1 1/2 tbsp olive oil
- 5 oz frozen shrimp, peeled
- 1 cup rice, rinsed and drained
- 1 cup frozen carrots and peas
- 3 garlic cloves, minced
- Pepper
- Salt

Directions:
1. Add 1 tbsp oil in instant pot and set the pot on sauté mode.
2. Add egg into the pot and cook until scramble.
3. Transfer scrambled egg to a plate and set aside.
4. Add remaining oil, garlic, and onion and sauté for 2 minutes.
5. Add carrots, peas, shrimp, rice, water, ginger, soy sauce, pepper, and salt. Stir well.
6. Seal pot with lid and cook on manual high pressure for 5 minutes.
7. Once done then release pressure using the quick-release method than open the lid.
8. Add scrambled egg and stir well.
9. Serve and enjoy.

Nutritional Value (Amount per Serving):
Calories 601; Fat 15 g; Carbohydrates 88.8 g; Sugar 5.5 g; Protein 27.8 g; Cholesterol 188 mg

Balsamic Salmon

Preparation Time: 10 minutes; Cooking Time: 3 minutes; Serve: 2

Ingredients:
- 2 salmon fillets
- 1 cup of water
- 2 tbsp balsamic vinegar
- 1 1/2 tbsp honey
- Pepper
- Salt

Directions:
1. Season salmon with pepper and salt.
2. Mix together vinegar and honey.
3. Brush fish fillets with vinegar honey mixture.
4. Pour water into the instant pot then place trivet into the pot.
5. Place fish fillets on top of the trivet.
6. Seal pot with lid and cook on manual high pressure for 3 minutes.
7. Once done then release pressure using the quick-release method than open the lid.
8. Garnish with parsley and serve.

Nutritional Value (Amount per Serving):
Calories 287; Fat 11 g; Carbohydrates 13.2 g; Sugar 13 g; Protein 34.6 g; Cholesterol 78 mg

Shrimp Scampi

Preparation Time: 10 minutes; Cooking Time: 2 minutes; Serve: 2
Ingredients:
- 1 lb shrimp, peeled and deveined
- 1 cup of water
- 1/4 tsp red chili flakes
- 3 garlic cloves, minced
- 2 tbsp butter
- 2 tbsp lemon juice
- Pepper
- Salt

Directions:
1. Add butter into the instant pot and set the pot on sauté mode.
2. Add garlic, pepper, red chili flakes, and salt to the pot and sauté for 2 minutes.
3. Add shrimp and water. Stir well.
4. Seal pot with lid and cook on manual high pressure for 2 minutes.
5. Once done then release pressure using the quick-release method than open the lid.
6. Stir in lemon juice and serve.

Nutritional Value (Amount per Serving):
Calories 382; Fat 15.5 g; Carbohydrates 5.3 g; Sugar 0.4 g; Protein 52.2 g; Cholesterol 508 mg

Dijon Fish Fillets

Preparation Time: 10 minutes; Cooking Time: 3 minutes; Serve: 2
Ingredients:
- 2 halibut fillets
- 1 tbsp Dijon mustard
- 1 1/2 cups water
- Pepper
- Salt

Directions:
1. Pour water into the instant pot then place steamer basket in the pot.
2. Season fish fillets with pepper and salt and brush with Dijon mustard.
3. Place fish fillets in the steamer basket.
4. Seal pot with lid and cook on manual high pressure for 3 minutes.
5. Once done then release pressure using the quick-release method than open the lid.
6. Serve and enjoy.

Nutritional Value (Amount per Serving):
Calories 323; Fat 7 g; Carbohydrates 0.5 g; Sugar 0.1 g; Protein 60.9 g; Cholesterol 93 mg

Old Bay Seasoned Haddock

Preparation Time: 10 minutes; Cooking Time: 7 minutes; Serve: 2

Ingredients:

- 1/2 lb haddock
- 1 tbsp fresh lemon juice
- 1/4 cup water
- 1 tbsp mayonnaise
- 1/4 tsp old bay seasoning
- 1/2 tsp olive oil
- 1/4 tsp dill, chopped

Directions:

1. Add water, mayonnaise, seasoning, olive oil, dill, and lemon juice in instant pot and stir well.
2. Place fish fillets in the pot.
3. Seal pot with lid and cook on manual high pressure for 7 minutes.
4. Once done then release pressure using the quick-release method than open the lid.
5. Serve and enjoy.

Nutritional Value (Amount per Serving):

Calories 168; Fat 4.7 g; Carbohydrates 2 g; Sugar 0.6 g; Protein 27.7 g; Cholesterol 86 mg

Shrimp Mac n Cheese

Preparation Time: 10 minutes; Cooking Time: 10 minutes; Serve: 2

Ingredients:

- 1 1/4 cups elbow macaroni
- 1 tbsp butter
- 2/3 cup milk
- 1 bell pepper, chopped
- 15 shrimp
- 1 tbsp Cajun spice
- 1/2 cup flour
- 1 cup cheddar cheese, shredded

Directions:

1. Add butter in instant pot and set the pot on sauté mode.
2. Add bell pepper and sauté for minutes.
3. Add water and pasta and stir well.
4. Seal pot with lid and cook on manual high pressure for 3 minutes.
5. Once done then release pressure using the quick-release method than open the lid.
6. Add Cajun spices and flour and stir well.
7. Set pot on sauté mode. Add shrimp and cook for 2 minutes.
8. Add cheese and milk and stir well.
9. Serve and enjoy.

Nutritional Value (Amount per Serving):

Calories 843; Fat 30.2 g; Carbohydrates 74.8 g; Sugar 8.4 g; Protein 65.1 g; Cholesterol 429 mg

Salmon Rice Pilaf

Preparation Time: 10 minutes; Cooking Time: 5 minutes; Serve: 2

Ingredients:

- 2 salmon fillets
- 1 cup chicken stock
- 1 tbsp butter
- 1/2 cup of rice
- 1/4 cup vegetable soup mix
- 1/4 tsp sea salt

Directions:

1. Add all ingredients except fish fillets into the instant pot and stir well.
2. Place steamer rack on top of rice mixture.
3. Place fish fillets on top of rack and season with pepper and salt.
4. Seal pot with lid and cook on manual high pressure for 5 minutes.

5. Once done then release pressure using the quick-release method than open the lid.
6. Serve and enjoy.

Nutritional Value (Amount per Serving):

Calories 474; Fat 17.4 g; Carbohydrates 40 g; Sugar 0.8 g; Protein 39 g; Cholesterol 94 mg

Perfect Salmon Dinner

Preparation Time: 10 minutes; Cooking Time: 2 minutes; Serve: 3

Ingredients:

- 1 lb salmon fillet, cut into three pieces
- 2 garlic cloves, minced
- 1/2 tsp ground cumin
- 1 tsp red chili powder
- Pepper
- Salt

Directions:

1. Pour 1 1/2 cups water into the instant pot then place trivet into the pot.
2. In a small bowl, mix together garlic, cumin, chili powder, pepper, and salt.
3. Rub salmon with spice mixture and place on top of the trivet.
4. Seal pot with lid and cook on steam mode for 2 minutes.
5. Once done then release pressure using the quick-release method than open the lid.
6. Serve and enjoy.

Nutritional Value (Amount per Serving):

Calories 207; Fat 9.6 g; Carbohydrates 1.3 g; Sugar 0.1 g; Protein 29.6 g; Cholesterol 67 mg

Steam Clams

Preparation Time: 10 minutes; Cooking Time: 3 minutes; Serve: 3

Ingredients:

- 1 lb mushy shell clams
- 2 tbsp butter, melted
- 1/4 cup white wine
- 1/2 tsp garlic powder
- 1/4 cup fresh lemon juice

Directions:

1. Add white wine, lemon juice, garlic powder, and butter into the instant pot.
2. Place trivet into the pot.
3. Arrange clams on top of the trivet.
4. Seal pot with lid and cook on manual high pressure for 3 minutes.
5. Once done then allow to release pressure naturally then open the lid.
6. Serve and enjoy.

Nutritional Value (Amount per Serving):

Calories 336; Fat 18.5 g; Carbohydrates 24.8 g; Sugar 2.8 g; Protein 13.1 g; Cholesterol 20 mg

Mahi Mahi Fillets

Preparation Time: 10 minutes; Cooking Time: 13 minutes; Serve: 4

Ingredients:

- 6 mahi-mahi fillets
- 29 oz can tomatoes, diced
- 1/2 onion, sliced
- 2 tbsp lemon juice
- 1/2 tsp dried oregano
- 3 tbsp butter
- Pepper
- Salt

Directions:

1. Add butter into the instant pot and set the pot on sauté mode.
2. Add onion and sauté for 2 minutes.
3. Add remaining ingredients except for fish fillets and sauté for 3 minutes.

4. Place fish fillets into the pot.
5. Seal pot with lid and cook on manual high pressure for 8 minutes.
6. Once done then release pressure using the quick-release method than open the lid.
7. Serve and enjoy.

Nutritional Value (Amount per Serving):
Calories 263; Fat 8.7 g; Carbohydrates 12.1 g; Sugar 7.8 g; Protein 33.7 g; Cholesterol 83 mg

Easy Garlic Lemon Shrimp

Preparation Time: 10 minutes; Cooking Time: 5 minutes; Serve: 3
Ingredients:
- 1 lb large shrimp
- 2 garlic cloves, minced
- 3 tbsp butter
- 1/2 tsp paprika
- 2 lemons, sliced

Directions:
1. Add butter into the pot and set the pot on sauté mode.
2. Add garlic and sauté for 1 minute.
3. Add shrimp, paprika, and lemon slices, and stirs well.
4. Seal pot with lid and cook on manual high pressure for 4 minutes.
5. Once done then allow to release pressure naturally then open the lid.
6. Serve and enjoy.

Nutritional Value (Amount per Serving):
Calories 229; Fat 11.6 g; Carbohydrates 4 g; Sugar 0.2 g; Protein 28.7 g; Cholesterol 247 mg

Cheesy Tilapia

Preparation Time: 10 minutes; Cooking Time: 10 minutes; Serve: 2
Ingredients:
- 2 tilapia fillets
- 3/4 cup parmesan cheese, grated
- 2 tbsp fresh lemon juice
- 2 tbsp mayonnaise
- Pepper
- Salt

Directions:
1. In a bowl, mix together mayo, lemon juice, pepper, and salt and marinate fish fillets in this mixture.
2. Place marinated tilapia fillets into the instant pot.
3. Seal pot with lid and cook on manual high pressure for 7 minutes.
4. Once done then allow to release pressure naturally then open the lid.
5. Top with cheese and cook on sauté mode for 3 minutes.
6. Serve and enjoy.

Nutritional Value (Amount per Serving):
Calories 244; Fat 12.1 g; Carbohydrates 4.9 g; Sugar 1.3 g; Protein 30.3 g; Cholesterol 485 mg

Scallops Curry

Preparation Time: 10 minutes; Cooking Time: 9 minutes; Serve: 4
Ingredients:
- 1 lb scallops
- 1 cup of coconut milk
- 1/2 tsp soy sauce
- 1/4 tsp nutmeg powder
- 1/2 cup red curry paste
- 1 1/2 cup chicken broth
- 1/2 tsp curry powder
- 1 tsp vinegar
- 1 tbsp olive oil
- 1/2 tsp salt

Directions:
1. Add oil into the instant pot and set the pot on sauté mode.
2. Add scallops and sauté for 3 minutes.
3. Add remaining ingredients and stir well.
4. Seal pot with lid and cook on manual high pressure for 6 minutes.
5. Once done then release pressure using the quick-release method than open the lid.
6. Serve and enjoy.

Nutritional Value (Amount per Serving):
Calories 404; Fat 28.3 g; Carbohydrates 12.6 g; Sugar 2.3 g; Protein 22.3 g; Cholesterol 37 mg

Healthy Shrimp Boil

Preparation Time: 10 minutes; Cooking Time: 1 minute; Serve: 6
Ingredients:
- 2 lbs frozen shrimp, deveined
- 1 onion, chopped
- 1/2 tsp red pepper flakes
- 1 tbsp old bay seasoning
- 10 oz sausage, sliced
- 5 frozen half corn on the cobs
- 3 garlic cloves, crushed
- 1 cup chicken stock
- 1/2 tsp salt

Directions:
1. Add all ingredients into the instant pot and stir well.
2. Seal pot with lid and cook on manual high pressure for 1 minute.
3. Once done then release pressure using the quick-release method than open the lid.
4. Stir and serve.

Nutritional Value (Amount per Serving):
Calories 407; Fat 17.1 g; Carbohydrates 19.6 g; Sugar 5.1 g; Protein 43 g; Cholesterol 267 mg

Asparagus Shrimp Risotto

Preparation Time: 10 minutes; Cooking Time: 16 minutes; Serve: 6
Ingredients:
- 1 1/2 cups Arborio rice
- 1 tbsp butter
- 3 1/2 cups chicken stock
- 1/2 cup white wine
- 1 cup mushrooms, sliced
- 1/4 cup parmesan cheese, grated
- 1 lb shrimp, cooked
- 1 cup asparagus, chopped
- 1/2 onion, diced
- 2 tsp olive oil
- 1/2 tsp pepper
- Salt

Directions:
1. Add oil into the instant pot and set the pot on sauté mode.
2. Add onion to the pot and sauté for 2-3 minutes.
3. Add mushrooms and cook for 5 minutes.
4. Add rice and cook until lightly brown.
5. Add stock and wine and stir well.
6. Seal pot with lid and cook on manual high pressure for 6 minutes,
7. Once done then release pressure using the quick-release method than open the lid.
8. Add asparagus and butter and cook on sauté mode for 1 minute.
9. Add shrimp and cook for 1 minute.
10. Stir in cheese and serve.

Nutritional Value (Amount per Serving):

Calories 339; Fat 6.4 g; Carbohydrates 42.3 g; Sugar 1.6 g; Protein 23.3 g; Cholesterol 168 mg

Basil Tilapia

Preparation Time: 10 minutes; Cooking Time: 4 minutes; Serve: 4
Ingredients:
- 4 tilapia fillets
- 3 garlic cloves, minced
- 2 tomatoes, chopped
- 2 tbsp olive oil
- 1/2 cup basil, chopped
- 1/8 tsp pepper
- 1/4 tsp salt

Directions:
1. Pour half cup of water into the instant pot.
2. Add fish fillets into the steamer basket and season with pepper and salt.
3. Place a steamer basket into the pot.
4. Seal pot with lid and cook on manual high pressure for 2 minutes.
5. Once done then release pressure using the quick-release method than open the lid.
6. In a bowl, mix together tomatoes, basil, oil, garlic, pepper, and salt.
7. Place cooked fish fillets on serving plate and top with tomato mixture.
8. Serve and enjoy.

Nutritional Value (Amount per Serving):
Calories 168; Fat 8.2 g; Carbohydrates 3.3 g; Sugar 1.7 g; Protein 21.8 g; Cholesterol 55 mg

Delicious Shrimp Risotto

Preparation Time: 10 minutes; Cooking Time: 17 minutes; Serve: 4
Ingredients:
- 1 lb shrimp, peeled, deveined, and chopped
- 1 1/2 cups Arborio rice
- 1/2 tbsp paprika
- 1/2 tbsp oregano, minced
- 1 red pepper, chopped
- 1 onion, chopped
- 1/2 cup parmesan cheese, grated
- 1 cup clam juice
- 3 cups chicken stock
- 1/4 cup dry sherry
- 2 tbsp butter
- 1/4 tsp pepper
- 1/2 tsp salt

Directions:
1. Add butter into the instant pot and set the pot on sauté mode.
2. Add onion and pepper and sauté until onion is softened.
3. Add paprika, oregano, pepper, and salt. Stir for minute.
4. Add rice and stir for a minute.
5. Add sherry, clam juice, and stock. Stir well.
6. Seal pot with lid and cook on manual high pressure for 10 minutes.
7. Once done then release pressure using the quick-release method than open the lid.
8. Add shrimp and cook on sauté mode for 2 minutes.
9. Stir in cheese and serve.

Nutritional Value (Amount per Serving):
Calories 530; Fat 10.4 g; Carbohydrates 71.6 g; Sugar 5.3 g; Protein 34.5 g; Cholesterol 259 mg

Cajun Shrimp

Preparation Time: 10 minutes; Cooking Time: 2 minutes; Serve: 4
Ingredients:
- 1 lb shrimp, peeled and deveined
- 15 asparagus spear

- 1 tbsp Cajun seasoning
- 1 tsp olive oil

Directions:
1. Pour 1 cup of water in instant pot then place the steam rack inside the pot.
2. Arrange asparagus on a steam rack in a layer.
3. Place shrimp on the top of asparagus.
4. Sprinkle Cajun seasoning over shrimp and drizzle with olive oil.
5. Seal pot with lid and cook on steam mode for 2 minutes.
6. Once done then release pressure using the quick-release method than open the lid.
7. Serve and enjoy.

Nutritional Value (Amount per Serving):
Calories 163; Fat 3.2 g; Carbohydrates 5.2 g; Sugar 1.7 g; Protein 27.8 g; Cholesterol 239 mg

Quick & Easy Shrimp

Preparation Time: 10 minutes; Cooking Time: 1 minute; Serve: 6
Ingredients:
- 30 oz frozen shrimp, deveined
- 1/2 cup chicken stock
- 1/2 cup apple cider vinegar

Directions:
1. Add all ingredients into the instant pot and stir well.
2. Seal pot with lid and cook on manual high pressure for 1 minute.
3. Once done then release pressure using the quick-release method than open the lid.
4. Serve and enjoy.

Nutritional Value (Amount per Serving):
Calories 156; Fat 2.6 g; Carbohydrates 1.5 g; Sugar 0.1 g; Protein 29 g; Cholesterol 213 mg

Chessey Shrimp Grits

Preparation Time: 10 minutes; Cooking Time: 7 minutes; Serve: 6
Ingredients:
- 1 lb shrimp, thawed
- 1/2 cup cheddar cheese, shredded
- 1/2 cup quick grits
- 1 tbsp butter
- 1 1/2 cups chicken broth
- 1/4 tsp red pepper flakes
- 1/2 tsp paprika
- 2 tbsp cilantro, chopped
- 1 tbsp coconut oil
- 1/2 tsp kosher salt

Directions:
1. Add oil into the instant pot and set the pot on sauté mode.
2. Add shrimp and cook until shrimp is no longer pink. Season with red pepper flakes and salt.
3. Remove shrimp from the pot and set aside.
4. Add remaining ingredients into the pot and stir well.
5. Seal pot with lid and cook on manual high pressure for 7 minutes.
6. Once done then allow to release pressure naturally then open the lid.
7. Stir in cheese and top with shrimp.

Nutritional Value (Amount per Serving):
Calories 221; Fat 9.1 g; Carbohydrates 12 g; Sugar 0.3 g; Protein 21.9 g; Cholesterol 174 mg

Healthy Salmon Chowder

Preparation Time: 10 minutes; Cooking Time: 8 minutes; Serve: 4
Ingredients:
- 1 lb frozen salmon
- 2 garlic cloves, minced

- 2 tbsp butter
- 2 celery stalks, chopped
- 1 onion, chopped
- 1 cup corn
- 1 medium potato, cubed
- 2 cups half and half
- 4 cups chicken broth

Directions:
1. Add butter into the instant pot and select sauté.
2. Add onion and garlic into the pot and sauté for 3-4 minutes.
3. Add remaining ingredients except for the half and a half and stir well.
4. Seal pot with lid and cook on manual high pressure for 5 minutes.
5. Once done then allow to release pressure naturally then open the lid.
6. Add half and half and stir well.
7. Serve and enjoy.

Nutritional Value (Amount per Serving):
Calories 571; Fat 35.1 g; Carbohydrates 26 g; Sugar 3.9 g; Protein 36.9 g; Cholesterol 133 mg

Shrimp with Sausage

Preparation Time: 10 minutes; Cooking Time: 5 minutes; Serve: 6
Ingredients:
- 1 lb frozen shrimp
- 1 1/2 cups sausage, sliced
- 3 ears corn, cut in thirds
- 1 lemon, wedges
- 2 cups chicken broth
- 1 1/2 tbsp old bay seasoning
- 1/4 cup parsley, chopped
- 5 small potatoes, diced
- 2 garlic cloves, minced
- 1 onion, chopped

Directions:
1. Add all ingredients into the instant pot and stir well.
2. Seal pot with lid and cook on manual high pressure for 5 minutes.
3. Once done then release pressure using the quick-release method than open the lid.
4. Serve and enjoy.

Nutritional Value (Amount per Serving):
Calories 290; Fat 4.8 g; Carbohydrates 40.1 g; Sugar 5.2 g; Protein 23.6 g; Cholesterol 119 mg

Chapter 9: Appetizers

Spinach Artichoke Dip

Preparation Time: 10 minutes; Cooking Time: 4 minutes; Serve: 10
Ingredients:

- 10 oz spinach
- 1 tsp onion powder
- 2 garlic cloves
- ½ cup mayonnaise
- ½ cup sour cream
- 14 oz artichoke hearts
- ½ cup chicken broth
- 8 oz mozzarella cheese, shredded
- 15 oz parmesan cheese, shredded
- 8 oz cream cheese

Directions:
1. Add all ingredients except parmesan and mozzarella cheese into the instant pot and stir well.
2. Seal pot with lid and cook on manual high pressure for 4 minutes.
3. Once done then release pressure using the quick-release method than open the lid.
4. Stir in cheese and serve.

Nutritional Value (Amount per Serving):
Calories 379; Fat 27 g; Carbohydrates 11.9 g; Sugar 1.5 g; Protein 24.7 g; Cholesterol 75 mg

Delicious White Dip

Preparation Time: 10 minutes; Cooking Time: 20 minutes; Serve: 10
Ingredients:

- 1 cup of water
- 1 tsp oregano
- 1 tbsp milk
- 1 can Rotel
- 1 tbsp garlic
- 8 oz cream cheese
- 1 tbsp butter
- 1 cup queso cheese mix, shredded
- 1 lb white American cheese, sliced

Directions:
1. Pour 1 cup of water into the instant pot then place the trivet in the pot.
2. In oven-safe bowl, add all ingredients and stir well. Cover bowl with foil and place on top of the trivet.
3. Seal pot with lid and cook on manual high pressure for 18 minutes.
4. Once done then release pressure using the quick-release method than open the lid.
5. Uncover the bowl and stir well and serve.

Nutritional Value (Amount per Serving):
Calories 92; Fat 9.1 g; Carbohydrates 1.1 g; Sugar 0.1 g; Protein 1.8 g; Cholesterol 28 mg

Easy Buffalo Chicken Dip

Preparation Time: 10 minutes; Cooking Time: 7 minutes; Serve: 12
Ingredients:

- 2 chicken breasts, skinless and boneless
- ¼ cup of water
- ½ cup buffalo sauce
- 4 oz cream cheese
- Pepper
- Salt

Directions:
1. Add all ingredients into the instant pot and stir well.
2. Seal pot with lid and cook on manual mode for 7 minutes.
3. Once done then allow to release pressure naturally then open the lid.

4. Shred the chicken using a fork.
5. Stir well and serve.

Nutritional Value (Amount per Serving):

Calories 79; Fat 5.1 g; Carbohydrates 0.3 g; Sugar 0 g; Protein 7.8 g; Cholesterol 32 mg

Chili Queso Dip

Preparation Time: 10 minutes; Cooking Time: 10 minutes; Serve: 10

Ingredients:

- 2 lb Velveeta cheese, cut into chunks
- 1 cup of water
- 1 tbsp chili powder
- 1 packet taco seasoning
- 14 oz can tomatoes, diced
- 10 oz Rotel
- 3 garlic cloves, minced
- 1 onion, diced
- 1 ½ lbs ground chuck

Directions:

1. Set instant pot on sauté mode.
2. Add meat and onion to the pot and cook until meat is browned.
3. Add all ingredients and stir well.
4. Seal pot with lid and cook on manual high pressure for 5 minutes.
5. Once done then allow to release pressure naturally for 5 minutes then release using quick-release method. Open the lid.
6. Stir well and serve.

Nutritional Value (Amount per Serving):

Calories 317; Fat 22.1 g; Carbohydrates 13.7 g; Sugar 8.3 g; Protein 20.8 g; Cholesterol 78 mg

Mexican Queso Dip

Preparation Time: 10 minutes; Cooking Time: 10 minutes; Serve: 16

Ingredients:

- 1 lb ground beef
- 32 oz Velveeta cheese, cut into cubes
- 10 oz Rotel
- 2 tbsp taco seasoning
- 1 onion, diced

Directions:

1. Set instant pot on sauté mode.
2. Add meat, onion, Rotel, and taco seasoning to the pot and sauté until meat is no longer pink.
3. Add cheese and stir well. Seal pot with lid and cook on manual high pressure for 4 minutes.
4. Once done then release pressure using the quick-release method than open the lid.
5. Stir well and serve.

Nutritional Value (Amount per Serving):

Calories 217; Fat 13.9 g; Carbohydrates 6.7 g; Sugar 4.3 g; Protein 18.8 g; Cholesterol 66 mg

Creamy Cauliflower Chicken

Preparation Time: 10 minutes; Cooking Time: 10 minutes; Serve: 12

Ingredients:

- 1 cauliflower head, chopped
- 2 cups cheddar cheese, shredded
- 4 oz cream cheese, cubed
- 1 tsp paprika
- ¼ cup ranch dressing
- ½ cup buffalo sauce
- 2 cups chicken, cooked

Directions:

1. Add all ingredients except cream cheese and cheddar cheese into the instant pot and stir well.
2. Seal pot with lid and cook on manual mode for 5 minutes.
3. Once done then release pressure using the quick-release method than open the lid.
4. Stir in cream cheese and cheddar cheese.
5. Serve and enjoy.

Nutritional Value (Amount per Serving):
Calories 152; Fat 10.3 g; Carbohydrates 2 g; Sugar 0.8 g; Protein 12.7 g; Cholesterol 48 mg

Onion Dip

Preparation Time: 10 minutes; Cooking Time: 15 minutes; Serve: 8
Ingredients:
- 8 oz cream cheese
- 1 cup onion, grated
- 1 cup mayonnaise
- 1 cup Swiss cheese, grated

Directions:
1. Add all ingredients into the oven-safe bowl and stir well. Cover bowl with foil.
2. Pour 1 cup of water into the instant pot then place the trivet in the pot.
3. Place bowl on top of the trivet.
4. Seal pot with lid and cook on manual high pressure for 15 minutes.
5. Once done then release pressure using the quick-release method than open the lid.
6. Uncover the bowl and stir everything well.
7. Serve and enjoy.

Nutritional Value (Amount per Serving):
Calories 271; Fat 23.5 g; Carbohydrates 9.8 g; Sugar 2.7 g; Protein 6.2 g; Cholesterol 51 mg

Spicy Potatoes

Preparation Time: 10 minutes; Cooking Time: 5 minutes; Serve: 4
Ingredients:
- 1 lb potatoes, cut into 1-inch cubes
- 2 tbsp lemon juice
- 1 1/2 tbsp Moroccan spice mix
- 2 tbsp olive oil

Directions:
1. Pour 1 cup water into the instant pot and then place a steamer basket into the pot.
2. Place potatoes into the steamer basket.
3. Seal pot with lid and cook on manual high pressure for 5 minutes.
4. Once done then allow to release pressure naturally then open the lid.
5. Transfer potatoes on a plate.
6. Add oil into the instant pot and set the pot on sauté mode.
7. Add potatoes to the pot and sprinkle with the spice mix and cook until potatoes are browned.
8. Drizzle with lemon juice and serve.

Nutritional Value (Amount per Serving):
Calories 205; Fat 10.6 g; Carbohydrates 25.5 g; Sugar 2 g; Protein 2.9 g; Cholesterol 0 mg

Cheesy Corn Dip

Preparation Time: 10 minutes; Cooking Time: 10 minutes; Serve: 4
Ingredients:
- 4 ears corn
- 1/4 tsp cayenne
- 1/2 tsp cumin
- 1/2 tsp garlic powder
- 1 tsp paprika
- 1 1/2 tsp chili powder

- 1 cup of water
- 1/4 cup basil, minced
- 1/4 cup cilantro, minced
- 1 tbsp lime juice
- 1/4 cup mayonnaise
- 4 oz cream cheese
- 1/2 tsp pepper
- 1 1/2 tsp salt

Directions:
1. Pour water into the instant pot then place trivet into the pot.
2. Place corn on top of the trivet.
3. Seal pot with lid and cook manual high pressure for 5 minutes.
4. Once done then release pressure using the quick-release method than open the lid.
5. Drain corn and cut corn from the cob.
6. Add corn kernels, cayenne, cumin, garlic, paprika, chili powder, mayonnaise, cream cheese, pepper, and salt into the instant pot.
7. Seal pot with lid and cook on manual high pressure for 5 minutes.
8. Once done then release pressure using the quick-release method than open the lid.
9. Add basil, cilantro, and lime juice and stir well.
10. Serve with chips and enjoy.

Nutritional Value (Amount per Serving):
Calories 299; Fat 17 g; Carbohydrates 35.7 g; Sugar 6.4 g; Protein 7.7 g; Cholesterol 35 mg

Cheese Fondue

Preparation Time: 10 minutes; Cooking Time: 4 minutes; Serve: 10
Ingredients:
- 1/2 cup cheddar cheese, shredded
- 1/4 cup milk
- 1/4 cup heavy cream
- 1/2 tsp chili powder
- 1 tsp garlic salt
- 4 oz can chilies, diced
- 1 can cheddar cheese soup
- 1/4 tsp salt

Directions:
1. Add all ingredients into the oven-safe bowl and stir everything well. Cover bowl with foil.
2. Pour 2 cups of water into the instant pot then place the trivet in the pot.
3. Place bowl on top of the trivet.
4. Seal pot with lid and cook on manual high pressure for 4 minutes.
5. Once done then release pressure using the quick-release method than open the lid.
6. Stir well and serve.

Nutritional Value (Amount per Serving):
Calories 78; Fat 5.7 g; Carbohydrates 3.8 g; Sugar 0.7 g; Protein 3.1 g; Cholesterol 18 mg

Easy Spinach Dip

Preparation Time: 10 minutes; Cooking Time: 4 minutes; Serve: 15
Ingredients:
- 10 oz frozen spinach
- 1/2 cup vegetable broth
- 1/2 cup onion, chopped
- 1 cup sour cream
- 3 garlic cloves, minced
- 12 oz parmesan cheese, shredded
- 12 oz Monterey jack cheese, shredded
- 8 oz cream cheese
- 1/4 tsp pepper
- 1/2 tsp salt

Directions:
1. Add all ingredients except parmesan and Monterey jack cheese into the instant pot and stir well.
2. Seal pot with lid and cook on manual high pressure for 4 minutes.
3. Once done then release pressure using the quick-release method than open the lid.

4. Add parmesan and Monterey jack cheese and stir to combine.
5. Serve and enjoy.

Nutritional Value (Amount per Serving):
Calories 251; Fat 20.3 g; Carbohydrates 3.3 g; Sugar 0.4 g; Protein 15.2 g; Cholesterol 60 mg

Tahini Garlic Hummus

Preparation Time: 10 minutes; Cooking Time: 40 minutes; Serve: 10

Ingredients:
- 1 1/2 cups dry garbanzo beans, rinsed
- 5 garlic cloves, minced
- 1/2 cup tahini
- 6 cups of water
- 1/2 cup fresh lemon juice
- 2 tbsp olive oil
- 1 tsp salt

Directions:
1. Add water, garbanzo beans, and salt into the instant pot.
2. Seal pot with lid and cook on manual high pressure for 40 minutes.
3. Once done then allow to release pressure naturally then open the lid. Drain beans.
4. Add cooked beans, garlic, salt, lemon juice, olive oil, and tahini to a food processor.
5. Add 1 cup reserved bean water and blend until smooth.
6. Serve and enjoy.

Nutritional Value (Amount per Serving):
Calories 210; Fat 11.2 g; Carbohydrates 21.5 g; Sugar 3.6 g; Protein 8 g; Cholesterol 0 mg

Black Bean Dip

Preparation Time: 10 minutes; Cooking Time: 30 minutes; Serve: 24

Ingredients:
- 1 1/2 cups dry black beans, rinsed
- 1 1/2 tsp ground cumin
- 1 fresh lime juice
- 1 1/2 tbsp olive oil
- 1 3/4 cup vegetable broth
- 13.5 oz can tomatoes, diced
- 2 jalapeno peppers, chopped
- 1/2 tsp ground coriander
- 1/2 tsp chili powder
- 1 tsp paprika
- 2 garlic cloves, minced
- 1 onion, diced
- 3/4 tsp sea salt

Directions:
1. Add all ingredients to the instant pot and stir well.
2. Seal pot with lid and cook on manual high pressure for 30 minutes.
3. Once done then allow to release pressure naturally for 10 minutes then release using quick-release method. Open the lid.
4. Transfer bean mixture into the food processor and process until smooth.
5. Serve and enjoy.

Nutritional Value (Amount per Serving):
Calories 59; Fat 1.2 g; Carbohydrates 9.3 g; Sugar 1.1 g; Protein 3.3 g; Cholesterol 0 mg

Dairy Free Queso

Preparation Time: 10 minutes; Cooking Time: 5 minutes; Serve: 4

Ingredients
- 1 lb cauliflower florets
- 1/4 tsp turmeric
- 1/2 tsp ground cumin
- 1/2 tsp garlic powder
- 2 tsp vinegar
- 4 tbsp nutritional yeast
- 3 garlic cloves, peeled
- 1/3 cup onion, diced

- 1 jalapeno pepper, diced
- 1 cup vegetable broth
- 1/2 carrots, sliced
- 1 1/2 tsp salt

Directions:
1. Add cauliflower, broth, onion, carrots, and jalapeno pepper into the instant pot and stir well.
2. Seal pot with lid and cook on manual mode for 5 minutes.
3. Once done then release pressure using the quick-release method than open the lid.
4. Transfer pot mixture to the food processor along with remaining ingredients and process until smooth.
5. Serve and enjoy.

Nutritional Value (Amount per Serving):
Calories 88; Fat 1.1 g; Carbohydrates 13.9 g; Sugar 3.9 g; Protein 8.5 g; Cholesterol 0 mg

Eggplant Caviar

Preparation Time: 10 minutes; Cooking Time: 25 minutes; Serve: 8

Ingredients
- 1 large eggplant
- 1/2 cup fresh cilantro, chopped
- 1 tsp brown sugar
- 2 tbsp vinegar
- 2 tbsp olive oil
- 1 cup can tomatoes, diced
- 1 large carrot, chopped
- 1 bell pepper, chopped
- 2 garlic cloves, chopped
- 1 onion, chopped
- 1/2 tsp salt

Directions:
1. Add all ingredients except cilantro into the instant pot and stir well.
2. Seal pot with lid and cook on manual high pressure for 15 minutes.
3. Once done then release pressure using the quick-release method than open the lid.
4. Set pot on sauté mode and cook for 10 minutes or until all liquid evaporates.
5. Add cilantro and stir well.
6. Serve and enjoy.

Nutritional Value (Amount per Serving):
Calories 68; Fat 3.7 g; Carbohydrates 8.9 g; Sugar 4.9 g; Protein 1.3 g; Cholesterol 0 mg

Creamy Ranch Chicken Dip

Preparation Time: 10 minutes; Cooking Time: 15 minutes; Serve: 16

Ingredients:
- 2 lbs chicken breast, skinless and boneless
- 2 oz ranch seasoning
- 1 stick butter
- 2 cups cheddar cheese, shredded
- 15 oz buffalo sauce
- 8 oz cream cheese

Directions:
1. Add chicken, butter, buffalo sauce, and cream cheese into the instant pot.
2. Seal pot with lid and cook on manual mode for 15 minutes.
3. Once done then release pressure using the quick-release method than open the lid.
4. Stir in cheese and ranch seasoning.
5. Serve and enjoy.

Nutritional Value (Amount per Serving):
Calories 244; Fat 16.8 g; Carbohydrates 2.3 g; Sugar 0.1 g; Protein 16.7 g; Cholesterol 82 mg

Southern Peanuts

Preparation Time: 10 minutes; Cooking Time: 1 hour 30 minutes; Serve: 6

Ingredients:

- 1 lb raw peanuts, rinsed
- 1/4 cup sea salt
- Water

Directions:

1. Add peanuts and salt into the instant pot.
2. Place trivet on top of peanuts.
3. Pour enough water to the pot to cover peanuts.
4. Seal the pot with a lid and cook on manual mode for 1 hour 30 minutes.
5. Once done then release pressure using the quick-release method than open the lid.
6. Stir well and serve.

Nutritional Value (Amount per Serving):

Calories 429; Fat 37.2 g; Carbohydrates 12.2 g; Sugar 3 g; Protein 19.5 g; Cholesterol 0 mg

Ranch Potatoes

Preparation Time: 10 minutes; Cooking Time: 7 minutes; Serve: 4

Ingredients:

- 2 lbs potatoes, cut into 1-inch chunks
- 1/2 cup vegetable broth
- 1/2 cup water
- 1 cup parmesan cheese, shredded
- 1 oz ranch seasoning
- 1/2 tsp salt

Directions:

1. Add water, potatoes, ranch seasoning, salt, and potatoes into the pot and stir well.
2. Seal pot with lid and cook on manual high pressure for 7 minutes.
3. Once done then release pressure using the quick-release method than open the lid.
4. Add cheese and stir until cheese is melted.
5. Serve and enjoy.

Nutritional Value (Amount per Serving):

Calories 228; Fat 3.4 g; Carbohydrates 36.2 g; Sugar 2.7 g; Protein 8.9 g; Cholesterol 10 mg

Sweet Glazed Carrots

Preparation Time: 10 minutes; Cooking Time: 4 minutes; Serve: 6

Ingredients:

- 2 lbs baby carrots
- 1/2 cup water
- 1/2 tsp cinnamon
- 1/3 cup brown sugar
- 1/3 cup butter
- 1/4 tsp salt

Directions:

1. Add all ingredients into the instant pot and stir well.
2. Seal pot with lid and cook on manual mode for 4 minutes.
3. Once done then release pressure using the quick-release method than open the lid.
4. Stir and serve.

Nutritional Value (Amount per Serving):

Calories 174; Fat 10.4 g; Carbohydrates 20.5 g; Sugar 15 g; Protein 1.1 g; Cholesterol 27 mg

Creamy Hummus

Preparation Time: 10 minutes; Cooking Time: 35 minutes; Serve: 10

Ingredients:

- 3 cups garbanzo beans, cooked
- 12 cups water

- 1/4 tsp paprika
- 1/2 tsp ground cumin
- 1 lemon juice
- 3 garlic cloves

- 1/4 cup tahini
- 1/2 cup warm water
- 1/4 cup olive oil
- 1 tsp salt

Directions:
1. Add beans and water into the instant pot.
2. Seal pot with lid and cook on manual high pressure for 35 minutes.
3. Once done then allow to release pressure naturally then open the lid.
4. Drain beans well. Transfer beans into the food processor with remaining ingredients except for oil and process until smooth.
5. Add oil and stir well.
6. Serve and enjoy.

Nutritional Value (Amount per Serving):
Calories 300; Fat 12 g; Carbohydrates 38.1 g; Sugar 6.6 g; Protein 12.7 g; Cholesterol 0 mg

Red Bean Dip

Preparation Time: 10 minutes; Cooking Time: 15 minutes; Serve: 6
Ingredients:
- 1 cup red beans, soaked in water for overnight
- 1 cup cheddar cheese, shredded
- 1/2 tsp dried oregano
- 1 tsp chili powder

- 14 oz can tomatoes
- 1 tbsp olive oil
- 2 garlic cloves
- 1 small onion
- 2 cups of water

Directions:
1. Add all ingredients into the instant pot and stir well.
2. Seal pot with lid and cook on manual high pressure for 15 minutes.
3. Once done then allow to release pressure naturally then open the lid.
4. Blend bean mixture using immersion blender until smooth.
5. Serve and enjoy.

Nutritional Value (Amount per Serving):
Calories 221; Fat 9 g; Carbohydrates 24.2 g; Sugar 3.5 g; Protein 12.5 g; Cholesterol 20 mg

Simple Baked Potato

Preparation Time: 10 minutes; Cooking Time: 14 minutes; Serve: 4
Ingredients:
- 4 medium potatoes, scrubbed and poke with a fork all over
- 1 cup of water

- Pepper
- Salt

Directions:
1. Pour 1 cup of water into the instant pot then place the trivet in the pot.
2. Place potatoes on top of the trivet.
3. Seal pot with lid and cook on manual high pressure for 14 minutes.
4. Once done then allow to release pressure naturally then open the lid.
5. Season potatoes with pepper and salt and serve.

Nutritional Value (Amount per Serving):
Calories 147; Fat 0.2 g; Carbohydrates 33.5 g; Sugar 2.5 g; Protein 3.5 g; Cholesterol 0 mg

Italian Mix Vegetables

Preparation Time: 10 minutes; Cooking Time: 14 minutes; Serve: 4

Ingredients:
- 1 onion, sliced
- 1 potato, peeled and sliced
- 1 eggplant, peeled and sliced
- 1 bell pepper, diced
- 1 zucchini, sliced
- 8 oz mushrooms, sliced
- 1 tbsp olive oil
- 1/2 cup parmesan cheese, grated
- 1/4 tsp red pepper flakes
- 3 tbsp water
- 1 tsp basil
- 1/2 tsp oregano
- 1 tbsp tomato paste
- 2 garlic cloves, minced
- Pepper
- Salt

Directions:
1. Add oil into the instant pot and set the pot on sauté mode.
2. Add garlic, onion, and potatoes and sauté for 4 minutes.
3. Add remaining ingredients except for cheese and stir well.
4. Seal pot with lid and cook on manual high pressure for 10 minutes.
5. Once done then allow to release pressure naturally then open the lid.
6. Add cheese and stir well.
7. Serve and enjoy.

Nutritional Value (Amount per Serving):
Calories 150; Fat 4.9 g; Carbohydrates 24.1 g; Sugar 8.8 g; Protein 6.4 g; Cholesterol 3 mg

Black Bean Dip

Preparation Time: 10 minutes; Cooking Time: 18 minutes; Serve: 6
Ingredients:
- 2 cups black beans, soaked in water overnight
- 2 cup cheddar cheese, shredded
- 1 tsp dried oregano
- 2 tsp chili powder
- 2 cups tomatoes
- 2 tbsp olive oil
- 5 garlic cloves, minced
- 1 medium onion, sliced
- 4 cups of water
- Pepper
- Salt

Directions:
1. Add all ingredients into the instant pot and stir well.
2. Seal pot with lid and cook on manual high pressure for 18 minutes.
3. Once done then allow to release pressure naturally then open the lid.
4. Blend the beans mixture using immersion blender until smooth.
5. Serve and enjoy.

Nutritional Value (Amount per Serving):
Calories 438; Fat 18.4 g; Carbohydrates 46.3 g; Sugar 4 g; Protein 24.4 g; Cholesterol 40 mg

Corn on the Cob

Preparation Time: 10 minutes; Cooking Time: 4 minutes; Serve: 8
Ingredients:
- 8 ears corn on the cob, remove husk and silk
- 4 tbsp butter
- Pepper
- Salt

Directions:
1. Pour 2 cups of water into the instant pot then place rack in the pot.
2. Place corn on the rack. Seal pot with lid and cook on manual high pressure for 4 minutes.
3. Once done then allow to release pressure naturally then open the lid.
4. Remove corn from pot and season with pepper and salt.

5. Top with butter and serve.

Nutritional Value (Amount per Serving):
Calories 110; Fat 6.2 g; Carbohydrates 14.1 g; Sugar 2.3 g; Protein 2 g; Cholesterol 15 mg

Stuffed Bell Peppers

Preparation Time: 10 minutes; Cooking Time: 36 minutes; Serve: 4
Ingredients:
- 4 large bell peppers, cut in half
- 1/4 cup feta cheese, crumbled
- 2 tsp dried oregano
- 2 cups of water
- 3 tbsp pine nuts, roasted
- 1 cup couscous
- 1/4 tsp pepper
- 1 tsp salt

Directions:
1. Add water and couscous into the instant pot and stir well.
2. Seal pot with lid and cook on manual high pressure for 3 minutes.
3. Once done then allow to release pressure naturally then open the lid.
4. Add remaining ingredients except for bell peppers to the pot and cook on sauté mode for 3 minutes.
5. Stuff couscous mixture into the bell peppers and place on a baking tray.
6. Bake at 375 F for 30 minutes.
7. Serve and enjoy.

Nutritional Value (Amount per Serving):
Calories 271; Fat 7.1 g; Carbohydrates 44.3 g; Sugar 6.6 g; Protein 9 g; Cholesterol 8 mg

Healthy Steamed Vegetables

Preparation Time: 10 minutes; Cooking Time: 2 minutes; Serve: 6
Ingredients:
- 1/2 lb yellow beans, cut into pieces
- 1/2 lb green beans, cut into pieces
- 1 tbsp butter
- 1 tsp garlic powder
- 1/4 cup water
- 1 cauliflower head, cut into florets
- Pepper
- Salt

Directions:
1. Add all ingredients into the instant pot and stir well.
2. Seal pot with lid and cook on manual high pressure for 2 minutes.
3. Once done then release pressure using the quick-release method than open the lid.
4. Stir well and serve with your favorite dip.

Nutritional Value (Amount per Serving):
Calories 96; Fat 2.4 g; Carbohydrates 14.9 g; Sugar 1.7 g; Protein 5.1 g; Cholesterol 5 mg

Simple Pepper & salt Baby Potatoes

Preparation Time: 10 minutes; Cooking Time: 10 minutes; Serve: 4
Ingredients:
- 1 lb baby potatoes
- 1 1/2 cup water
- Pepper
- Salt

Directions:
1. Pour water into the instant pot the place trivet in the pot.
2. Arrange baby potatoes on top of the trivet.
3. Seal pot with lid and cook on manual high pressure for 10 minutes.
4. Once done then allow to release pressure naturally then open the lid.
5. Season potatoes with pepper and salt and serve.

Nutritional Value (Amount per Serving):

Calories 1985; Fat 0 g; Carbohydrates 453.6 g; Sugar 85.1 g; Protein 56.7 g; Cholesterol 0 mg

Baby Back Ribs

Preparation Time: 10 minutes; Cooking Time: 20 minutes; Serve: 6

Ingredients:

- 1 1/2 lbs baby back ribs
- 2 cups BBQ sauce
- 1 cup of water
- 1/2 tsp cayenne
- 1/2 tsp mustard powder
- 1/2 tsp paprika
- 1 tsp garlic powder
- 1/3 cup brown sugar
- 1/4 tsp pepper
- 2 tsp kosher salt

Directions:

1. In a small bowl, whisk together brown sugar, cayenne, mustard powder, paprika, pepper, garlic powder, pepper, and salt.
2. Rub ribs with brown sugar mixture.
3. Pour water into the instant pot then place the trivet in the pot.
4. Place ribs on top of the trivet. Seal pot with lid and cook on high pressure for 20 minutes.
5. Once done then release pressure using the quick-release method than open the lid.
6. Remove ribs from pot and place on a baking dish and brush with BBQ sauce.
7. Serve and enjoy.

Nutritional Value (Amount per Serving):

Calories 413; Fat 14.2 g; Carbohydrates 38.8 g; Sugar 29.7 g; Protein 30.1 g; Cholesterol 87 mg

Healthy Beet Hummus

Preparation Time: 10 minutes; Cooking Time: 40 minutes; Serve: 16

Ingredients:

- 1 cup chickpeas
- 1/3 cup water
- 1/4 cup olive oil
- 1/4 cup fresh lemon juice
- 3 beets, peeled and diced
- 2 garlic cloves, peeled
- 1/4 cup sunflower seeds
- 1 1/2 tsp kosher salt

Directions:

1. Add beets, chickpeas, 1 tsp salt, 3 cups water, garlic, and sunflower seeds into the instant pot.
2. Seal pot with lid and cook on manual high pressure for 40 minutes.
3. Strain beet, chickpeas, garlic, and sunflower seeds and place in a food processor along with lemon juice and remaining salt and process until smooth.
4. Add oil and 1/3 cup water and process until smooth.
5. Serve and enjoy.

Nutritional Value (Amount per Serving):

Calories 86; Fat 4.3 g; Carbohydrates 9.8 g; Sugar 2.9 g; Protein 2.9 g; Cholesterol 0 mg

Chicken Jalapeno Popper Dip

Preparation Time: 10 minutes; Cooking Time: 14 minutes; Serve: 10

Ingredients:

- 1 lb chicken breast, boneless
- 1/2 cup water
- 1/2 cup breadcrumbs
- 3/4 cup sour cream
- 3 jalapeno pepper, sliced
- 8 oz cream cheese
- 8 oz cheddar cheese

Directions:

1. add chicken, jalapeno, water, and cream cheese into the instant pot.
2. Seal pot with lid and cook on manual high pressure for 12 minutes.
3. Once done then release pressure using the quick-release method than open the lid.
4. Stir in cream and cheddar cheese.
5. Transfer instant pot mixture to the baking dish and top with breadcrumbs and broil for 2 minutes.
6. Serve and enjoy.

Nutritional Value (Amount per Serving):
Calories 282; Fat 20.5 g; Carbohydrates 5.8 g; Sugar 0.7 g; Protein 18.3 g; Cholesterol 85 mg

Jalapeno Hummus

Preparation Time: 10 minutes; Cooking Time: 25 minutes; Serve: 4
Ingredients:
- 1 cup chickpeas
- 1 tsp dried onion, minced
- 1 tsp ground cumin
- 1/4 cup jalapeno, diced
- 1/2 cup fresh cilantro
- 1 tbsp tahini
- 1/2 cup avocado oil
- 1/2 tsp sea salt

Directions:
1. Add chickpeas and 2 cups water into the instant pot.
2. Seal pot with lid and cook on manual high pressure for 25 minutes.
3. Once done then allow to release pressure naturally then open the lid.
4. Transfer chickpeas to the food processor along with remaining ingredients and process until smooth.
5. Serve and enjoy.

Nutritional Value (Amount per Serving):
Calories 246; Fat 8.8 g; Carbohydrates 33.4 g; Sugar 5.7 g; Protein 10.9 g; Cholesterol 0 mg

Flavorful Salsa

Preparation Time: 10 minutes; Cooking Time: 30 minutes; Serve: 8
Ingredients:
- 12 cups fresh tomatoes, peeled, seeded, and diced
- 3 tbsp cayenne pepper
- 2 tbsp garlic powder
- 3 tbsp sugar
- 1/2 cup vinegar
- 12 oz can tomato paste
- 1 cup jalapeno pepper, chopped
- 3 onions, chopped
- 2 green peppers, chopped
- 1 tbsp salt

Directions:
1. Add all ingredients into the instant pot and stir well.
2. Seal pot with lid and cook on manual high pressure for 30 minutes.
3. Once done then allow to release pressure naturally then open the lid.
4. Allow to cool completely then serve or store.

Nutritional Value (Amount per Serving):
Calories 145; Fat 1.1 g; Carbohydrates 32.5 g; Sugar 20.3 g; Protein 5.1 g; Cholesterol 0 mg

Cheddar Cheese Dip

Preparation Time: 10 minutes; Cooking Time: 9 minutes; Serve: 16
Ingredients:
- 1 lb bacon slices, cooked and crumbled
- 1 green onion, sliced
- 1/4 cup heavy cream

- 2 cups cheddar cheese, shredded
- 1 cup non-alcoholic beer
- 1 tsp garlic powder
- 1 1/2 tbsp Dijon mustard
- 1/4 cup sour cream
- 18 oz cream cheese, softened

Directions:

1. Add cream cheese, bacon, beer, garlic powder, mustard, and sour cream into the instant pot and stir well.
2. Seal pot with lid and cook on manual high pressure for 5 minutes.
3. Once done then release pressure using the quick-release method than open the lid.
4. Stir in heavy cream and cheese and cook on sauté mode for 3-4 minutes.
5. Garnish with green onion and serve.

Nutritional Value (Amount per Serving):

Calories 195; Fat 17.4 g; Carbohydrates 2 g; Sugar 0.2 g; Protein 6.3 g; Cholesterol 54 mg

Creamy Eggplant Dip

Preparation Time: 10 minutes; Cooking Time: 20 minutes; Serve: 4

Ingredients:

- 1 eggplant
- 1/8 tsp paprika
- 1/2 tbsp olive oil
- 1/2 lemon juice
- 2 tbsp tahini
- 1 garlic clove
- 1 cup of water
- 1/8 tsp salt

Directions:

1. Pour water into the instant pot then place eggplant into the pot.
2. Seal pot with lid and cook on manual mode for 20 minutes.
3. Once done then release pressure using the quick-release method than open the lid.
4. Remove eggplant from the pot and let it cool.
5. Remove the skin of the eggplant and place eggplant flesh into the food processor.
6. Add remaining ingredients into the food processor and process until smooth.
7. Serve and enjoy.

Nutritional Value (Amount per Serving):

Calories 91; Fat 6.1 g; Carbohydrates 8.7 g; Sugar 3.6 g; Protein 2.5 g; Cholesterol 0 mg

Delicious Nacho Dip

Preparation Time: 10 minutes; Cooking Time: 20 minutes; Serve: 10

Ingredients:

- 1 lb ground beef
- 1 cup Mexican cheese
- 4 oz cream cheese
- 14 oz salsa
- 15 oz can black beans, drained
- 1/4 cup water
- 2 tsp cayenne pepper
- 1 1/2 tsp ground cumin
- 1 1/2 tsp chili powder
- 3 garlic cloves, chopped
- 1 jalapeno pepper, chopped
- 1 small onion, chopped
- 1 tbsp olive oil
- 1 tsp salt

Directions:

1. Add oil into the instant pot and set the pot on sauté mode.
2. Add jalapeno peppers and onion and sauté for 5 minutes.
3. Add garlic and sauté for a minute.
4. Add ground beef, cayenne, cumin, chili powder, and salt and sauté until browned.
5. Add water and stir well.
6. Add salsa and beans and stir well.
7. Seal pot with lid and cook on manual high pressure for 10 minutes.

8. Once done then allow to release pressure naturally then open the lid.
9. Stir in cheese and sour cream.
10. Serve and enjoy.

Nutritional Value (Amount per Serving):

Calories 214; Fat 10.4 g; Carbohydrates 12.1 g; Sugar 2 g; Protein 19 g; Cholesterol 58 mg

Spinach Dip

Preparation Time: 10 minutes; Cooking Time: 4 minutes; Serve: 10

Ingredients:
- 1 lb fresh spinach
- 1 tsp onion powder
- 1 cup mozzarella cheese, shredded
- 7.5 oz cream cheese, cubed
- 1/2 cup mayonnaise
- 1/2 cup sour cream
- 1/2 cup chicken broth
- 1 tbsp olive oil
- 2 garlic cloves, minced
- 1/4 tsp pepper
- 1/2 tsp salt

Directions:
1. Add oil into the instant pot and set the pot on sauté mode.
2. Add spinach and garlic and sauté until spinach is wilted. Drain excess liquid.
3. Add remaining ingredients and stir well.
4. Seal pot with lid and cook on manual high pressure for 4 minutes.
5. Once done then release pressure using the quick-release method than open the lid.
6. Stir well and serve.

Nutritional Value (Amount per Serving):

Calories 179; Fat 15.9 g; Carbohydrates 6.1 g; Sugar 1.1 g; Protein 4.5 g; Cholesterol 33 mg

Chipotle Bean Dip

Preparation Time: 10 minutes; Cooking Time: 43 minutes; Serve: 6

Ingredients:
- 1 cup dry pinto beans, rinsed
- 1/2 tsp cumin
- 1 tsp liquid smoke
- 1/2 cup salsa
- 2 garlic cloves, peeled
- 2 chipotle peppers in adobo sauce
- 5 cups of water
- 1/4 tsp pepper
- 1 tsp salt

Directions:
1. Add water, beans, chipotle peppers, and garlic into the instant pot.
2. Seal pot with lid and cook on manual high pressure for 43 minutes.
3. Once done then allow to release pressure naturally then open the lid.
4. Transfer beans to the blender and blends until smooth.
5. Add remaining ingredients and blend until just mixed.
6. Serve and enjoy.

Nutritional Value (Amount per Serving):

Calories 124; Fat 0.8 g; Carbohydrates 22.3 g; Sugar 1.4 g; Protein 7.7 g; Cholesterol 2 mg

Asian Boiled Peanuts

Preparation Time: 10 minutes; Cooking Time: 60 minutes; Serve: 4

Ingredients:
- 1 lb raw peanuts
- 3 dried red chili peppers
- 3 garlic cloves
- 2 cinnamon stick
- 3 whole star anise
- 3 tbsp kosher salt

Directions:
1. Add all ingredients into the instant pot and stir well.
2. Pour enough water to the pot to cover peanuts.
3. Seal pot with lid and cook on manual high pressure for 60 minutes.
4. Once done then allow to release pressure naturally then open the lid.
5. Serve and enjoy.

Nutritional Value (Amount per Serving):
Calories 672; Fat 55.9 g; Carbohydrates 24.3 g; Sugar 4.8 g; Protein 30.3 g; Cholesterol 0 mg

Mexican Pinto Bean Dip

Preparation Time: 10 minutes; Cooking Time: 45 minutes; Serve: 6

Ingredients:
- 1 cup dry pinto beans
- 1 1/2 tsp chili powder
- 4 chilies
- 4 cups of water
- 1 tsp salt

Directions:
1. Add water, chilies, and beans into the instant pot.
2. Seal pot with lid and cook on manual high pressure for 45 minutes.
3. Once done then allow to release pressure naturally for 10 minutes then release using quick-release method. Open the lid.
4. Transfer beans into the blender along with chili powder and salt and blends until smooth.
5. Serve and enjoy.

Nutritional Value (Amount per Serving):
Calories 115; Fat 0.5 g; Carbohydrates 20.7 g; Sugar 0.9 g; Protein 7 g; Cholesterol 0 mg

Chapter 10: Desserts

Orange Strawberry Compote

Preparation Time: 10 minutes; Cooking Time: 2 minutes; Serve: 4
Ingredients:

- 1 lb fresh strawberries, rinsed and cut into cubes
- 1 tsp chia seeds
- ¼ cup of orange juice

Directions:

1. Add all ingredients into the instant pot and cook on sauté mode for 2 minutes.
2. Pour compote in glass container and place in the fridge.
3. Serve chilled and enjoy.

Nutritional Value (Amount per Serving):
Calories 43; Fat 0.4 g; Carbohydrates 10 g; Sugar 6.9 g; Protein 0.9 g; Cholesterol 0 mg

Apple Rice Pudding

Preparation Time: 10 minutes; Cooking Time: 30 minutes; Serve: 6
Ingredients:

- 3 apples, peeled and diced
- 2 cups Arborio rice
- 2/3 cup dried cherries
- 4 tbsp almonds, sliced
- ½ cup brown sugar
- 4 cups of milk
- 1 ½ cup apple juice
- 1 ½ tsp cinnamon
- 3 tbsp butter
- ½ tsp salt

Directions:

1. Add butter into the instant pot and set the pot on sauté mode.
2. Add rice and cook for 2-3 minutes.
3. Add spices, brown sugar, and apples and stir well.
4. Stir in apple juice and milk.
5. Seal pot with lid and cook on manual high pressure for 6 minutes.
6. Once done then release pressure using the quick-release method than open the lid.
7. Top with dried cherries and almonds.
8. Serve and enjoy.

Nutritional Value (Amount per Serving):
Calories 517; Fat 11.7 g; Carbohydrates 93.9 g; Sugar 36.8 g; Protein 10.8 g; Cholesterol 29 mg

Cherry Apple Risotto

Preparation Time: 10 minutes; Cooking Time: 15 minutes; Serve: 4
Ingredients:

- 1 ½ cups Arborio rice
- 3 tbsp almonds, sliced
- ½ cup dried cherries
- 3 cups of milk
- 1 cup apple juice
- 1/3 cup brown sugar
- 1 tsp cinnamon
- 2 apples, diced
- 2 tbsp butter
- ¼ tsp salt

Directions:

1. Add butter into the instant pot and set the pot on sauté mode.
2. Add rice and cook for 4 minutes.
3. Add apples, sugar, and spices and stir well.
4. Seal pot with lid and cook on manual high pressure for 6 minutes.
5. Once done then release pressure using the quick-release method than open the lid.

6. Top with cherries and almonds.
7. Serve and enjoy.

Nutritional Value (Amount per Serving):
Calories 558; Fat 12.4 g; Carbohydrates 101.3 g; Sugar 37.8 g; Protein 12.1 g; Cholesterol 30 mg

Poached Pears

Preparation Time: 10 minutes; Cooking Time: 15 minutes; Serve: 6

Ingredients:

- 6 firm pears, peel
- 2 cup of sugar
- 1 stick cinnamon
- 1 tsp ginger, grated
- 1 bottle red wine

Directions:
1. Add sugar, ginger, cinnamon, and wine into the instant pot and stir well.
2. Place pears to the pot. Seal pot with lid and cook on manual high pressure for 7 minutes.
3. Once done then allow to release pressure naturally then open the lid.
4. Serve and enjoy.

Nutritional Value (Amount per Serving):
Calories 372; Fat 0.3 g; Carbohydrates 98.7 g; Sugar 87.1 g; Protein 0.8 g; Cholesterol 0 mg

Brownie Cake

Preparation Time: 10 minutes; Cooking Time: 20 minutes; Serve: 6

Ingredients:

- 2 eggs
- 2 tbsp powdered sugar
- 1/2 tsp baking powder
- 1 cup of water
- 1/4 cup pecans, chopped
- 1/4 cup chocolate chips
- 1/3 cup sugar
- 1/3 cup cocoa powder
- 1/3 cup all-purpose flour
- 4 tbsp butter
- Pinch of salt

Directions:
1. In a bowl, whisk together eggs, sugar, cocoa powder, baking powder, flour, butter, and salt.
2. Add pecans and chocolate chips and stir well.
3. Spray cake pan with cooking spray.
4. Pour batter into the prepared pan and cover the pan with foil.
5. Pour water into the instant pot then place the trivet in the pot.
6. Place cake pan on top of the trivet.
7. Seal pot with lid and cook on manual high pressure for 20 minutes.
8. Once done then allow to release pressure naturally for 5 minutes then release using quick release method. Open the lid.
9. Sprinkle powdered sugar on top of brownie cake.
10. Slice and serve.

Nutritional Value (Amount per Serving):
Calories 278; Fat 18.1 g; Carbohydrates 27.2 g; Sugar 17.7 g; Protein 4.9 g; Cholesterol 77 mg

Thai Black Rice Pudding

Preparation Time: 10 minutes; Cooking Time: 22 minutes; Serve: 4

Ingredients:

- 1 cup black rice, rinsed and drained
- 1/2 cup sugar
- 5 cups of coconut milk
- 1 cup of water
- 1/2 tsp salt

Directions:
1. Add all ingredients into the instant pot and stir well.
2. Seal pot with lid and cook on manual high pressure for 22 minutes.
3. Once done then allow to release pressure naturally for 15 minutes then release using the quick-release method. Open the lid.
4. Stir well and serve.

Nutritional Value (Amount per Serving):
Calories 831; Fat 71.8 g; Carbohydrates 51.4 g; Sugar 35.3 g; Protein 8.6 g; Cholesterol 1 mg

Coconut Rice Pudding

Preparation Time: 10 minutes; Cooking Time: 5 minutes; Serve: 8
Ingredients:
- 1 cup Arborio rice, rinsed
- 1 tbsp coconut flakes
- 1/2 tsp vanilla
- 2 eggs, lightly beaten
- 1/2 cup sugar
- 3/4 cup heavy cream
- 1 tbsp coconut cream
- 14 oz coconut milk
- 1/4 tsp cinnamon
- 1 1/2 cups water
- Pinch of salt

Directions:
1. Whisk together eggs, heavy cream, and coconut milk until frothy.
2. Add rice, vanilla, water, egg mixture, sugar, coconut cream, cinnamon, and salt to the pot and stir well.
3. Seal pot with lid and cook on high pressure for 5 minutes.
4. Once done then allow to release pressure naturally for 10 minutes then release using the quick-release method. Open the lid.
5. Add coconut flakes and stir well.
6. Serve and enjoy.

Nutritional Value (Amount per Serving):
Calories 201; Fat 6.8 g; Carbohydrates 32.2 g; Sugar 12.7 g; Protein 3.3 g; Cholesterol 56 mg

Healthy Sweet Potato Rice Pudding

Preparation Time: 10 minutes; Cooking Time: 8 minutes; Serve: 8
Ingredients:
- 1 cup Arborio rice
- 1/4 cup raisins
- 1 medium sweet potato, peeled and shredded
- 1/4 tsp cardamom
- 1 tsp vanilla
- 1/2 tsp cinnamon
- 1 1/2 cups water
- 1/2 cup honey
- 12 oz milk
- 13.5 oz coconut milk
- 1 tbsp butter
- 1 tsp salt

Directions:
1. Add butter into the instant pot and set the pot on sauté mode.
2. Stir in honey, water, milk, and coconut milk.
3. Add vanilla, cardamom, cinnamon, and salt. Stir and cook until it comes to simmer.
4. Add rice and sweet potato and stir well.
5. Seal pot with lid and cook on manual high pressure for 8 minutes.
6. Once done then release pressure using the quick-release method than open the lid.
7. Add resins and stir well.
8. Serve and enjoy.

Nutritional Value (Amount per Serving):
Calories 323; Fat 13.9 g; Carbohydrates 47.9 g; Sugar 24.6 g; Protein 4.6 g; Cholesterol 7 mg

Quinoa Pudding

Preparation Time: 10 minutes; Cooking Time: 50 minutes; Serve: 2
Ingredients:
- 1/2 cup quinoa, rinsed
- 1/8 cup ground almonds
- 4 tbsp sweetened condensed milk
- 2 1/2 cups milk
- 2 tsp ghee
- 1/8 tsp ground cardamom

Directions:
1. Add ghee into the instant pot and set the pot on sauté mode.
2. Add quinoa to the pot and cook for 2 minutes.
3. Add milk and stir well.
4. Seal pot with lid and cook on manual high pressure for 10 minutes.
5. Once done then allow to release pressure naturally then open the lid.
6. Add cardamom, condensed milk, and almonds and stir well.
7. Select slow cook mode and cook for 30 minutes or until get the desired consistency.
8. Serve and enjoy.

Nutritional Value (Amount per Serving):
Calories 504; Fat 19.4 g; Carbohydrates 64.4 g; Sugar 34.8 g; Protein 20.3 g; Cholesterol 49 mg

Apple Crisp

Preparation Time: 10 minutes; Cooking Time: 8 minutes; Serve: 4
Ingredients:
- 5 cups apples, peeled and cubed
- 1/4 cup brown sugar
- 1/4 cup flour
- 1 cup old fashioned oats
- 1/2 cup butter, melted
- 1 tbsp maple syrup
- 1/2 cup water
- 2 tsp ground cinnamon

Directions:
1. Add apples into the instant pot.
2. Sprinkle cinnamon on top of apples.
3. Add maple syrup and water to the pot and stir well.
4. In a bowl, mix together melted butter flour, oats, and brown sugar.
5. Spread butter oats mixture on top of apples.
6. Seal pot with lid and cook on manual high pressure for 8 minutes.
7. Once done then allow to release pressure naturally then open the lid.
8. Serve and enjoy.

Nutritional Value (Amount per Serving):
Calories 583; Fat 26.2 g; Carbohydrates 84.5 g; Sugar 41.9 g; Protein 6.9 g; Cholesterol 61 mg

Healthy Carrot Cake

Preparation Time: 10 minutes; Cooking Time: 45 minutes; Serve: 8
Ingredients:
- 4 eggs
- 1 tbsp baking powder
- 1 cup almond flour
- 1 1/2 cup coconut flour
- 1/2 tsp vanilla
- 3/4 cup coconut oil, melted
- 1/2 cup swerve
- 1 cup pecan, chopped
- 2 1/4 cup carrots, grated
- 1/2 tbsp cinnamon
- Pinch of salt

Directions:

1. Spray cake pan with cooking spray and set aside.
2. Pour two cups of water into the instant pot then place a trivet in the pot.
3. In a bowl, mix together swerve, vanilla, and coconut oil. Add eggs and stir to combine.
4. Add coconut flour, cinnamon, baking powder, almond flour, and salt and stir to combine.
5. Add grated carrots and pecans and fold well.
6. Pour batter into the prepared cake pan and cover with foil.
7. Place cake pan on top of the trivet.
8. Seal pot with lid and cook on steam mode for 45 minutes.
9. Once done then release pressure using the quick-release method than open the lid.
10. Carefully remove the cake from the pot and let it cool completely.
11. Slice and serve.

Nutritional Value (Amount per Serving):
Calories 410; Fat 32.8 g; Carbohydrates 22.9 g; Sugar 1.8 g; Protein 9.2 g; Cholesterol 82 mg

Chocolate Cake

Preparation Time: 10 minutes; Cooking Time: 50 minutes; Serve: 8
Ingredients:

- 2 eggs, lightly beaten
- 1/2 tsp vanilla
- 2 tbsp coconut oil, melted
- 1/4 cup milk
- 1 tbsp sugar
- 1/2 tsp baking soda
- 1 cup almond flour
- 1 cup of chocolate chips
- Pinch of salt

Directions:

1. Spray cake pan with cooking spray and set aside.
2. Pour two cups of water into the instant pot then place a trivet in the pot.
3. Add chocolate chips and milk in a saucepan and heat over low heat until chocolate is melted. Stir well.
4. Add coconut oil in melted chocolate chip mixture and stir to combine.
5. Remove saucepan from heat and let it cool completely.
6. In a large bowl, mix together all dry ingredients.
7. Add vanilla and eggs to the chocolate mixture and stir well.
8. Slowly add a dry ingredient and mix well.
9. Pour batter into the prepared cake pan and place the pan on top of the trivet.
10. Seal pot with lid and cook on manual mode for 40 minutes.
11. Once done then allow to release pressure naturally for 10 minutes then release using quick-release method. Open the lid.
12. Carefully remove the cake from the pot and let it cool completely.
13. Slice and serve.

Nutritional Value (Amount per Serving):
Calories 188; Fat 12.6 g; Carbohydrates 15.2 g; Sugar 12.9 g; Protein 4 g; Cholesterol 46 mg

Coconut Custard

Preparation Time: 10 minutes; Cooking Time: 30 minutes; Serve: 8
Ingredients:

- 5 eggs
- 1 tbsp swerve
- 2 cups of coconut milk
- 1 tsp vanilla extract

Directions:

1. In a large bowl, add all ingredients and beat using a blender for until well combined.
2. Pour 2 cups of water into the instant pot then place a trivet in the pot.
3. Pour custard mixture into the ramekins. Cover ramekins with foil and place on top of the trivet.
4. Seal pot with lid and cook on manual high pressure for 30 minutes.
5. Once done then allow to release pressure naturally then open the lid.
6. Remove from pot and let it cool completely.
7. Place in refrigerator for 1 hour.
8. Serve and enjoy.

Nutritional Value (Amount per Serving):
Calories 179; Fat 17 g; Carbohydrates 5.5 g; Sugar 4.2 g; Protein 4.8 g; Cholesterol 102 mg

Choco Mug Cake

Preparation Time: 10 minutes; Cooking Time: 5 minutes; Serve: 1
Ingredients:
- 3 tbsp almond flour
- 1 tbsp powdered sugar
- 1/4 tsp vanilla
- 1/2 tsp baking powder
- 3 tbsp coconut oil
- 1 tbsp chocolate chips
- 1 tbsp cocoa powder

Directions:
1. Pour 1 cup of water into the instant pot then place a trivet in the pot.
2. In a small bowl, mix together all ingredients until well combined.
3. Pour batter into the heat-safe mug. Cover with foil and place on top of the trivet.
4. Seal pot with lid and cook on manual high pressure for 5 minutes.
5. Once done then release pressure using the quick-release method than open the lid.
6. Serve and enjoy.

Nutritional Value (Amount per Serving):
Calories 936; Fat 86.6 g; Carbohydrates 36.5 g; Sugar 16.5 g; Protein 19.8 g; Cholesterol 2 mg

Brown Rice Pudding

Preparation Time: 10 minutes; Cooking Time: 20 minutes; Serve: 4
Ingredients:
- 1 1/2 cups almond milk
- 1/2 tsp vanilla
- 3/4 cup brown rice
- 1 cup of water
- 1 1/2 tsp ground cinnamon
- Pinch of salt

Directions:
1. Add rice, cinnamon, vanilla, water, almond milk, and salt into the instant pot and stir well.
2. Seal pot with lid and cook on porridge mode for 20 minutes.
3. Once done then allow to release pressure naturally then open the lid.
4. Stir well and serve.

Nutritional Value (Amount per Serving):
Calories 340; Fat 22.4 g; Carbohydrates 32.9 g; Sugar 3.1 g; Protein 4.8 g; Cholesterol 0 mg

Sweet Tapioca Pudding

Preparation Time: 10 minutes; Cooking Time: 8 minutes; Serve: 4
Ingredients:
- 1/2 cup pearl tapioca
- 1 can coconut milk
- 1/2 cup water
- 4 tbsp maple syrup

- 1 cup almond milk
- Pinch of cardamom

Directions:
1. Soak tapioca in almond milk for 1 hour.
2. Combine together all ingredients except water into the heat-safe bowl and cover bowl with foil.
3. Pour 1/2 cup water into the instant pot the place trivet into the pot.
4. Place bowl on top of the trivet.
5. Seal pot with lid and cook on manual high pressure for 8 minutes.
6. Once done then allow to release pressure naturally then open the lid.
7. Stir well. Place in refrigerator for 1 hour.
8. Serve and enjoy.

Nutritional Value (Amount per Serving):

Calories 313; Fat 18.1 g; Carbohydrates 38.4 g; Sugar 18.5 g; Protein 2.4 g; Cholesterol 1 mg

Vanilla Bread Pudding

Preparation Time: 10 minutes; Cooking Time: 15 minutes; Serve: 4

Ingredients:
- 3 eggs, lightly beaten
- 1 tsp coconut oil
- 1 tsp vanilla
- 4 cup bread cube
- 1/2 tsp cinnamon
- 1/4 cup raisins
- 1/4 cup chocolate chips
- 2 cup milk
- 1/4 tsp salt

Directions:
1. Pour water into the instant pot then place trivet into the pot.
2. Add bread cubes in baking dish.
3. In a large bowl, mix together remaining ingredients.
4. Pour bowl mixture into the baking dish on top of bread cubes and cover dish with foil.
5. Place baking dish on top of the trivet.
6. Seal pot with lid and cook on steam mode for 15 minutes.
7. Once done then allow to release pressure naturally then open the lid.
8. Carefully remove baking dish from the pot.
9. Serve and enjoy.

Nutritional Value (Amount per Serving):

Calories 230; Fat 10.1 g; Carbohydrates 25 g; Sugar 16.7 g; Protein 9.2 g; Cholesterol 135 mg

Chocolate Mousse

Preparation Time: 10 minutes; Cooking Time: 6 minutes; Serve: 5

Ingredients:
- 4 egg yolks
- 1/4 cup water
- 1/2 cup sugar
- 1 tsp vanilla
- 1 cup heavy cream
- 1/2 cup cocoa powder
- 1/2 cup milk
- 1/4 tsp sea salt

Directions:
1. Whisk egg yolk in a bowl until combined.
2. In a saucepan, add cocoa, water, and sugar and whisk over medium heat until sugar is melted.
3. Add milk and cream to the saucepan and whisk to combine. Do not boil.
4. Add vanilla and salt and stir well.
5. Pour 1 1/2 cups water into the instant pot then place a trivet in the pot.

6. Pour mixture into the ramekins and place on top of the trivet.
7. Seal pot with lid and cook on manual mode for 6 minutes.
8. Once done then release pressure using the quick-release method than open the lid.
9. Serve and enjoy.

Nutritional Value (Amount per Serving):

Calories 235; Fat 14.1 g; Carbohydrates 27.2 g; Sugar 21.5 g; Protein 5 g; Cholesterol 203 mg

Blueberry Cupcakes

Preparation Time: 10 minutes; Cooking Time: 25 minutes; Serve: 6

Ingredients:

- 2 eggs, lightly beaten
- 1/4 cup butter, softened
- 1/2 tsp baking soda
- 1 tsp baking powder
- 1 tsp vanilla extract
- 1/2 fresh lemon juice
- 1 lemon zest
- 1/4 cup sour cream
- 1/4 cup milk
- 1 cup of sugar
- 3/4 cup fresh blueberries
- 1 cup all-purpose flour
- 1/4 tsp salt

Directions:

1. Add all ingredients into the large bowl and mix well.
2. Pour 1 cup water into the instant pot then place trivet into the pot.
3. Pour batter into the silicone cupcake mold and place on top of the trivet.
4. Seal pot with lid and cook manual high pressure for 25 minutes.
5. Once done then allow to release pressure naturally then open the lid.
6. Serve and enjoy.

Nutritional Value (Amount per Serving):

Calories 330; Fat 11.6 g; Carbohydrates 53.6 g; Sugar 36 g; Protein 4.9 g; Cholesterol 80 mg

Moist Pumpkin Brownie

Preparation Time: 10 minutes; Cooking Time: 35 minutes; Serve: 4

Ingredients:

- 2 eggs, lightly beaten
- 3/4 cup pumpkin puree
- 1/2 tsp baking powder
- 1/3 cup cocoa powder
- 1/2 cup almond flour
- 1 tbsp vanilla
- 1/4 cup milk
- 1 cup maple syrup

Directions:

1. Add all ingredients into the large bowl and mix until well combined.
2. Spray spring-form pan with cooking spray.
3. Pour batter into the pan and cover the pan with foil.
4. Pour 2 cups water into the instant pot and place trivet into the pot.
5. Place cake pan on top of the trivet.
6. Seal pot with lid and cook on manual mode for 35 minutes.
7. Once done then release pressure using the quick-release method than open the lid.
8. Slice and serve.

Nutritional Value (Amount per Serving):

Calories 306; Fat 5.5 g; Carbohydrates 62.9 g; Sugar 49.9 g; Protein 5.8 g; Cholesterol 83 mg

Mini Choco Cake

Preparation Time: 10 minutes; Cooking Time: 9 minutes; Serve: 2

Ingredients:

- 2 eggs
- 2 tbsp swerve
- 1/4 cup cocoa powder
- 1/2 tsp vanilla
- 1/2 tsp baking powder
- 2 tbsp heavy cream

Directions for Cooking:
1. In a bowl, mix together all dry ingredients until combined.
2. Add all wet ingredients to the dry mixture and whisk until smooth.
3. Spray two ramekins with cooking spray.
4. Pour 1 cup water into the instant pot then place trivet to the pot.
5. Pour batter into the ramekins and place ramekins on top of the trivet.
6. Seal pot with lid and cook on manual high pressure for 9 minutes.
7. Once done then release pressure using the quick-release method than open the lid.
8. Carefully remove ramekins from the pot and let it cool.
9. Serve and enjoy.

Nutritional Value (Amount per Serving):
Calories 143; Fat 11.3 g; Carbohydrates 22.4 g; Sugar 15.7 g; Protein 7.8 g; Cholesterol 184 mg

Cinnamon Pears

Preparation Time: 10 minutes; Cooking Time: 7 minutes; Serve: 4
Ingredients:
- 4 firm pears, peel
- 1/2 tsp nutmeg
- 1/3 cup sugar
- 1 tsp ginger
- 1 1/2 tsp cinnamon
- 1 cinnamon stick
- 1 cup of orange juice

Directions:
1. Add orange juice and all spices into the instant pot.
2. Place trivet into the pot.
3. Arrange pears on top of the trivet.
4. Seal pot with lid and cook on manual high pressure for 7 minutes.
5. Once done then allow to release pressure naturally then open the lid.
6. Carefully remove pears from pot and set aside.
7. Discard cinnamon stick and cloves from the pot.
8. Add sugar to the pot and set the pot on sauté mode.
9. Cook sauce until thickened.
10. Pour sauce over pears and serve.

Nutritional Value (Amount per Serving):
Calories 221; Fat 0.6 g; Carbohydrates 57.5 g; Sugar 42.4 g; Protein 1.3 g; Cholesterol 0 mg

Delicious Pumpkin Pudding

Preparation Time: 10 minutes; Cooking Time: 20 minutes; Serve: 6
Ingredients:
- 2 large eggs, lightly beaten
- 1/2 cup milk
- 1/2 tsp vanilla
- 1 tsp pumpkin pie spice
- 14 oz pumpkin puree
- 3/4 cup Swerve

Directions:
1. Grease baking dish with cooking spray and set aside.
2. In a large bowl, whisk eggs with remaining ingredients.
3. Pour 1 1/2 cups of water into the instant pot then place a steamer rack in the pot.
4. Pour mixture into the prepared dish and cover with foil.
5. Place dish on top of steamer rack.

6. Seal pot with lid and cook on manual high pressure for 20 minutes.
7. Once done then allow to release pressure naturally for 10 minutes then release using quick-release method. Open the lid.
8. Carefully remove the dish from the pot and let it cool.
9. Place pudding dish in the refrigerator for 7-8 hours.
10. Serve and enjoy.

Nutritional Value (Amount per Serving):
Calories 58; Fat 2.3 g; Carbohydrates 36.7 g; Sugar 33.3 g; Protein 3.5 g; Cholesterol 64 mg

Saffron Rice Pudding

Preparation Time: 10 minutes; Cooking Time: 10 minutes; Serve: 6
Ingredients:

- 1/2 cup rice
- 1/2 tsp cardamom powder
- 3 tbsp almonds, chopped
- 3 tbsp walnuts, chopped
- 4 cups of milk
- 1/2 cup sugar
- 2 tbsp shredded coconut
- 1 tsp saffron
- 3 tbsp raisins
- 1 tbsp ghee
- 1/8 tsp salt

Directions:
1. Add ghee into the pot and set the pot on sauté mode.
2. Add rice and cook for 30 seconds.
3. Add 3 cups milk, coconut, raisins, saffron, nuts, cardamom powder, sugar, 1/2 cup water, and salt and stir well.
4. Seal pot with lid and cook on manual high pressure for 10 minutes.
5. Once done then allow to release pressure naturally for 15 minutes then release using quick-release method. Open the lid.
6. Add remaining milk and stir well and cook on sauté mode for 2 minutes.
7. Serve and enjoy.

Nutritional Value (Amount per Serving):
Calories 280; Fat 9.9 g; Carbohydrates 42.1 g; Sugar 27 g; Protein 8.2 g; Cholesterol 19 mg

Flavorful Carrot Halva

Preparation Time: 10 minutes; Cooking Time: 10 minutes; Serve: 6
Ingredients:

- 2 cups carrots, shredded
- 2 tbsp ghee
- 1/2 tsp cardamom
- 3 tbsp ground cashews
- 1/4 cup sugar
- 1 cup milk
- 4 tbsp raw cashews
- 3 tbsp raisins

Directions:
1. Add ghee to the instant pot and set the pot on sauté mode.
2. Add raisins and cashews and cook until lightly golden brown.
3. Add remaining ingredients except for cardamom and stir well.
4. Seal pot with lid and cook on manual high pressure for 10 minutes.
5. Once done then allow to release pressure naturally then open the lid.
6. Add cardamom and stir well and serve.

Nutritional Value (Amount per Serving):
Calories 171; Fat 9.3 g; Carbohydrates 20.5 g; Sugar 15.2 g; Protein 3.3 g; Cholesterol 14 mg

Vermicelli Pudding

Preparation Time: 10 minutes; Cooking Time: 2 minutes; Serve: 6

Ingredients:
- 1/3 cup vermicelli, roasted
- 6 dates, pitted, sliced
- 3 tbsp cashews, slice
- 2 tbsp pistachios, slice
- 1/4 tsp vanilla
- 1/2 tsp saffron
- 1/3 cup sugar
- 5 cups of milk
- 3 tbsp shredded coconut
- 2 tbsp raisins
- 3 tbsp almonds
- 2 tbsp ghee

Directions:
1. Add ghee to the instant pot and set the pot on sauté mode.
2. Add dates, cashews, pistachios, and almonds into the pot and cook for a minute.
3. Add raisins, coconut, and vermicelli. Stir well.
4. Add 3 cups milk, saffron, and sugar. Stir well.
5. Seal pot with lid and cook on manual high pressure for 2 minutes.
6. Once done then allow to release pressure naturally then open the lid.
7. Stir remaining milk and vanilla.
8. Serve and enjoy.

Nutritional Value (Amount per Serving):

Calories 283; Fat 13.4 g; Carbohydrates 34.9 g; Sugar 28.1 g; Protein 9 g; Cholesterol 28 mg

Simple Raspberry Mug Cake

Preparation Time: 10 minutes; Cooking Time: 10 minutes; Serve: 3

Ingredients:
- 3 eggs
- 1 cup almond flour
- 1/2 tsp vanilla
- 1 tbsp swerve
- 2 tbsp chocolate chips
- 1/2 cup raspberries
- Pinch of salt

Directions:
1. Add all ingredients into the large bowl and mix until well combined.
2. Pour 2 cups of water into the instant pot then place a trivet in the pot.
3. Pour batter into the heat-safe mugs. Cover with foil and place on top of the trivet.
4. Seal pot with lid and cook on manual high pressure for 10 minutes.
5. Once done then release pressure using the quick-release method than open the lid.
6. Serve and enjoy.

Nutritional Value (Amount per Serving):

Calories 326; Fat 25.3 g; Carbohydrates 20 g; Sugar 11.3 g; Protein 11.3 g; Cholesterol 165 mg

Yogurt Custard

Preparation Time: 10 minutes; Cooking Time: 20 minutes; Serve: 6

Ingredients:
- 1 cup plain yogurt
- 1 1/2 tsp ground cardamom
- 1 cup sweetened condensed milk
- 1 cup milk

Directions:
1. Add all ingredients into the heat-safe bowl and stir to combine.
2. Cover bowl with foil.
3. Pour 2 cups of water into the instant pot then place trivet in the pot.
4. Place bowl on top of the trivet.
5. Seal pot with lid and cook on manual high pressure for 20 minutes.

6. Once done then allow to release pressure naturally for 20 minutes then release using quick-release method. Open the lid.
7. Once custard bowl is cool then place in the refrigerator for 1 hour.
8. Serve and enjoy.

Nutritional Value (Amount per Serving):
Calories 215; Fat 5.8 g; Carbohydrates 33 g; Sugar 32.4 g; Protein 7.7 g; Cholesterol 23 mg

Cardamom Zucchini Pudding

Preparation Time: 10 minutes; Cooking Time: 10 minutes; Serve: 4

Ingredients:
- 1 3/4 cups zucchini, shredded
- 5 oz half and half
- 5.5 oz milk
- 1 tsp cardamom powder
- 1/3 cup sugar

Directions:
1. Add all ingredients except cardamom into the instant pot and stir well.
2. Seal pot with lid and cook on manual high pressure for 10 minutes.
3. Once done then allow to release pressure naturally for 10 minutes then release using quick-release method. Open the lid.
4. Stir in cardamom and serve.

Nutritional Value (Amount per Serving):
Calories 138; Fat 5 g; Carbohydrates 22.1 g; Sugar 19.4 g; Protein 3 g; Cholesterol 16 mg

Yummy Strawberry Cobbler

Preparation Time: 10 minutes; Cooking Time: 12 minutes; Serve: 3

Ingredients:
- 1 cup strawberries, sliced
- 1/2 tsp vanilla
- 1/3 cup butter
- 1 cup milk
- 1 tsp baking powder
- 1/2 cup granulated sugar
- 1 1/4 cup all-purpose flour

Directions:
1. In a large bowl, add all ingredients except strawberries and stir to combine.
2. Add sliced strawberries and fold well.
3. Grease ramekins with cooking spray then pour batter into the ramekins.
4. Pour 1 1/2 cups water into the instant pot then place trivet in the pot.
5. Place ramekins on top of the trivet.
6. Seal pot with lid and cook on manual high pressure for 12 minutes.
7. Once done then allow to release pressure naturally for 10 minutes then release using quick-release method. Open the lid.
8. Serve and enjoy.

Nutritional Value (Amount per Serving):
Calories 555; Fat 22.8 g; Carbohydrates 81.7 g; Sugar 39.6 g; Protein 8.6 g; Cholesterol 61 mg

Peach Cobbler

Preparation Time: 10 minutes; Cooking Time: 20 minutes; Serve: 6

Ingredients:
- 20 oz can peach pie filling
- 1 1/2 tsp cinnamon
- 1/4 tsp nutmeg
- 14.5 oz vanilla cake mix
- 1/2 cup butter, melted

Directions:

1. Add peach pie filling into the instant pot.
2. In a large bowl, mix together remaining ingredients and spread over peach pie filling.
3. Seal pot with lid and cook on manual high pressure for 10 minutes.
4. Once done then allow to release pressure naturally for 10 minutes then release using quick-release method. Open the lid.
5. Serve and enjoy.

Nutritional Value (Amount per Serving):
Calories 445; Fat 15.4 g; Carbohydrates 76.1 g; Sugar 47.7 g; Protein 0.2 g; Cholesterol 41 mg

Hazelnuts Brownies

Preparation Time: 10 minutes; Cooking Time: 25 minutes; Serve: 6
Ingredients:

- 4 eggs
- 1 cup almond flour
- 4 tbsp hazelnuts, chopped
- 1/4 cup Swerve
- ¼ cup of cocoa powder
- 2 tbsp butter
- 1/2 tsp vanilla
- 1/2 cup mascarpone
- 1/2 cup flaxseed meal

Directions:
1. In a large bowl, add all ingredients and beat until well combined.
2. Spray baking dish with cooking spray.
3. Pour 1 cup of water into the instant pot then place a trivet in the pot.
4. Pour batter into the baking dish and place dish on top of the trivet.
5. Seal pot with lid and cook on manual high pressure for 25 minutes.
6. Once done then release pressure using the quick-release method than open the lid.
7. Slice and serve.

Nutritional Value (Amount per Serving):
Calories 289; Fat 23.6 g; Carbohydrates 18.1 g; Sugar 11.3 g; Protein 12.3 g; Cholesterol 130 mg

Apple Pear Crisp

Preparation Time: 10 minutes; Cooking Time: 20 minutes; Serve: 4
Ingredients:

- 4 apples, peel and cut into chunks
- 1 cup steel-cut oats
- 2 pears, cut into chunks
- 1 1/2 cup water
- 1/2 tsp cinnamon
- 1/4 cup maple syrup

Directions:
1. Add all ingredients into the instant pot and stir well.
2. Seal pot with lid and cook on manual high for 10 minutes.
3. Once done then allow to release pressure naturally for 10 minutes then release using quick-release method. Open the lid.
4. Serve warm and enjoy.

Nutritional Value (Amount per Serving):
Calories 306; Fat 1.9 g; Carbohydrates 74 g; Sugar 45.3 g; Protein 3.7 g; Cholesterol 0 mg

Vanilla Peanut Butter Fudge

Preparation Time: 10 minutes; Cooking Time: 90 minutes; Serve: 12
Ingredients:

- 1 cup of chocolate chips
- 8.5 oz cream cheese
- 1/4 cup peanut butter
- 1/2 tsp vanilla
- 1/4 cup swerve

Directions:
1. Add all ingredients into the instant pot and stir well.
2. Seal pot with lid and cook on slow cook mode for 60 minutes.
3. Once done then release pressure using the quick-release method than open the lid.
4. Stir until smooth and cook for 30 minutes more on sauté mode.
5. Pour mixture into the baking pan and place in the fridge until set.
6. Slice and serve.

Nutritional Value (Amount per Serving):
Calories 177; Fat 13.9 g; Carbohydrates 14.9 g; Sugar 12.8 g; Protein 3.9 g; Cholesterol 25 mg

Walnut Carrot Cake

Preparation Time: 10 minutes; Cooking Time: 40 minutes; Serve: 8
Ingredients:

- 3 eggs
- 1 tsp baking powder
- 2/3 cup Swerve
- 1 cup almond flour
- 3/4 cup walnuts, chopped
- 1 cup carrot, shredded
- 1/2 cup heavy cream
- 1/4 cup coconut oil
- 1 tsp apple pie spice

Directions:
1. Spray a baking dish with cooking spray and set aside.
2. Add all ingredients into the large bowl and mix with a hand mixer until well combined.
3. Pour batter into the baking dish and cover dish with foil.
4. Pour 2 cups of water into the instant pot then place a trivet in the pot.
5. Place cake dish on top of the trivet.
6. Seal pot with lid and cook on manual high pressure for 40 minutes.
7. Once done then allow to release pressure naturally for 10 minutes then release using quick-release method. Open the lid.
8. Carefully remove the dish from the pot and let it cool.
9. Slice and serve.

Nutritional Value (Amount per Serving):
Calories 208; Fat 19.9 g; Carbohydrates 24.1 g; Sugar 21.1 g; Protein 5.9 g; Cholesterol 72 mg

Chapter 11: 1000-Day Meal Plan

DAY	BREAKFAST	LUNCH / DINNER	DESSERT
1	Delicious French Toast Casserole	Spicy Chickpea Curry	Orange Strawberry Compote
2	Easy Breakfast Grits	Flavorful Ramen	Apple Rice Pudding
3	Pumpkin Oatmeal	Delicious Black-Eyed Peas Curry	Cherry Apple Risotto
4	Roasted Baby Potatoes	Rich & Creamy Alfredo Sauce	Poached Pears
5	Easy Cinnamon Apples	Indian Curried Cauliflower Potato	Brownie Cake
6	Ranch Potatoes	Carrot Potato Medley	Thai Black Rice Pudding
7	Quick & Easy Oatmeal	Lentil Chickpea Curry	Coconut Rice Pudding
8	Creamy Mashed Potatoes	Creamy Sweet Potato Curry	Healthy Sweet Potato Rice Pudding
9	Delicious Chocolate Oatmeal	Steamed Broccoli	Quinoa Pudding
10	Hearty Polenta Porridge	Quick & Easy Shrimp	Apple Crisp
11	Peach Oatmeal	Cheesy Shrimp Grits	Healthy Carrot Cake
12	Apple Cinnamon Oatmeal	Healthy Salmon Chowder	Chocolate Cake
13	Chocó Banana Oatmeal	Shrimp with Sausage	Coconut Custard
14	Healthy Almond Oatmeal	Curried Spinach Quinoa	Choco Mug Cake
15	Spinach Frittata	Healthy Vegan Chili	Brown Rice Pudding
16	Broccoli Frittata	Cabbage with Coconut	Sweet Tapioca Pudding
17	Quinoa Porridge	Roasted Baby Potatoes	Vanilla Bread Pudding
18	Creamy Walnut Grits	Spicy Chickpea Curry	Chocolate Mousse
19	Healthy Wheat Porridge	Tasty Mushroom Stroganoff	Blueberry Cupcakes
20	Quinoa Pumpkin Porridge	Quick & Healthy Kale	Moist Pumpkin Brownie
21	Blueberry Oatmeal	Perfect & Healthy Carrots	Mini Choco Cake
22	Mushroom Frittata	Vegan Collard Greens	Cinnamon Pears
23	Quick Brussels Sprouts	Potato Curry	Delicious Pumpkin Pudding
24	Oatmeal Porridge	Garlic Mushrooms	Easy Egg Custard
25	Healthy Breakfast Porridge	Parmesan Broccoli	Cinnamon Lemon Pears
26	Strawberry Oatmeal	Perfect Green Beans	Sliced Apples with Nuts
27	Berry Oatmeal	Perfect Instant Pot Cabbage	Peanut Butter Brownies
28	Perfect Breakfast Casserole	Delicious Cheesy Cauliflower	Cheesecake
29	Delicious Breakfast Casserole	Healthy & Easy Instant Pot Zucchini	Saffron Rice Pudding
30	Sweet Potato Breakfast	Sweet & Sour Red Cabbage	Flavorful Carrot Halva
31	Banana Peanut Butter Oats	Sugar Snap Peas	Vermicelli Pudding
32	Jalapeno Cheddar Grits	Southern Okra & Tomatoes	Simple Raspberry Mug Cake
33	Fruit Compote	Garlic Mushrooms	Yogurt Custard
34	Carrot Oatmeal	Tasty Tikka Masala Chickpeas	Cardamom Zucchini Pudding
35	Slow Cook Cherry Oatmeal	Cheesy & Creamy Ziti	Yummy Strawberry Cobbler

36	Ham Cheese Breakfast Casserole	Classic Mac n Cheese	Peach Cobbler
37	Cranberry Apple Breakfast Grains	Sticky Noodles	Hazelnuts Brownies
38	Sausage Casserole	Crispy Roasted Potatoes	Apple Pear Crisp
39	Blueberry French Toast Casserole	Sweet Potato Mash	Vanilla Peanut Butter Fudge
40	Oat Millet Porridge	Cheesy Spaghetti	Walnut Carrot Cake
41	Baked Apples	Sautéed vegetables	Yummy Strawberry Cobbler
42	Quinoa Blueberry Bowl	Healthy Veggie Curry	Yogurt Custard
43	Savory Barley	Braised Parsnips	Walnut Carrot Cake
44	Fajita Casserole	Healthy Ratatouille	Vermicelli Pudding
45	Latte Oatmeal	Herb Mushrooms	Vanilla Peanut Butter Fudge
46	Coconut Blueberry Oatmeal	Creamy Squash Puree	Vanilla Bread Pudding
47	Pumpkin Cranberry Oatmeal	Cheesy Cauliflower Rice	Thai Black Rice Pudding
48	Cranberry Farro	Delicious Baby Carrots	Sweet Tapioca Pudding
49	Tropical Oatmeal	Lemon Haddock	Sliced Apples with Nuts
50	Simple & Easy Breakfast Casserole	Quick Coconut Shrimp Curry	Simple Raspberry Mug Cake
51	Creamy Mac n Cheese	Yummy Fish Tacos	Saffron Rice Pudding
52	Cherry Risotto	Delicious Scallops	Quinoa Pudding
53	Almond Coconut Risotto	Healthy Shrimp Rice	Poached Pears
54	Creamy Polenta	Balsamic Salmon	Peanut Butter Brownies
55	Sweet Cherry Chocolate Oat	Shrimp Scampi	Peach Cobbler
56	Coconut Lime Breakfast Quinoa	Dijon Fish Fillets	Orange Strawberry Compote
57	Quick & Easy Farro	Macaroni with Cauliflower Broccoli	Moist Pumpkin Brownie
58	Farro Breakfast Risotto	Spicy Cabbage	Mini Choco Cake
59	Tapioca Pudding	Instant Pot Artichokes	Healthy Sweet Potato Rice Pudding
60	Sweetened Breakfast Oats	Flavorful Ranch Cauliflower Mashed	Healthy Carrot Cake
61	Cauliflower Mash	Kale Curry	Hazelnuts Brownies
62	Chia Oatmeal	Buttery Carrots & Parsnips	Flavorful Carrot Halva
63	Blueberry Lemon Oatmeal	Creamy Parsnip Mash	Easy Egg Custard
64	Breakfast Cobbler	Red Bean Rice	Delicious Pumpkin Pudding
65	Tomato Corn Risotto	Tender Pinto Beans	Coconut Rice Pudding
66	Tropical Oatmeal	Tomatillo White Beans	Coconut Custard
67	Tomato Corn Risotto	Flavorful Refried Beans	Cinnamon Pears
68	Tapioca Pudding	Delicious Beans & Rice	Cinnamon Lemon Pears
69	Sweetened Breakfast Oats	Indian Red Kidney Beans	Chocolate Mousse
70	Sweet Potato Breakfast	Mexican Black Beans	Chocolate Cake
71	Sweet Cherry Chocolate Oat	Ham & Pinto Beans	Choco Mug Cake

72	Strawberry Oatmeal	Rosemary Salmon	Cherry Apple Risotto
73	Spinach Frittata	Crab Legs	Cheesecake
74	Slow Cook Cherry Oatmeal	Lemon Garlic Mussels	Cardamom Zucchini Pudding
75	Simple & Easy Breakfast Casserole	Zesty Salmon	Brownie Cake
76	Savory Barley	Delicious Basa Fillets	Brown Rice Pudding
77	Sausage Casserole	Indian Fried Prawns	Blueberry Cupcakes
78	Roasted Baby Potatoes	Spicy Salmon	Apple Rice Pudding
79	Ranch Potatoes	Basil Salmon	Apple Pear Crisp
80	Quinoa Pumpkin Porridge	Lemon Pepper Cod	Apple Crisp
81	Quinoa Porridge	Easy Salmon Stew	Apple Crisp
82	Quinoa Blueberry Bowl	Sweet Baked Beans	Apple Pear Crisp
83	Quick Brussels Sprouts	Easy Baked Beans	Apple Rice Pudding
84	Quick & Easy Oatmeal	Sweet & Tender Lima Beans	Blueberry Cupcakes
85	Quick & Easy Farro	Flavorful Onion Rice	Brown Rice Pudding
86	Pumpkin Oatmeal	Healthy Chicken Noodle Soup	Brownie Cake
87	Pumpkin Cranberry Oatmeal	Nutritious Lentil Soup	Cardamom Zucchini Pudding
88	Perfect Breakfast Casserole	Cheesy Broccoli Soup	Cheesecake
89	Peach Oatmeal	Carrot Ginger Soup	Cherry Apple Risotto
90	Oatmeal Porridge	Cabbage Soup	Choco Mug Cake
91	Oat Millet Porridge	Zucchini Corn Soup	Chocolate Cake
92	Mushroom Frittata	Lentil Sausage Stew	Chocolate Mousse
93	Latte Oatmeal	Black Bean Rice	Cinnamon Lemon Pears
94	Jalapeno Cheddar Grits	Nutritious Lentils Rice	Cinnamon Pears
95	Hearty Polenta Porridge	Cheesy Beef Rice	Coconut Custard
96	Healthy Wheat Porridge	Coconut Beans & Rice	Coconut Rice Pudding
97	Healthy Breakfast Porridge	Mushroom Brown Rice	Delicious Pumpkin Pudding
98	Healthy Almond Oatmeal	Simple & Delicious Parmesan Rice	Easy Egg Custard
99	Ham Cheese Breakfast Casserole	Chicken Cheese Rice	Flavorful Carrot Halva
100	Fruit Compote	Flavorful Fajita Rice	Hazelnuts Brownies
101	Farro Breakfast Risotto	Creamy Pea Risotto	Healthy Carrot Cake
102	Fajita Casserole	Quick & Easy Chicken Rice	Healthy Sweet Potato Rice Pudding
103	Easy Cinnamon Apples	Garlic Turmeric Rice	Mini Choco Cake
104	Easy Breakfast Grits	Flavorful Rice Pilaf	Moist Pumpkin Brownie
105	Delicious French Toast Casserole	Perfect Jasmine Rice	Orange Strawberry Compote
106	Delicious Chocolate Oatmeal	Broccoli Rice	Peach Cobbler
107	Delicious Breakfast Casserole	Spanish rice	Peanut Butter Brownies
108	Creamy Walnut Grits	Onion Pepper Couscous	Poached Pears
109	Creamy Polenta	Lemon Snap Pea Couscous	Quinoa Pudding

110	Creamy Mashed Potatoes	Pearl Barley	Saffron Rice Pudding
111	Creamy Mac n Cheese	Spanish Quinoa	Simple Raspberry Mug Cake
112	Cranberry Farro	Buttery Scallions Risotto	Sliced Apples with Nuts
113	Cranberry Apple Breakfast Grains	Simple Paprika Rice	Sweet Tapioca Pudding
114	Coconut Lime Breakfast Quinoa	Delicious Potato Risotto	Thai Black Rice Pudding
115	Coconut Blueberry Oatmeal	Jalapeno Brown Rice	Vanilla Bread Pudding
116	Choco Banana Oatmeal	Herb Garlic Chicken	Vanilla Peanut Butter Fudge
117	Chia Oatmeal	Delicious Chicken Burrito Bowl	Vermicelli Pudding
118	Cherry Risotto	Chicken Cheese Spaghetti	Walnut Carrot Cake
119	Cauliflower Mash	Moist & Tender Chicken	Yogurt Custard
120	Carrot Oatmeal	Simple BBQ Chicken	Yummy Strawberry Cobbler
121	Broccoli Frittata	Flavorful Chicken Curry	Orange Strawberry Compote
122	Breakfast Cobbler	Spicy Chicken Wings	Apple Rice Pudding
123	Blueberry Oatmeal	BBQ Honey Chicken Wings	Cherry Apple Risotto
124	Blueberry Lemon Oatmeal	Honey Mustard Chicken	Poached Pears
125	Blueberry French Toast Casserole	Tortellini Tomato Soup	Brownie Cake
126	Berry Oatmeal	Healthy Split Pea Soup	Thai Black Rice Pudding
127	Banana Peanut Butter Oats	Barley Mushroom Soup	Coconut Rice Pudding
128	Baked Apples	Creamy Mushroom Soup	Healthy Sweet Potato Rice Pudding
129	Apple Cinnamon Oatmeal	Sweet Potato Soup	Quinoa Pudding
130	Almond Coconut Risotto	Healthy Vegetable Soup	Apple Crisp
131	Almond Coconut Risotto	Onion Soup	Healthy Carrot Cake
132	Apple Cinnamon Oatmeal	Teriyaki Chicken Drumsticks	Chocolate Cake
133	Baked Apples	Mexican Salsa Chicken	Coconut Custard
134	Banana Peanut Butter Oats	Artichoke Chicken	Choco Mug Cake
135	Berry Oatmeal	Creamy Peanut Butter Chicken	Brown Rice Pudding
136	Blueberry French Toast Casserole	BBQ Pulled Chicken	Sweet Tapioca Pudding
137	Blueberry Lemon Oatmeal	Buffalo Chicken Breasts	Vanilla Bread Pudding
138	Blueberry Oatmeal	Enchilada Chicken	Chocolate Mousse
139	Breakfast Cobbler	Moist & Tender Turkey Breast	Blueberry Cupcakes
140	Broccoli Frittata	Cafe Rio Chicken	Moist Pumpkin Brownie
141	Carrot Oatmeal	Marinara Chicken	Mini Choco Cake
142	Cauliflower Mash	Veggie Chicken Soup	Cinnamon Pears
143	Cherry Risotto	Zucchini Soup	Delicious Pumpkin Pudding
144	Chia Oatmeal	Curried Cauliflower Soup	Easy Egg Custard
145	Choco Banana Oatmeal	Summer Veggie Soup	Cinnamon Lemon Pears

146	Coconut Blueberry Oatmeal	Vegetable Chicken Stew	Sliced Apples with Nuts
147	Coconut Lime Breakfast Quinoa	Thai Sweet Potato Stew	Peanut Butter Brownies
148	Cranberry Apple Breakfast Grains	Chicken Taco Soup	Cheesecake
149	Cranberry Farro	Tasty Chicken Rice Soup	Saffron Rice Pudding
150	Creamy Mac n Cheese	Cabbage Pork Soup	Flavorful Carrot Halva
151	Creamy Mashed Potatoes	Chicken Adobo	Vermicelli Pudding
152	Creamy Polenta	Tasty BBQ Ranch Chicken	Simple Raspberry Mug Cake
153	Creamy Walnut Grits	Indian Chicken Tikka Masala	Yogurt Custard
154	Delicious Breakfast Casserole	Bacon Pineapple Chicken	Cardamom Zucchini Pudding
155	Delicious Chocolate Oatmeal	Flavorful Chicken Cacciatore	Yummy Strawberry Cobbler
156	Delicious French Toast Casserole	Sweet Potato Chicken Curry	Peach Cobbler
157	Easy Breakfast Grits	Chicken Chili	Hazelnuts Brownies
158	Easy Cinnamon Apples	Chicken Meatballs	Apple Pear Crisp
159	Fajita Casserole	Easy Adobo Chicken	Vanilla Peanut Butter Fudge
160	Farro Breakfast Risotto	Yummy Orange Chicken	Walnut Carrot Cake
161	Fruit Compote	Thai Chicken	Yummy Strawberry Cobbler
162	Ham Cheese Breakfast Casserole	Curried Chicken	Yogurt Custard
163	Healthy Almond Oatmeal	Olive Chicken	Walnut Carrot Cake
164	Healthy Breakfast Porridge	Sweet Mango Chicken	Vermicelli Pudding
165	Healthy Wheat Porridge	Herb Chicken	Vanilla Peanut Butter Fudge
166	Hearty Polenta Porridge	Creamy Pesto Chicken	Vanilla Bread Pudding
167	Jalapeno Cheddar Grits	Healthy Shrimp Boil	Thai Black Rice Pudding
168	Latte Oatmeal	Asparagus Shrimp Risotto	Sweet Tapioca Pudding
169	Mushroom Frittata	Basil Tilapia	Sliced Apples with Nuts
170	Oat Millet Porridge	Delicious Shrimp Risotto	Simple Raspberry Mug Cake
171	Oatmeal Porridge	Cajun Shrimp	Saffron Rice Pudding
172	Peach Oatmeal	Lemon Butter chicken	Quinoa Pudding
173	Perfect Breakfast Casserole	Instant Pot Turkey Breast	Poached Pears
174	Pumpkin Cranberry Oatmeal	Ranch Chicken	Peanut Butter Brownies
175	Pumpkin Oatmeal	Orange BBQ Chicken	Peach Cobbler
176	Quick & Easy Farro	Mustard Chicken	Orange Strawberry Compote
177	Quick & Easy Oatmeal	Delicious Beef Tips	Moist Pumpkin Brownie
178	Quick Brussels Sprouts	Shredded Mexican Beef	Mini Choco Cake
179	Quinoa Blueberry Bowl	Korean Beef	Healthy Sweet Potato Rice Pudding
180	Quinoa Porridge	Italian Beef	Healthy Carrot Cake
181	Quinoa Pumpkin Porridge	Beef Stroganoff	Hazelnuts Brownies
182	Ranch Potatoes	Asian Pot Roast	Flavorful Carrot Halva

183	Roasted Baby Potatoes	Italian Ribs	Easy Egg Custard
184	Sausage Casserole	Shredded Thai Beef	Delicious Pumpkin Pudding
185	Savory Barley	Healthy Spinach Lentil Soup	Coconut Rice Pudding
186	Simple & Easy Breakfast Casserole	Mushroom Soup	Coconut Custard
187	Slow Cook Cherry Oatmeal	Spinach Soup	Cinnamon Pears
188	Spinach Frittata	Hearty Beef Stew	Cinnamon Lemon Pears
189	Strawberry Oatmeal	Spinach Chickpea Stew	Chocolate Mousse
190	Sweet Cherry Chocolate Oat	Healthy Eggplant Stew	Chocolate Cake
191	Sweet Potato Breakfast	Squash Cauliflower Soup	Choco Mug Cake
192	Sweetened Breakfast Oats	Corn Soup	Cherry Apple Risotto
193	Tapioca Pudding	Carrot Pea Soup	Cheesecake
194	Tomato Corn Risotto	Mexican Barbecue	Cardamom Zucchini Pudding
195	Tropical Oatmeal	Korean Beef Tacos	Brownie Cake
196	Delicious French Toast Casserole	Delicious Italian Beef	Brown Rice Pudding
197	Easy Breakfast Grits	Flavorful Barbacoa	Blueberry Cupcakes
198	Pumpkin Oatmeal	Asian Beef	Apple Rice Pudding
199	Roasted Baby Potatoes	Tasty Steak Bites	Apple Pear Crisp
200	Easy Cinnamon Apples	Smoky Beef	Apple Crisp
201	Ranch Potatoes	Flank Steak	Apple Crisp
202	Quick & Easy Oatmeal	Moist & Tender Ribs	Apple Pear Crisp
203	Creamy Mashed Potatoes	Spicy Beef Curry	Apple Rice Pudding
204	Delicious Chocolate Oatmeal	Pork Tenderloin	Blueberry Cupcakes
205	Hearty Polenta Porridge	Tasty Beef Chili	Brown Rice Pudding
206	Peach Oatmeal	Chipotle Chili	Brownie Cake
207	Apple Cinnamon Oatmeal	Veggie Beef Roast	Cardamom Zucchini Pudding
208	Choco Banana Oatmeal	Meatballs	Cheesecake
209	Healthy Almond Oatmeal	Mongolian Beef	Cherry Apple Risotto
210	Spinach Frittata	Flavors Taco Meat	Choco Mug Cake
211	Broccoli Frittata	Leg of Lamb	Chocolate Cake
212	Quinoa Porridge	Flavors Lamb Shanks	Chocolate Mousse
213	Creamy Walnut Grits	Perfect Dinner Lamb	Cinnamon Lemon Pears
214	Healthy Wheat Porridge	Flavorful Taco Mince	Cinnamon Pears
215	Quinoa Pumpkin Porridge	Delicious Lamb Curry	Coconut Custard
216	Blueberry Oatmeal	Eastern Lamb Stew	Coconut Rice Pudding
217	Mushroom Frittata	Sweet & Sour Fish	Delicious Pumpkin Pudding
218	Quick Brussels Sprouts	Spicy Shrimp Noodles	Easy Egg Custard
219	Oatmeal Porridge	Nutritious Salmon	Flavorful Carrot Halva
220	Healthy Breakfast Porridge	Vegetable Fish Curry	Hazelnuts Brownies
221	Strawberry Oatmeal	Tuna Pasta	Healthy Carrot Cake
222	Berry Oatmeal	Cajun Seafood Gumbo	Healthy Sweet Potato Rice Pudding
223	Perfect Breakfast Casserole	Lemon Pepper Salmon	Mini Choco Cake

224	Delicious Breakfast Casserole	Lemon Garlic Salmon	Moist Pumpkin Brownie
225	Sweet Potato Breakfast	Dill Salmon	Orange Strawberry Compote
226	Banana Peanut Butter Oats	Irish Lamb Stew	Peach Cobbler
227	Jalapeno Cheddar Grits	Soy Honey Pork Tenderloin	Peanut Butter Brownies
228	Fruit Compote	Creamy Pork Chops	Poached Pears
229	Carrot Oatmeal	Juicy & Tender Pork Chops	Quinoa Pudding
230	Slow Cook Cherry Oatmeal	Filipino Pork Adobo	Saffron Rice Pudding
231	Ham Cheese Breakfast Casserole	Korean Pork Chops	Simple Raspberry Mug Cake
232	Cranberry Apple Breakfast Grains	Simple Lamb Curry	Sliced Apples with Nuts
233	Sausage Casserole	Herb Seasoned Lamb	Sweet Tapioca Pudding
234	Blueberry French Toast Casserole	Flavorful Lamb Korma	Thai Black Rice Pudding
235	Oat Millet Porridge	Tasty & Spicy Lamb	Vanilla Bread Pudding
236	Baked Apples	Lamb Stew	Vanilla Peanut Butter Fudge
237	Quinoa Blueberry Bowl	Lamb Shanks	Vermicelli Pudding
238	Savory Barley	Asian Lamb Curry	Walnut Carrot Cake
239	Fajita Casserole	Indian Lamb Curry	Yogurt Custard
240	Latte Oatmeal	Rogan Josh	Yummy Strawberry Cobbler
241	Coconut Blueberry Oatmeal	Cheesy Lamb Chops	Saffron Rice Pudding
242	Pumpkin Cranberry Oatmeal	Garlicky Lamb	Vanilla Bread Pudding
243	Cranberry Farro	Teriyaki Pork	Chocolate Mousse
244	Tropical Oatmeal	Easy & Tasty Ribs	Blueberry Cupcakes
245	Simple & Easy Breakfast Casserole	Shredded Pork	Moist Pumpkin Brownie
246	Creamy Mac n Cheese	Pork Curry	Mini Choco Cake
247	Cherry Risotto	Meatloaf	Cinnamon Pears
248	Almond Coconut Risotto	Cajun Beef	Delicious Pumpkin Pudding
249	Creamy Polenta	Old Bay Seasoned Haddock	Easy Egg Custard
250	Sweet Cherry Chocolate Oat	Shrimp Mac n Cheese	Cinnamon Lemon Pears
251	Coconut Lime Breakfast Quinoa	Salmon Rice Pilaf	Orange Strawberry Compote
252	Quick & Easy Farro	Perfect Salmon Dinner	Apple Rice Pudding
253	Farro Breakfast Risotto	Steam Clams	Cherry Apple Risotto
254	Tapioca Pudding	Mahi Mahi Fillets	Poached Pears
255	Sweetened Breakfast Oats	Curried Lentil Stew	Brownie Cake
256	Cauliflower Mash	Savory Butternut Squash Soup	Thai Black Rice Pudding
257	Chia Oatmeal	Potato Ham Soup	Coconut Rice Pudding
258	Blueberry Lemon Oatmeal	Northern Bean Soup	Healthy Sweet Potato Rice Pudding
259	Breakfast Cobbler	Squash Apple Soup	Quinoa Pudding

260	Tomato Corn Risotto	Delicious Tortilla Chicken Soup	Apple Crisp
261	Delicious French Toast Casserole	Hamburger Soup	Healthy Carrot Cake
262	Easy Breakfast Grits	Tasty Taco Soup	Chocolate Cake
263	Pumpkin Oatmeal	Easy Garlic Lemon Shrimp	Coconut Custard
264	Roasted Baby Potatoes	Cheesy Tilapia	Choco Mug Cake
265	Easy Cinnamon Apples	Scallops Curry	Brown Rice Pudding
266	Ranch Potatoes	Cheesy Beef	Sweet Tapioca Pudding
267	Quick & Easy Oatmeal	Corned Beef	Vanilla Bread Pudding
268	Creamy Mashed Potatoes	Pork Posole	Chocolate Mousse
269	Delicious Chocolate Oatmeal	Sauerkraut Pork	Blueberry Cupcakes
270	Hearty Polenta Porridge	Pork Adobo	Moist Pumpkin Brownie
271	Peach Oatmeal	Easy Pork Chops	Mini Choco Cake
272	Apple Cinnamon Oatmeal	Garlicky Pork Roast	Cinnamon Pears
273	Chocó Banana Oatmeal	Orange pulled pork	Delicious Pumpkin Pudding
274	Healthy Almond Oatmeal	Pork with Cabbage	Easy Egg Custard
275	Spinach Frittata	Salsa Pork	Cinnamon Lemon Pears
276	Broccoli Frittata	Spicy Chickpea Curry	Sliced Apples with Nuts
277	Quinoa Porridge	Flavorful Ramen	Peanut Butter Brownies
278	Creamy Walnut Grits	Delicious Black Eyed Peas Curry	Cheesecake
279	Healthy Wheat Porridge	Rich & Creamy Alfredo Sauce	Saffron Rice Pudding
280	Quinoa Pumpkin Porridge	Indian Curried Cauliflower Potato	Flavorful Carrot Halva
281	Blueberry Oatmeal	Carrot Potato Medley	Vermicelli Pudding
282	Mushroom Frittata	Lentil Chickpea Curry	Simple Raspberry Mug Cake
283	Quick Brussels Sprouts	Creamy Sweet Potato Curry	Yogurt Custard
284	Oatmeal Porridge	Steamed Broccoli	Cardamom Zucchini Pudding
285	Healthy Breakfast Porridge	Quick & Easy Shrimp	Yummy Strawberry Cobbler
286	Strawberry Oatmeal	Cheesy Shrimp Grits	Peach Cobbler
287	Berry Oatmeal	Healthy Salmon Chowder	Hazelnuts Brownies
288	Perfect Breakfast Casserole	Shrimp with Sausage	Apple Pear Crisp
289	Delicious Breakfast Casserole	Curried Spinach Quinoa	Vanilla Peanut Butter Fudge
290	Sweet Potato Breakfast	Healthy Vegan Chili	Walnut Carrot Cake
291	Banana Peanut Butter Oats	Cabbage with Coconut	Yummy Strawberry Cobbler
292	Jalapeno Cheddar Grits	Roasted Baby Potatoes	Yogurt Custard
293	Fruit Compote	Spicy Chickpea Curry	Walnut Carrot Cake
294	Carrot Oatmeal	Tasty Mushroom Stroganoff	Vermicelli Pudding
295	Slow Cook Cherry Oatmeal	Quick & Healthy Kale	Vanilla Peanut Butter Fudge
296	Ham Cheese Breakfast Casserole	Perfect & Healthy Carrots	Vanilla Bread Pudding
297	Cranberry Apple Breakfast Grains	Vegan Collard Greens	Thai Black Rice Pudding

298	Sausage Casserole	Potato Curry	Sweet Tapioca Pudding
299	Blueberry French Toast Casserole	Garlic Mushrooms	Sliced Apples with Nuts
300	Oat Millet Porridge	Parmesan Broccoli	Simple Raspberry Mug Cake
301	Baked Apples	Perfect Green Beans	Saffron Rice Pudding
302	Quinoa Blueberry Bowl	Perfect Instant Pot Cabbage	Quinoa Pudding
303	Savory Barley	Delicious Cheesy Cauliflower	Poached Pears
304	Fajita Casserole	Healthy & Easy Instant Pot Zucchini	Peanut Butter Brownies
305	Latte Oatmeal	Sweet & Sour Red Cabbage	Peach Cobbler
306	Coconut Blueberry Oatmeal	Sugar Snap Peas	Orange Strawberry Compote
307	Pumpkin Cranberry Oatmeal	Southern Okra & Tomatoes	Moist Pumpkin Brownie
308	Cranberry Farro	Garlic Mushrooms	Mini Choco Cake
309	Tropical Oatmeal	Tasty Tikka Masala Chickpeas	Healthy Sweet Potato Rice Pudding
310	Simple & Easy Breakfast Casserole	Cheesy & Creamy Ziti	Healthy Carrot Cake
311	Creamy Mac n Cheese	Classic Mac n Cheese	Hazelnuts Brownies
312	Cherry Risotto	Sticky Noodles	Flavorful Carrot Halva
313	Almond Coconut Risotto	Crispy Roasted Potatoes	Easy Egg Custard
314	Creamy Polenta	Sweet Potato Mash	Delicious Pumpkin Pudding
315	Sweet Cherry Chocolate Oat	Cheesy Spaghetti	Coconut Rice Pudding
316	Coconut Lime Breakfast Quinoa	Sautéed vegetables	Coconut Custard
317	Quick & Easy Farro	Healthy Veggie Curry	Cinnamon Pears
318	Farro Breakfast Risotto	Braised Parsnips	Cinnamon Lemon Pears
319	Tapioca Pudding	Healthy Ratatouille	Chocolate Mousse
320	Sweetened Breakfast Oats	Herb Mushrooms	Chocolate Cake
321	Cauliflower Mash	Creamy Squash Puree	Choco Mug Cake
322	Chia Oatmeal	Cheesy Cauliflower Rice	Cherry Apple Risotto
323	Blueberry Lemon Oatmeal	Delicious Baby Carrots	Cheesecake
324	Breakfast Cobbler	Lemon Haddock	Cardamom Zucchini Pudding
325	Tomato Corn Risotto	Quick Coconut Shrimp Curry	Brownie Cake
326	Tropical Oatmeal	Yummy Fish Tacos	Brown Rice Pudding
327	Tomato Corn Risotto	Delicious Scallops	Blueberry Cupcakes
328	Tapioca Pudding	Healthy Shrimp Rice	Apple Rice Pudding
329	Sweetened Breakfast Oats	Balsamic Salmon	Apple Pear Crisp
330	Sweet Potato Breakfast	Shrimp Scampi	Apple Crisp
331	Sweet Cherry Chocolate Oat	Dijon Fish Fillets	Apple Crisp
332	Strawberry Oatmeal	Macaroni with Cauliflower Broccoli	Apple Pear Crisp

333	Spinach Frittata	Spicy Cabbage	Apple Rice Pudding
334	Slow Cook Cherry Oatmeal	Instant Pot Artichokes	Blueberry Cupcakes
335	Simple & Easy Breakfast Casserole	Flavorful Ranch Cauliflower Mashed	Brown Rice Pudding
336	Savory Barley	Kale Curry	Brownie Cake
337	Sausage Casserole	Buttery Carrots & Parsnips	Cardamom Zucchini Pudding
338	Roasted Baby Potatoes	Creamy Parsnip Mash	Cheesecake
339	Ranch Potatoes	Red Bean Rice	Cherry Apple Risotto
340	Quinoa Pumpkin Porridge	Tender Pinto Beans	Choco Mug Cake
341	Quinoa Porridge	Tomatillo White Beans	Chocolate Cake
342	Quinoa Blueberry Bowl	Flavorful Refried Beans	Chocolate Mousse
343	Quick Brussels Sprouts	Delicious Beans & Rice	Cinnamon Lemon Pears
344	Quick & Easy Oatmeal	Indian Red Kidney Beans	Cinnamon Pears
345	Quick & Easy Farro	Mexican Black Beans	Coconut Custard
346	Pumpkin Oatmeal	Ham & Pinto Beans	Coconut Rice Pudding
347	Pumpkin Cranberry Oatmeal	Rosemary Salmon	Delicious Pumpkin Pudding
348	Perfect Breakfast Casserole	Crab Legs	Easy Egg Custard
349	Peach Oatmeal	Lemon Garlic Mussels	Flavorful Carrot Halva
350	Oatmeal Porridge	Zesty Salmon	Hazelnuts Brownies
351	Oat Millet Porridge	Delicious Basa Fillets	Healthy Carrot Cake
352	Mushroom Frittata	Indian Fried Prawns	Healthy Sweet Potato Rice Pudding
353	Latte Oatmeal	Spicy Salmon	Mini Choco Cake
354	Jalapeno Cheddar Grits	Basil Salmon	Moist Pumpkin Brownie
355	Hearty Polenta Porridge	Lemon Pepper Cod	Orange Strawberry Compote
356	Healthy Wheat Porridge	Easy Salmon Stew	Peach Cobbler
357	Healthy Breakfast Porridge	Sweet Baked Beans	Peanut Butter Brownies
358	Healthy Almond Oatmeal	Easy Baked Beans	Poached Pears
359	Ham Cheese Breakfast Casserole	Sweet & Tender Lima Beans	Quinoa Pudding
360	Fruit Compote	Flavorful Onion Rice	Saffron Rice Pudding
361	Farro Breakfast Risotto	Healthy Chicken Noodle Soup	Simple Raspberry Mug Cake
362	Fajita Casserole	Nutritious Lentil Soup	Sliced Apples with Nuts
363	Easy Cinnamon Apples	Cheesy Broccoli Soup	Sweet Tapioca Pudding
364	Easy Breakfast Grits	Carrot Ginger Soup	Thai Black Rice Pudding
365	Delicious French Toast Casserole	Cabbage Soup	Vanilla Bread Pudding
366	Delicious Chocolate Oatmeal	Zucchini Corn Soup	Vanilla Peanut Butter Fudge
367	Delicious Breakfast Casserole	Lentil Sausage Stew	Vermicelli Pudding
368	Creamy Walnut Grits	Black Bean Rice	Walnut Carrot Cake
369	Creamy Polenta	Nutritious Lentils Rice	Yogurt Custard
370	Creamy Mashed Potatoes	Cheesy Beef Rice	Yummy Strawberry Cobbler

371	Creamy Mac n Cheese	Coconut Beans & Rice	Orange Strawberry Compote
372	Cranberry Farro	Mushroom Brown Rice	Apple Rice Pudding
373	Cranberry Apple Breakfast Grains	Simple & Delicious Parmesan Rice	Cherry Apple Risotto
374	Coconut Lime Breakfast Quinoa	Chicken Cheese Rice	Poached Pears
375	Coconut Blueberry Oatmeal	Flavorful Fajita Rice	Brownie Cake
376	Choco Banana Oatmeal	Creamy Pea Risotto	Thai Black Rice Pudding
377	Chia Oatmeal	Quick & Easy Chicken Rice	Coconut Rice Pudding
378	Cherry Risotto	Garlic Turmeric Rice	Healthy Sweet Potato Rice Pudding
379	Cauliflower Mash	Flavorful Rice Pilaf	Quinoa Pudding
380	Carrot Oatmeal	Perfect Jasmine Rice	Apple Crisp
381	Broccoli Frittata	Broccoli Rice	Healthy Carrot Cake
382	Breakfast Cobbler	Spanish rice	Chocolate Cake
383	Blueberry Oatmeal	Onion Pepper Couscous	Coconut Custard
384	Blueberry Lemon Oatmeal	Lemon Snap Pea Couscous	Choco Mug Cake
385	Blueberry French Toast Casserole	Pearl Barley	Brown Rice Pudding
386	Berry Oatmeal	Spanish Quinoa	Sweet Tapioca Pudding
387	Banana Peanut Butter Oats	Buttery Scallions Risotto	Vanilla Bread Pudding
388	Baked Apples	Simple Paprika Rice	Chocolate Mousse
389	Apple Cinnamon Oatmeal	Delicious Potato Risotto	Blueberry Cupcakes
390	Almond Coconut Risotto	Jalapeno Brown Rice	Moist Pumpkin Brownie
391	Almond Coconut Risotto	Herb Garlic Chicken	Mini Choco Cake
392	Apple Cinnamon Oatmeal	Delicious Chicken Burrito Bowl	Cinnamon Pears
393	Baked Apples	Chicken Cheese Spaghetti	Delicious Pumpkin Pudding
394	Banana Peanut Butter Oats	Moist & Tender Chicken	Easy Egg Custard
395	Berry Oatmeal	Simple BBQ Chicken	Cinnamon Lemon Pears
396	Blueberry French Toast Casserole	Flavorful Chicken Curry	Sliced Apples with Nuts
397	Blueberry Lemon Oatmeal	Spicy Chicken Wings	Peanut Butter Brownies
398	Blueberry Oatmeal	BBQ Honey Chicken Wings	Cheesecake
399	Breakfast Cobbler	Honey Mustard Chicken	Saffron Rice Pudding
400	Broccoli Frittata	Tortellini Tomato Soup	Flavorful Carrot Halva
401	Carrot Oatmeal	Healthy Split Pea Soup	Vermicelli Pudding
402	Cauliflower Mash	Barley Mushroom Soup	Simple Raspberry Mug Cake
403	Cherry Risotto	Creamy Mushroom Soup	Yogurt Custard
404	Chia Oatmeal	Sweet Potato Soup	Cardamom Zucchini Pudding
405	Choco Banana Oatmeal	Healthy Vegetable Soup	Yummy Strawberry Cobbler
406	Coconut Blueberry Oatmeal	Onion Soup	Peach Cobbler
407	Coconut Lime Breakfast Quinoa	Teriyaki Chicken Drumsticks	Hazelnuts Brownies

408	Cranberry Apple Breakfast Grains	Mexican Salsa Chicken	Apple Pear Crisp
409	Cranberry Farro	Artichoke Chicken	Vanilla Peanut Butter Fudge
410	Creamy Mac n Cheese	Creamy Peanut Butter Chicken	Walnut Carrot Cake
411	Creamy Mashed Potatoes	BBQ Pulled Chicken	Yummy Strawberry Cobbler
412	Creamy Polenta	Buffalo Chicken Breasts	Yogurt Custard
413	Creamy Walnut Grits	Enchilada Chicken	Walnut Carrot Cake
414	Delicious Breakfast Casserole	Moist & Tender Turkey Breast	Vermicelli Pudding
415	Delicious Chocolate Oatmeal	Cafe Rio Chicken	Vanilla Peanut Butter Fudge
416	Delicious French Toast Casserole	Marinara Chicken	Vanilla Bread Pudding
417	Easy Breakfast Grits	Veggie Chicken Soup	Thai Black Rice Pudding
418	Easy Cinnamon Apples	Zucchini Soup	Sweet Tapioca Pudding
419	Fajita Casserole	Curried Cauliflower Soup	Sliced Apples with Nuts
420	Farro Breakfast Risotto	Summer Veggie Soup	Simple Raspberry Mug Cake
421	Fruit Compote	Vegetable Chicken Stew	Saffron Rice Pudding
422	Ham Cheese Breakfast Casserole	Thai Sweet Potato Stew	Quinoa Pudding
423	Healthy Almond Oatmeal	Chicken Taco Soup	Poached Pears
424	Healthy Breakfast Porridge	Tasty Chicken Rice Soup	Peanut Butter Brownies
425	Healthy Wheat Porridge	Cabbage Pork Soup	Peach Cobbler
426	Hearty Polenta Porridge	Chicken Adobo	Orange Strawberry Compote
427	Jalapeno Cheddar Grits	Tasty BBQ Ranch Chicken	Moist Pumpkin Brownie
428	Latte Oatmeal	Indian Chicken Tikka Masala	Mini Choco Cake
429	Mushroom Frittata	Bacon Pineapple Chicken	Healthy Sweet Potato Rice Pudding
430	Oat Millet Porridge	Flavorful Chicken Cacciatore	Healthy Carrot Cake
431	Oatmeal Porridge	Sweet Potato Chicken Curry	Hazelnuts Brownies
432	Peach Oatmeal	Chicken Chili	Flavorful Carrot Halva
433	Perfect Breakfast Casserole	Chicken Meatballs	Easy Egg Custard
434	Pumpkin Cranberry Oatmeal	Easy Adobo Chicken	Delicious Pumpkin Pudding
435	Pumpkin Oatmeal	Yummy Orange Chicken	Coconut Rice Pudding
436	Quick & Easy Farro	Thai Chicken	Coconut Custard
437	Quick & Easy Oatmeal	Curried Chicken	Cinnamon Pears
438	Quick Brussels Sprouts	Olive Chicken	Cinnamon Lemon Pears
439	Quinoa Blueberry Bowl	Sweet Mango Chicken	Chocolate Mousse
440	Quinoa Porridge	Herb Chicken	Chocolate Cake
441	Quinoa Pumpkin Porridge	Creamy Pesto Chicken	Choco Mug Cake
442	Ranch Potatoes	Healthy Shrimp Boil	Cherry Apple Risotto
443	Roasted Baby Potatoes	Asparagus Shrimp Risotto	Cheesecake

444	Sausage Casserole	Basil Tilapia	Cardamom Zucchini Pudding
445	Savory Barley	Delicious Shrimp Risotto	Brownie Cake
446	Simple & Easy Breakfast Casserole	Cajun Shrimp	Brown Rice Pudding
447	Slow Cook Cherry Oatmeal	Lemon Butter chicken	Blueberry Cupcakes
448	Spinach Frittata	Instant Pot Turkey Breast	Apple Rice Pudding
449	Strawberry Oatmeal	Ranch Chicken	Apple Pear Crisp
450	Sweet Cherry Chocolate Oat	Orange BBQ Chicken	Apple Crisp
451	Sweet Potato Breakfast	Mustard Chicken	Apple Crisp
452	Sweetened Breakfast Oats	Delicious Beef Tips	Apple Pear Crisp
453	Tapioca Pudding	Shredded Mexican Beef	Apple Rice Pudding
454	Tomato Corn Risotto	Korean Beef	Blueberry Cupcakes
455	Tropical Oatmeal	Italian Beef	Brown Rice Pudding
456	Delicious French Toast Casserole	Beef Stroganoff	Brownie Cake
457	Easy Breakfast Grits	Asian Pot Roast	Cardamom Zucchini Pudding
458	Pumpkin Oatmeal	Italian Ribs	Cheesecake
459	Roasted Baby Potatoes	Shredded Thai Beef	Cherry Apple Risotto
460	Easy Cinnamon Apples	Healthy Spinach Lentil Soup	Choco Mug Cake
461	Ranch Potatoes	Mushroom Soup	Chocolate Cake
462	Quick & Easy Oatmeal	Spinach Soup	Chocolate Mousse
463	Creamy Mashed Potatoes	Hearty Beef Stew	Cinnamon Lemon Pears
464	Delicious Chocolate Oatmeal	Spinach Chickpea Stew	Cinnamon Pears
465	Hearty Polenta Porridge	Healthy Eggplant Stew	Coconut Custard
466	Peach Oatmeal	Squash Cauliflower Soup	Coconut Rice Pudding
467	Apple Cinnamon Oatmeal	Corn Soup	Delicious Pumpkin Pudding
468	Choco Banana Oatmeal	Carrot Pea Soup	Easy Egg Custard
469	Healthy Almond Oatmeal	Mexican Barbecue	Flavorful Carrot Halva
470	Spinach Frittata	Korean Beef Tacos	Hazelnuts Brownies
471	Broccoli Frittata	Delicious Italian Beef	Healthy Carrot Cake
472	Quinoa Porridge	Flavorful Barbacoa	Healthy Sweet Potato Rice Pudding
473	Creamy Walnut Grits	Asian Beef	Mini Choco Cake
474	Healthy Wheat Porridge	Tasty Steak Bites	Moist Pumpkin Brownie
475	Quinoa Pumpkin Porridge	Smoky Beef	Orange Strawberry Compote
476	Blueberry Oatmeal	Flank Steak	Peach Cobbler
477	Mushroom Frittata	Moist & Tender Ribs	Peanut Butter Brownies
478	Quick Brussels Sprouts	Spicy Beef Curry	Poached Pears
479	Oatmeal Porridge	Pork Tenderloin	Quinoa Pudding
480	Healthy Breakfast Porridge	Tasty Beef Chili	Saffron Rice Pudding
481	Strawberry Oatmeal	Chipotle Chili	Simple Raspberry Mug Cake
482	Berry Oatmeal	Veggie Beef Roast	Sliced Apples with Nuts
483	Perfect Breakfast Casserole	Meatballs	Sweet Tapioca Pudding

484	Delicious Breakfast Casserole	Mongolian Beef	Thai Black Rice Pudding
485	Sweet Potato Breakfast	Flavors Taco Meat	Vanilla Bread Pudding
486	Banana Peanut Butter Oats	Leg of Lamb	Vanilla Peanut Butter Fudge
487	Jalapeno Cheddar Grits	Flavors Lamb Shanks	Vermicelli Pudding
488	Fruit Compote	Perfect Dinner Lamb	Walnut Carrot Cake
489	Carrot Oatmeal	Flavorful Taco Mince	Yogurt Custard
490	Slow Cook Cherry Oatmeal	Delicious Lamb Curry	Yummy Strawberry Cobbler
491	Ham Cheese Breakfast Casserole	Eastern Lamb Stew	Saffron Rice Pudding
492	Cranberry Apple Breakfast Grains	Sweet & Sour Fish	Vanilla Bread Pudding
493	Sausage Casserole	Spicy Shrimp Noodles	Chocolate Mousse
494	Blueberry French Toast Casserole	Nutritious Salmon	Blueberry Cupcakes
495	Oat Millet Porridge	Vegetable Fish Curry	Moist Pumpkin Brownie
496	Baked Apples	Tuna Pasta	Mini Choco Cake
497	Quinoa Blueberry Bowl	Cajun Seafood Gumbo	Cinnamon Pears
498	Savory Barley	Lemon Pepper Salmon	Delicious Pumpkin Pudding
499	Fajita Casserole	Lemon Garlic Salmon	Easy Egg Custard
500	Latte Oatmeal	Dill Salmon	Cinnamon Lemon Pears
501	Delicious French Toast Casserole	Spicy Chickpea Curry	Orange Strawberry Compote
502	Easy Breakfast Grits	Flavorful Ramen	Apple Rice Pudding
503	Pumpkin Oatmeal	Delicious Black Eyed Peas Curry	Cherry Apple Risotto
504	Roasted Baby Potatoes	Rich & Creamy Alfredo Sauce	Poached Pears
505	Easy Cinnamon Apples	Indian Curried Cauliflower Potato	Brownie Cake
506	Ranch Potatoes	Carrot Potato Medley	Thai Black Rice Pudding
507	Quick & Easy Oatmeal	Lentil Chickpea Curry	Coconut Rice Pudding
508	Creamy Mashed Potatoes	Creamy Sweet Potato Curry	Healthy Sweet Potato Rice Pudding
509	Delicious Chocolate Oatmeal	Steamed Broccoli	Quinoa Pudding
510	Hearty Polenta Porridge	Quick & Easy Shrimp	Apple Crisp
511	Peach Oatmeal	Cheesy Shrimp Grits	Healthy Carrot Cake
512	Apple Cinnamon Oatmeal	Healthy Salmon Chowder	Chocolate Cake
513	Chocó Banana Oatmeal	Shrimp with Sausage	Coconut Custard
514	Healthy Almond Oatmeal	Curried Spinach Quinoa	Choco Mug Cake
515	Spinach Frittata	Healthy Vegan Chili	Brown Rice Pudding
516	Broccoli Frittata	Cabbage with Coconut	Sweet Tapioca Pudding
517	Quinoa Porridge	Roasted Baby Potatoes	Vanilla Bread Pudding
518	Creamy Walnut Grits	Spicy Chickpea Curry	Chocolate Mousse
519	Healthy Wheat Porridge	Tasty Mushroom Stroganoff	Blueberry Cupcakes
520	Quinoa Pumpkin Porridge	Quick & Healthy Kale	Moist Pumpkin Brownie
521	Blueberry Oatmeal	Perfect & Healthy Carrots	Mini Choco Cake

522	Mushroom Frittata	Vegan Collard Greens	Cinnamon Pears
523	Quick Brussels Sprouts	Potato Curry	Delicious Pumpkin Pudding
524	Oatmeal Porridge	Garlic Mushrooms	Easy Egg Custard
525	Healthy Breakfast Porridge	Parmesan Broccoli	Cinnamon Lemon Pear
526	Strawberry Oatmeal	Perfect Green Beans	Sliced Apples with Nuts
527	Berry Oatmeal	Perfect Instant Pot Cabbage	Peanut Butter Brownies
528	Perfect Breakfast Casserole	Delicious Cheesy Cauliflower	Cheesecake
529	Delicious Breakfast Casserole	Healthy & Easy Instant Pot Zucchini	Saffron Rice Pudding
530	Sweet Potato Breakfast	Sweet & Sour Red Cabbage	Flavorful Carrot Halva
531	Banana Peanut Butter Oats	Sugar Snap Peas	Vermicelli Pudding
532	Jalapeno Cheddar Grits	Southern Okra & Tomatoes	Simple Raspberry Mug Cake
533	Fruit Compote	Garlic Mushrooms	Yogurt Custard
534	Carrot Oatmeal	Tasty Tikka Masala Chickpeas	Cardamom Zucchini Pudding
535	Slow Cook Cherry Oatmeal	Cheesy & Creamy Ziti	Yummy Strawberry Cobbler
536	Ham Cheese Breakfast Casserole	Classic Mac n Cheese	Peach Cobbler
537	Cranberry Apple Breakfast Grains	Sticky Noodles	Hazelnuts Brownies
538	Sausage Casserole	Crispy Roasted Potatoes	Apple Pear Crisp
539	Blueberry French Toast Casserole	Sweet Potato Mash	Vanilla Peanut Butter Fudge
540	Oat Millet Porridge	Cheesy Spaghetti	Walnut Carrot Cake
541	Baked Apples	Sautéed vegetables	Yummy Strawberry Cobbler
542	Quinoa Blueberry Bowl	Healthy Veggie Curry	Yogurt Custard
543	Savory Barley	Braised Parsnips	Walnut Carrot Cake
544	Fajita Casserole	Healthy Ratatouille	Vermicelli Pudding
545	Latte Oatmeal	Herb Mushrooms	Vanilla Peanut Butter Fudge
546	Coconut Blueberry Oatmeal	Creamy Squash Puree	Vanilla Bread Pudding
547	Pumpkin Cranberry Oatmeal	Cheesy Cauliflower Rice	Thai Black Rice Pudding
548	Cranberry Farro	Delicious Baby Carrots	Sweet Tapioca Pudding
549	Tropical Oatmeal	Lemon Haddock	Sliced Apples with Nuts
550	Simple & Easy Breakfast Casserole	Quick Coconut Shrimp Curry	Simple Raspberry Mug Cake
551	Creamy Mac n Cheese	Yummy Fish Tacos	Saffron Rice Pudding
552	Cherry Risotto	Delicious Scallops	Quinoa Pudding
553	Almond Coconut Risotto	Healthy Shrimp Rice	Poached Pears
554	Creamy Polenta	Balsamic Salmon	Peanut Butter Brownies
555	Sweet Cherry Chocolate Oat	Shrimp Scampi	Peach Cobbler
556	Coconut Lime Breakfast Quinoa	Dijon Fish Fillets	Orange Strawberry Compote
557	Quick & Easy Farro	Macaroni with Cauliflower Broccoli	Moist Pumpkin Brownie

558	Farro Breakfast Risotto	Spicy Cabbage	Mini Choco Cake
559	Tapioca Pudding	Instant Pot Artichokes	Healthy Sweet Potato Rice Pudding
560	Sweetened Breakfast Oats	Flavorful Ranch Cauliflower Mashed	Healthy Carrot Cake
561	Cauliflower Mash	Kale Curry	Hazelnuts Brownies
562	Chia Oatmeal	Buttery Carrots & Parsnips	Flavorful Carrot Halva
563	Blueberry Lemon Oatmeal	Creamy Parsnip Mash	Easy Egg Custard
564	Breakfast Cobbler	Red Bean Rice	Delicious Pumpkin Pudding
565	Tomato Corn Risotto	Tender Pinto Beans	Coconut Rice Pudding
566	Tropical Oatmeal	Tomatillo White Beans	Coconut Custard
567	Tomato Corn Risotto	Flavorful Refried Beans	Cinnamon Pears
568	Tapioca Pudding	Delicious Beans & Rice	Cinnamon Lemon Pears
569	Sweetened Breakfast Oats	Indian Red Kidney Beans	Chocolate Mousse
570	Sweet Potato Breakfast	Mexican Black Beans	Chocolate Cake
571	Sweet Cherry Chocolate Oat	Ham & Pinto Beans	Choco Mug Cake
572	Strawberry Oatmeal	Rosemary Salmon	Cherry Apple Risotto
573	Spinach Frittata	Crab Legs	Cheesecake
574	Slow Cook Cherry Oatmeal	Lemon Garlic Mussels	Cardamom Zucchini Pudding
575	Simple & Easy Breakfast Casserole	Zesty Salmon	Brownie Cake
576	Savory Barley	Delicious Basa Fillets	Brown Rice Pudding
577	Sausage Casserole	Indian Fried Prawns	Blueberry Cupcakes
578	Roasted Baby Potatoes	Spicy Salmon	Apple Rice Pudding
579	Ranch Potatoes	Basil Salmon	Apple Pear Crisp
580	Quinoa Pumpkin Porridge	Lemon Pepper Cod	Apple Crisp
581	Quinoa Porridge	Easy Salmon Stew	Apple Crisp
582	Quinoa Blueberry Bowl	Sweet Baked Beans	Apple Pear Crisp
583	Quick Brussels Sprouts	Easy Baked Beans	Apple Rice Pudding
584	Quick & Easy Oatmeal	Sweet & Tender Lima Beans	Blueberry Cupcakes
585	Quick & Easy Farro	Flavorful Onion Rice	Brown Rice Pudding
586	Pumpkin Oatmeal	Healthy Chicken Noodle Soup	Brownie Cake
587	Pumpkin Cranberry Oatmeal	Nutritious Lentil Soup	Cardamom Zucchini Pudding
588	Perfect Breakfast Casserole	Cheesy Broccoli Soup	Cheesecake
589	Peach Oatmeal	Carrot Ginger Soup	Cherry Apple Risotto
590	Oatmeal Porridge	Cabbage Soup	Choco Mug Cake
591	Oat Millet Porridge	Zucchini Corn Soup	Chocolate Cake
592	Mushroom Frittata	Lentil Sausage Stew	Chocolate Mousse
593	Latte Oatmeal	Black Bean Rice	Cinnamon Lemon Pears
594	Jalapeno Cheddar Grits	Nutritious Lentils Rice	Cinnamon Pears
595	Hearty Polenta Porridge	Cheesy Beef Rice	Coconut Custard
596	Healthy Wheat Porridge	Coconut Beans & Rice	Coconut Rice Pudding
597	Healthy Breakfast Porridge	Mushroom Brown Rice	Delicious Pumpkin Pudding

598	Healthy Almond Oatmeal	Simple & Delicious Parmesan Rice	Easy Egg Custard
599	Ham Cheese Breakfast Casserole	Chicken Cheese Rice	Flavorful Carrot Halva
600	Fruit Compote	Flavorful Fajita Rice	Hazelnuts Brownies
601	Farro Breakfast Risotto	Creamy Pea Risotto	Healthy Carrot Cake
602	Fajita Casserole	Quick & Easy Chicken Rice	Healthy Sweet Potato Rice Pudding
603	Easy Cinnamon Apples	Garlic Turmeric Rice	Mini Choco Cake
604	Easy Breakfast Grits	Flavorful Rice Pilaf	Moist Pumpkin Brownie
605	Delicious French Toast Casserole	Perfect Jasmine Rice	Orange Strawberry Compote
606	Delicious Chocolate Oatmeal	Broccoli Rice	Peach Cobbler
607	Delicious Breakfast Casserole	Spanish rice	Peanut Butter Brownies
608	Creamy Walnut Grits	Onion Pepper Couscous	Poached Pears
609	Creamy Polenta	Lemon Snap Pea Couscous	Quinoa Pudding
610	Creamy Mashed Potatoes	Pearl Barley	Saffron Rice Pudding
611	Creamy Mac n Cheese	Spanish Quinoa	Simple Raspberry Mug Cake
612	Cranberry Farro	Buttery Scallions Risotto	Sliced Apples with Nuts
613	Cranberry Apple Breakfast Grains	Simple Paprika Rice	Sweet Tapioca Pudding
614	Coconut Lime Breakfast Quinoa	Delicious Potato Risotto	Thai Black Rice Pudding
615	Coconut Blueberry Oatmeal	Jalapeno Brown Rice	Vanilla Bread Pudding
616	Choco Banana Oatmeal	Herb Garlic Chicken	Vanilla Peanut Butter Fudge
617	Chia Oatmeal	Delicious Chicken Burrito Bowl	Vermicelli Pudding
618	Cherry Risotto	Chicken Cheese Spaghetti	Walnut Carrot Cake
619	Cauliflower Mash	Moist & Tender Chicken	Yogurt Custard
620	Carrot Oatmeal	Simple BBQ Chicken	Yummy Strawberry Cobbler
621	Broccoli Frittata	Flavorful Chicken Curry	Orange Strawberry Compote
622	Breakfast Cobbler	Spicy Chicken Wings	Apple Rice Pudding
623	Blueberry Oatmeal	BBQ Honey Chicken Wings	Cherry Apple Risotto
624	Blueberry Lemon Oatmeal	Honey Mustard Chicken	Poached Pears
625	Blueberry French Toast Casserole	Tortellini Tomato Soup	Brownie Cake
626	Berry Oatmeal	Healthy Split Pea Soup	Thai Black Rice Pudding
627	Banana Peanut Butter Oats	Barley Mushroom Soup	Coconut Rice Pudding
628	Baked Apples	Creamy Mushroom Soup	Healthy Sweet Potato Rice Pudding
629	Apple Cinnamon Oatmeal	Sweet Potato Soup	Quinoa Pudding
630	Almond Coconut Risotto	Healthy Vegetable Soup	Apple Crisp
631	Almond Coconut Risotto	Onion Soup	Healthy Carrot Cake

632	Apple Cinnamon Oatmeal	Teriyaki Chicken Drumsticks	Chocolate Cake
633	Baked Apples	Mexican Salsa Chicken	Coconut Custard
634	Banana Peanut Butter Oats	Artichoke Chicken	Choco Mug Cake
635	Berry Oatmeal	Creamy Peanut Butter Chicken	Brown Rice Pudding
636	Blueberry French Toast Casserole	BBQ Pulled Chicken	Sweet Tapioca Pudding
637	Blueberry Lemon Oatmeal	Buffalo Chicken Breasts	Vanilla Bread Pudding
638	Blueberry Oatmeal	Enchilada Chicken	Chocolate Mousse
639	Breakfast Cobbler	Moist & Tender Turkey Breast	Blueberry Cupcakes
640	Broccoli Frittata	Cafe Rio Chicken	Moist Pumpkin Brownie
641	Carrot Oatmeal	Marinara Chicken	Mini Choco Cake
642	Cauliflower Mash	Veggie Chicken Soup	Cinnamon Pears
643	Cherry Risotto	Zucchini Soup	Delicious Pumpkin Pudding
644	Chia Oatmeal	Curried Cauliflower Soup	Easy Egg Custard
645	Choco Banana Oatmeal	Summer Veggie Soup	Cinnamon Lemon Pears
646	Coconut Blueberry Oatmeal	Vegetable Chicken Stew	Sliced Apples with Nuts
647	Coconut Lime Breakfast Quinoa	Thai Sweet Potato Stew	Peanut Butter Brownies
648	Cranberry Apple Breakfast Grains	Chicken Taco Soup	Cheesecake
649	Cranberry Farro	Tasty Chicken Rice Soup	Saffron Rice Pudding
650	Creamy Mac n Cheese	Cabbage Pork Soup	Flavorful Carrot Halva
651	Creamy Mashed Potatoes	Chicken Adobo	Vermicelli Pudding
652	Creamy Polenta	Tasty BBQ Ranch Chicken	Simple Raspberry Mug Cake
653	Creamy Walnut Grits	Indian Chicken Tikka Masala	Yogurt Custard
654	Delicious Breakfast Casserole	Bacon Pineapple Chicken	Cardamom Zucchini Pudding
655	Delicious Chocolate Oatmeal	Flavorful Chicken Cacciatore	Yummy Strawberry Cobbler
656	Delicious French Toast Casserole	Sweet Potato Chicken Curry	Peach Cobbler
657	Easy Breakfast Grits	Chicken Chili	Hazelnuts Brownies
658	Easy Cinnamon Apples	Chicken Meatballs	Apple Pear Crisp
659	Fajita Casserole	Easy Adobo Chicken	Vanilla Peanut Butter Fudge
660	Farro Breakfast Risotto	Yummy Orange Chicken	Walnut Carrot Cake
661	Fruit Compote	Thai Chicken	Yummy Strawberry Cobbler
662	Ham Cheese Breakfast Casserole	Curried Chicken	Yogurt Custard
663	Healthy Almond Oatmeal	Olive Chicken	Walnut Carrot Cake
664	Healthy Breakfast Porridge	Sweet Mango Chicken	Vermicelli Pudding
665	Healthy Wheat Porridge	Herb Chicken	Vanilla Peanut Butter Fudge
666	Hearty Polenta Porridge	Creamy Pesto Chicken	Vanilla Bread Pudding
667	Jalapeno Cheddar Grits	Healthy Shrimp Boil	Thai Black Rice Pudding

668	Latte Oatmeal	Asparagus Shrimp Risotto	Sweet Tapioca Pudding
669	Mushroom Frittata	Basil Tilapia	Sliced Apples with Nuts
670	Oat Millet Porridge	Delicious Shrimp Risotto	Simple Raspberry Mug Cake
671	Oatmeal Porridge	Cajun Shrimp	Saffron Rice Pudding
672	Peach Oatmeal	Lemon Butter chicken	Quinoa Pudding
673	Perfect Breakfast Casserole	Instant Pot Turkey Breast	Poached Pears
674	Pumpkin Cranberry Oatmeal	Ranch Chicken	Peanut Butter Brownies
675	Pumpkin Oatmeal	Orange BBQ Chicken	Peach Cobbler
676	Quick & Easy Farro	Mustard Chicken	Orange Strawberry Compote
677	Quick & Easy Oatmeal	Delicious Beef Tips	Moist Pumpkin Brownie
678	Quick Brussels Sprouts	Shredded Mexican Beef	Mini Choco Cake
679	Quinoa Blueberry Bowl	Korean Beef	Healthy Sweet Potato Rice Pudding
680	Quinoa Porridge	Italian Beef	Healthy Carrot Cake
681	Quinoa Pumpkin Porridge	Beef Stroganoff	Hazelnuts Brownies
682	Ranch Potatoes	Asian Pot Roast	Flavorful Carrot Halva
683	Roasted Baby Potatoes	Italian Ribs	Easy Egg Custard
684	Sausage Casserole	Shredded Thai Beef	Delicious Pumpkin Pudding
685	Savory Barley	Healthy Spinach Lentil Soup	Coconut Rice Pudding
686	Simple & Easy Breakfast Casserole	Mushroom Soup	Coconut Custard
687	Slow Cook Cherry Oatmeal	Spinach Soup	Cinnamon Pears
688	Spinach Frittata	Hearty Beef Stew	Cinnamon Lemon Pears
689	Strawberry Oatmeal	Spinach Chickpea Stew	Chocolate Mousse
690	Sweet Cherry Chocolate Oat	Healthy Eggplant Stew	Chocolate Cake
691	Sweet Potato Breakfast	Squash Cauliflower Soup	Choco Mug Cake
692	Sweetened Breakfast Oats	Corn Soup	Cherry Apple Risotto
693	Tapioca Pudding	Carrot Pea Soup	Cheesecake
694	Tomato Corn Risotto	Mexican Barbecue	Cardamom Zucchini Pudding
695	Tropical Oatmeal	Korean Beef Tacos	Brownie Cake
696	Delicious French Toast Casserole	Delicious Italian Beef	Brown Rice Pudding
697	Easy Breakfast Grits	Flavorful Barbacoa	Blueberry Cupcakes
698	Pumpkin Oatmeal	Asian Beef	Apple Rice Pudding
699	Roasted Baby Potatoes	Tasty Steak Bites	Apple Pear Crisp
700	Easy Cinnamon Apples	Smoky Beef	Apple Crisp
701	Ranch Potatoes	Flank Steak	Apple Crisp
702	Quick & Easy Oatmeal	Moist & Tender Ribs	Apple Pear Crisp
703	Creamy Mashed Potatoes	Spicy Beef Curry	Apple Rice Pudding
704	Delicious Chocolate Oatmeal	Pork Tenderloin	Blueberry Cupcakes
705	Hearty Polenta Porridge	Tasty Beef Chili	Brown Rice Pudding
706	Peach Oatmeal	Chipotle Chili	Brownie Cake

707	Apple Cinnamon Oatmeal	Veggie Beef Roast	Cardamom Zucchini Pudding
708	Choco Banana Oatmeal	Meatballs	Cheesecake
709	Healthy Almond Oatmeal	Mongolian Beef	Cherry Apple Risotto
710	Spinach Frittata	Flavors Taco Meat	Choco Mug Cake
711	Broccoli Frittata	Leg of Lamb	Chocolate Cake
712	Quinoa Porridge	Flavors Lamb Shanks	Chocolate Mousse
713	Creamy Walnut Grits	Perfect Dinner Lamb	Cinnamon Lemon Pears
714	Healthy Wheat Porridge	Flavorful Taco Mince	Cinnamon Pears
715	Quinoa Pumpkin Porridge	Delicious Lamb Curry	Coconut Custard
716	Blueberry Oatmeal	Eastern Lamb Stew	Coconut Rice Pudding
717	Mushroom Frittata	Sweet & Sour Fish	Delicious Pumpkin Pudding
718	Quick Brussels Sprouts	Spicy Shrimp Noodles	Easy Egg Custard
719	Oatmeal Porridge	Nutritious Salmon	Flavorful Carrot Halva
720	Healthy Breakfast Porridge	Vegetable Fish Curry	Hazelnuts Brownies
721	Strawberry Oatmeal	Tuna Pasta	Healthy Carrot Cake
722	Berry Oatmeal	Cajun Seafood Gumbo	Healthy Sweet Potato Rice Pudding
723	Perfect Breakfast Casserole	Lemon Pepper Salmon	Mini Choco Cake
724	Delicious Breakfast Casserole	Lemon Garlic Salmon	Moist Pumpkin Brownie
725	Sweet Potato Breakfast	Dill Salmon	Orange Strawberry Compote
726	Banana Peanut Butter Oats	Irish Lamb Stew	Peach Cobbler
727	Jalapeno Cheddar Grits	Soy Honey Pork Tenderloin	Peanut Butter Brownies
728	Fruit Compote	Creamy Pork Chops	Poached Pears
729	Carrot Oatmeal	Juicy & Tender Pork Chops	Quinoa Pudding
730	Slow Cook Cherry Oatmeal	Filipino Pork Adobo	Saffron Rice Pudding
731	Ham Cheese Breakfast Casserole	Korean Pork Chops	Simple Raspberry Mug Cake
732	Cranberry Apple Breakfast Grains	Simple Lamb Curry	Sliced Apples with Nuts
733	Sausage Casserole	Herb Seasoned Lamb	Sweet Tapioca Pudding
734	Blueberry French Toast Casserole	Flavorful Lamb Korma	Thai Black Rice Pudding
735	Oat Millet Porridge	Tasty & Spicy Lamb	Vanilla Bread Pudding
736	Baked Apples	Lamb Stew	Vanilla Peanut Butter Fudge
737	Quinoa Blueberry Bowl	Lamb Shanks	Vermicelli Pudding
738	Savory Barley	Asian Lamb Curry	Walnut Carrot Cake
739	Fajita Casserole	Indian Lamb Curry	Yogurt Custard
740	Latte Oatmeal	Rogan Josh	Yummy Strawberry Cobbler
741	Coconut Blueberry Oatmeal	Cheesy Lamb Chops	Saffron Rice Pudding
742	Pumpkin Cranberry Oatmeal	Garlicky Lamb	Vanilla Bread Pudding
743	Cranberry Farro	Teriyaki Pork	Chocolate Mousse
744	Tropical Oatmeal	Easy & Tasty Ribs	Blueberry Cupcakes

745	Simple & Easy Breakfast Casserole	Shredded Pork	Moist Pumpkin Brownie
746	Creamy Mac n Cheese	Pork Curry	Mini Choco Cake
747	Cherry Risotto	Meatloaf	Cinnamon Pears
748	Almond Coconut Risotto	Cajun Beef	Delicious Pumpkin Pudding
749	Creamy Polenta	Old Bay Seasoned Haddock	Easy Egg Custard
750	Sweet Cherry Chocolate Oat	Shrimp Mac n Cheese	Cinnamon Lemon Pears
751	Coconut Lime Breakfast Quinoa	Salmon Rice Pilaf	Orange Strawberry Compote
752	Quick & Easy Farro	Perfect Salmon Dinner	Apple Rice Pudding
753	Farro Breakfast Risotto	Steam Clams	Cherry Apple Risotto
754	Tapioca Pudding	Mahi Mahi Fillets	Poached Pears
755	Sweetened Breakfast Oats	Curried Lentil Stew	Brownie Cake
756	Cauliflower Mash	Savory Butternut Squash Soup	Thai Black Rice Pudding
757	Chia Oatmeal	Potato Ham Soup	Coconut Rice Pudding
758	Blueberry Lemon Oatmeal	Northern Bean Soup	Healthy Sweet Potato Rice Pudding
759	Breakfast Cobbler	Squash Apple Soup	Quinoa Pudding
760	Tomato Corn Risotto	Delicious Tortilla Chicken Soup	Apple Crisp
761	Delicious French Toast Casserole	Hamburger Soup	Healthy Carrot Cake
762	Easy Breakfast Grits	Tasty Taco Soup	Chocolate Cake
763	Pumpkin Oatmeal	Easy Garlic Lemon Shrimp	Coconut Custard
764	Roasted Baby Potatoes	Cheesy Tilapia	Choco Mug Cake
765	Easy Cinnamon Apples	Scallops Curry	Brown Rice Pudding
766	Ranch Potatoes	Cheesy Beef	Sweet Tapioca Pudding
767	Quick & Easy Oatmeal	Corned Beef	Vanilla Bread Pudding
768	Creamy Mashed Potatoes	Pork Posole	Chocolate Mousse
769	Delicious Chocolate Oatmeal	Sauerkraut Pork	Blueberry Cupcakes
770	Hearty Polenta Porridge	Pork Adobo	Moist Pumpkin Brownie
771	Peach Oatmeal	Easy Pork Chops	Mini Choco Cake
772	Apple Cinnamon Oatmeal	Garlicky Pork Roast	Cinnamon Pears
773	Chocó Banana Oatmeal	Orange pulled pork	Delicious Pumpkin Pudding
774	Healthy Almond Oatmeal	Pork with Cabbage	Easy Egg Custard
775	Spinach Frittata	Salsa Pork	Cinnamon Lemon Pears
776	Broccoli Frittata	Spicy Chickpea Curry	Sliced Apples with Nuts
777	Quinoa Porridge	Flavorful Ramen	Peanut Butter Brownies
778	Creamy Walnut Grits	Delicious Black Eyed Peas Curry	Cheesecake
779	Healthy Wheat Porridge	Rich & Creamy Alfredo Sauce	Saffron Rice Pudding
780	Quinoa Pumpkin Porridge	Indian Curried Cauliflower Potato	Flavorful Carrot Halva
781	Blueberry Oatmeal	Carrot Potato Medley	Vermicelli Pudding

782	Mushroom Frittata	Lentil Chickpea Curry	Simple Raspberry Mug Cake
783	Quick Brussels Sprouts	Creamy Sweet Potato Curry	Yogurt Custard
784	Oatmeal Porridge	Steamed Broccoli	Cardamom Zucchini Pudding
785	Healthy Breakfast Porridge	Quick & Easy Shrimp	Yummy Strawberry Cobbler
786	Strawberry Oatmeal	Cheesy Shrimp Grits	Peach Cobbler
787	Berry Oatmeal	Healthy Salmon Chowder	Hazelnuts Brownies
788	Perfect Breakfast Casserole	Shrimp with Sausage	Apple Pear Crisp
789	Delicious Breakfast Casserole	Curried Spinach Quinoa	Vanilla Peanut Butter Fudge
790	Sweet Potato Breakfast	Healthy Vegan Chili	Walnut Carrot Cake
791	Banana Peanut Butter Oats	Cabbage with Coconut	Yummy Strawberry Cobbler
792	Jalapeno Cheddar Grits	Roasted Baby Potatoes	Yogurt Custard
793	Fruit Compote	Spicy Chickpea Curry	Walnut Carrot Cake
794	Carrot Oatmeal	Tasty Mushroom Stroganoff	Vermicelli Pudding
795	Slow Cook Cherry Oatmeal	Quick & Healthy Kale	Vanilla Peanut Butter Fudge
796	Ham Cheese Breakfast Casserole	Perfect & Healthy Carrots	Vanilla Bread Pudding
797	Cranberry Apple Breakfast Grains	Vegan Collard Greens	Thai Black Rice Pudding
798	Sausage Casserole	Potato Curry	Sweet Tapioca Pudding
799	Blueberry French Toast Casserole	Garlic Mushrooms	Sliced Apples with Nuts
800	Oat Millet Porridge	Parmesan Broccoli	Simple Raspberry Mug Cake
801	Baked Apples	Perfect Green Beans	Saffron Rice Pudding
802	Quinoa Blueberry Bowl	Perfect Instant Pot Cabbage	Quinoa Pudding
803	Savory Barley	Delicious Cheesy Cauliflower	Poached Pears
804	Fajita Casserole	Healthy & Easy Instant Pot Zucchini	Peanut Butter Brownies
805	Latte Oatmeal	Sweet & Sour Red Cabbage	Peach Cobbler
806	Coconut Blueberry Oatmeal	Sugar Snap Peas	Orange Strawberry Compote
807	Pumpkin Cranberry Oatmeal	Southern Okra & Tomatoes	Moist Pumpkin Brownie
808	Cranberry Farro	Garlic Mushrooms	Mini Choco Cake
809	Tropical Oatmeal	Tasty Tikka Masala Chickpeas	Healthy Sweet Potato Rice Pudding
810	Simple & Easy Breakfast Casserole	Cheesy & Creamy Ziti	Healthy Carrot Cake
811	Creamy Mac n Cheese	Classic Mac n Cheese	Hazelnuts Brownies
812	Cherry Risotto	Sticky Noodles	Flavorful Carrot Halva
813	Almond Coconut Risotto	Crispy Roasted Potatoes	Easy Egg Custard
814	Creamy Polenta	Sweet Potato Mash	Delicious Pumpkin Pudding
815	Sweet Cherry Chocolate Oat	Cheesy Spaghetti	Coconut Rice Pudding
816	Coconut Lime Breakfast Quinoa	Sautéed vegetables	Coconut Custard

817	Quick & Easy Farro	Healthy Veggie Curry	Cinnamon Pears
818	Farro Breakfast Risotto	Braised Parsnips	Cinnamon Lemon Pears
819	Tapioca Pudding	Healthy Ratatouille	Chocolate Mousse
820	Sweetened Breakfast Oats	Herb Mushrooms	Chocolate Cake
821	Cauliflower Mash	Creamy Squash Puree	Choco Mug Cake
822	Chia Oatmeal	Cheesy Cauliflower Rice	Cherry Apple Risotto
823	Blueberry Lemon Oatmeal	Delicious Baby Carrots	Cheesecake
824	Breakfast Cobbler	Lemon Haddock	Cardamom Zucchini Pudding
825	Tomato Corn Risotto	Quick Coconut Shrimp Curry	Brownie Cake
826	Tropical Oatmeal	Yummy Fish Tacos	Brown Rice Pudding
827	Tomato Corn Risotto	Delicious Scallops	Blueberry Cupcakes
828	Tapioca Pudding	Healthy Shrimp Rice	Apple Rice Pudding
829	Sweetened Breakfast Oats	Balsamic Salmon	Apple Pear Crisp
830	Sweet Potato Breakfast	Shrimp Scampi	Apple Crisp
831	Sweet Cherry Chocolate Oat	Dijon Fish Fillets	Apple Crisp
832	Strawberry Oatmeal	Macaroni with Cauliflower Broccoli	Apple Pear Crisp
833	Spinach Frittata	Spicy Cabbage	Apple Rice Pudding
834	Slow Cook Cherry Oatmeal	Instant Pot Artichokes	Blueberry Cupcakes
835	Simple & Easy Breakfast Casserole	Flavorful Ranch Cauliflower Mashed	Brown Rice Pudding
836	Savory Barley	Kale Curry	Brownie Cake
837	Sausage Casserole	Buttery Carrots & Parsnips	Cardamom Zucchini Pudding
838	Roasted Baby Potatoes	Creamy Parsnip Mash	Cheesecake
839	Ranch Potatoes	Red Bean Rice	Cherry Apple Risotto
840	Quinoa Pumpkin Porridge	Tender Pinto Beans	Choco Mug Cake
841	Quinoa Porridge	Tomatillo White Beans	Chocolate Cake
842	Quinoa Blueberry Bowl	Flavorful Refried Beans	Chocolate Mousse
843	Quick Brussels Sprouts	Delicious Beans & Rice	Cinnamon Lemon Pears
844	Quick & Easy Oatmeal	Indian Red Kidney Beans	Cinnamon Pears
845	Quick & Easy Farro	Mexican Black Beans	Coconut Custard
846	Pumpkin Oatmeal	Ham & Pinto Beans	Coconut Rice Pudding
847	Pumpkin Cranberry Oatmeal	Rosemary Salmon	Delicious Pumpkin Pudding
848	Perfect Breakfast Casserole	Crab Legs	Easy Egg Custard
849	Peach Oatmeal	Lemon Garlic Mussels	Flavorful Carrot Halva
850	Oatmeal Porridge	Zesty Salmon	Hazelnuts Brownies
851	Oat Millet Porridge	Delicious Basa Fillets	Healthy Carrot Cake
852	Mushroom Frittata	Indian Fried Prawns	Healthy Sweet Potato Rice Pudding
853	Latte Oatmeal	Spicy Salmon	Mini Choco Cake
854	Jalapeno Cheddar Grits	Basil Salmon	Moist Pumpkin Brownie
855	Hearty Polenta Porridge	Lemon Pepper Cod	Orange Strawberry Compote

856	Healthy Wheat Porridge	Easy Salmon Stew	Peach Cobbler
857	Healthy Breakfast Porridge	Sweet Baked Beans	Peanut Butter Brownies
858	Healthy Almond Oatmeal	Easy Baked Beans	Poached Pears
859	Ham Cheese Breakfast Casserole	Sweet & Tender Lima Beans	Quinoa Pudding
860	Fruit Compote	Flavorful Onion Rice	Saffron Rice Pudding
861	Farro Breakfast Risotto	Healthy Chicken Noodle Soup	Simple Raspberry Mug Cake
862	Fajita Casserole	Nutritious Lentil Soup	Sliced Apples with Nuts
863	Easy Cinnamon Apples	Cheesy Broccoli Soup	Sweet Tapioca Pudding
864	Easy Breakfast Grits	Carrot Ginger Soup	Thai Black Rice Pudding
865	Delicious French Toast Casserole	Cabbage Soup	Vanilla Bread Pudding
866	Delicious Chocolate Oatmeal	Zucchini Corn Soup	Vanilla Peanut Butter Fudge
867	Delicious Breakfast Casserole	Lentil Sausage Stew	Vermicelli Pudding
868	Creamy Walnut Grits	Black Bean Rice	Walnut Carrot Cake
869	Creamy Polenta	Nutritious Lentils Rice	Yogurt Custard
870	Creamy Mashed Potatoes	Cheesy Beef Rice	Yummy Strawberry Cobbler
871	Creamy Mac n Cheese	Coconut Beans & Rice	Orange Strawberry Compote
872	Cranberry Farro	Mushroom Brown Rice	Apple Rice Pudding
873	Cranberry Apple Breakfast Grains	Simple & Delicious Parmesan Rice	Cherry Apple Risotto
874	Coconut Lime Breakfast Quinoa	Chicken Cheese Rice	Poached Pears
875	Coconut Blueberry Oatmeal	Flavorful Fajita Rice	Brownie Cake
876	Choco Banana Oatmeal	Creamy Pea Risotto	Thai Black Rice Pudding
877	Chia Oatmeal	Quick & Easy Chicken Rice	Coconut Rice Pudding
878	Cherry Risotto	Garlic Turmeric Rice	Healthy Sweet Potato Rice Pudding
879	Cauliflower Mash	Flavorful Rice Pilaf	Quinoa Pudding
880	Carrot Oatmeal	Perfect Jasmine Rice	Apple Crisp
881	Broccoli Frittata	Broccoli Rice	Healthy Carrot Cake
882	Breakfast Cobbler	Spanish rice	Chocolate Cake
883	Blueberry Oatmeal	Onion Pepper Couscous	Coconut Custard
884	Blueberry Lemon Oatmeal	Lemon Snap Pea Couscous	Choco Mug Cake
885	Blueberry French Toast Casserole	Pearl Barley	Brown Rice Pudding
886	Berry Oatmeal	Spanish Quinoa	Sweet Tapioca Pudding
887	Banana Peanut Butter Oats	Buttery Scallions Risotto	Vanilla Bread Pudding
888	Baked Apples	Simple Paprika Rice	Chocolate Mousse
889	Apple Cinnamon Oatmeal	Delicious Potato Risotto	Blueberry Cupcakes
890	Almond Coconut Risotto	Jalapeno Brown Rice	Moist Pumpkin Brownie
891	Almond Coconut Risotto	Herb Garlic Chicken	Mini Choco Cake

892	Apple Cinnamon Oatmeal	Delicious Chicken Burrito Bowl	Cinnamon Pears
893	Baked Apples	Chicken Cheese Spaghetti	Delicious Pumpkin Pudding
894	Banana Peanut Butter Oats	Moist & Tender Chicken	Easy Egg Custard
895	Berry Oatmeal	Simple BBQ Chicken	Cinnamon Lemon Pears
896	Blueberry French Toast Casserole	Flavorful Chicken Curry	Sliced Apples with Nuts
897	Blueberry Lemon Oatmeal	Spicy Chicken Wings	Peanut Butter Brownies
898	Blueberry Oatmeal	BBQ Honey Chicken Wings	Cheesecake
899	Breakfast Cobbler	Honey Mustard Chicken	Saffron Rice Pudding
900	Broccoli Frittata	Tortellini Tomato Soup	Flavorful Carrot Halva
901	Carrot Oatmeal	Healthy Split Pea Soup	Vermicelli Pudding
902	Cauliflower Mash	Barley Mushroom Soup	Simple Raspberry Mug Cake
903	Cherry Risotto	Creamy Mushroom Soup	Yogurt Custard
904	Chia Oatmeal	Sweet Potato Soup	Cardamom Zucchini Pudding
905	Choco Banana Oatmeal	Healthy Vegetable Soup	Yummy Strawberry Cobbler
906	Coconut Blueberry Oatmeal	Onion Soup	Peach Cobbler
907	Coconut Lime Breakfast Quinoa	Teriyaki Chicken Drumsticks	Hazelnuts Brownies
908	Cranberry Apple Breakfast Grains	Mexican Salsa Chicken	Apple Pear Crisp
909	Cranberry Farro	Artichoke Chicken	Vanilla Peanut Butter Fudge
910	Creamy Mac n Cheese	Creamy Peanut Butter Chicken	Walnut Carrot Cake
911	Creamy Mashed Potatoes	BBQ Pulled Chicken	Yummy Strawberry Cobbler
912	Creamy Polenta	Buffalo Chicken Breasts	Yogurt Custard
913	Creamy Walnut Grits	Enchilada Chicken	Walnut Carrot Cake
914	Delicious Breakfast Casserole	Moist & Tender Turkey Breast	Vermicelli Pudding
915	Delicious Chocolate Oatmeal	Cafe Rio Chicken	Vanilla Peanut Butter Fudge
916	Delicious French Toast Casserole	Marinara Chicken	Vanilla Bread Pudding
917	Easy Breakfast Grits	Veggie Chicken Soup	Thai Black Rice Pudding
918	Easy Cinnamon Apples	Zucchini Soup	Sweet Tapioca Pudding
919	Fajita Casserole	Curried Cauliflower Soup	Sliced Apples with Nuts
920	Farro Breakfast Risotto	Summer Veggie Soup	Simple Raspberry Mug Cake
921	Fruit Compote	Vegetable Chicken Stew	Saffron Rice Pudding
922	Ham Cheese Breakfast Casserole	Thai Sweet Potato Stew	Quinoa Pudding
923	Healthy Almond Oatmeal	Chicken Taco Soup	Poached Pears
924	Healthy Breakfast Porridge	Tasty Chicken Rice Soup	Peanut Butter Brownies
925	Healthy Wheat Porridge	Cabbage Pork Soup	Peach Cobbler
926	Hearty Polenta Porridge	Chicken Adobo	Orange Strawberry Compote
927	Jalapeno Cheddar Grits	Tasty BBQ Ranch Chicken	Moist Pumpkin Brownie

928	Latte Oatmeal	Indian Chicken Tikka Masala	Mini Choco Cake
929	Mushroom Frittata	Bacon Pineapple Chicken	Healthy Sweet Potato Rice Pudding
930	Oat Millet Porridge	Flavorful Chicken Cacciatore	Healthy Carrot Cake
931	Oatmeal Porridge	Sweet Potato Chicken Curry	Hazelnuts Brownies
932	Peach Oatmeal	Chicken Chili	Flavorful Carrot Halva
933	Perfect Breakfast Casserole	Chicken Meatballs	Easy Egg Custard
934	Pumpkin Cranberry Oatmeal	Easy Adobo Chicken	Delicious Pumpkin Pudding
935	Pumpkin Oatmeal	Yummy Orange Chicken	Coconut Rice Pudding
936	Quick & Easy Farro	Thai Chicken	Coconut Custard
937	Quick & Easy Oatmeal	Curried Chicken	Cinnamon Pears
938	Quick Brussels Sprouts	Olive Chicken	Cinnamon Lemon Pears
939	Quinoa Blueberry Bowl	Sweet Mango Chicken	Chocolate Mousse
940	Quinoa Porridge	Herb Chicken	Chocolate Cake
941	Quinoa Pumpkin Porridge	Creamy Pesto Chicken	Choco Mug Cake
942	Ranch Potatoes	Healthy Shrimp Boil	Cherry Apple Risotto
943	Roasted Baby Potatoes	Asparagus Shrimp Risotto	Cheesecake
944	Sausage Casserole	Basil Tilapia	Cardamom Zucchini Pudding
945	Savory Barley	Delicious Shrimp Risotto	Brownie Cake
946	Simple & Easy Breakfast Casserole	Cajun Shrimp	Brown Rice Pudding
947	Slow Cook Cherry Oatmeal	Lemon Butter chicken	Blueberry Cupcakes
948	Spinach Frittata	Instant Pot Turkey Breast	Apple Rice Pudding
949	Strawberry Oatmeal	Ranch Chicken	Apple Pear Crisp
950	Sweet Cherry Chocolate Oat	Orange BBQ Chicken	Apple Crisp
951	Sweet Potato Breakfast	Mustard Chicken	Apple Crisp
952	Sweetened Breakfast Oats	Delicious Beef Tips	Apple Pear Crisp
953	Tapioca Pudding	Shredded Mexican Beef	Apple Rice Pudding
954	Tomato Corn Risotto	Korean Beef	Blueberry Cupcakes
955	Tropical Oatmeal	Italian Beef	Brown Rice Pudding
956	Delicious French Toast Casserole	Beef Stroganoff	Brownie Cake
957	Easy Breakfast Grits	Asian Pot Roast	Cardamom Zucchini Pudding
958	Pumpkin Oatmeal	Italian Ribs	Cheesecake
959	Roasted Baby Potatoes	Shredded Thai Beef	Cherry Apple Risotto
960	Easy Cinnamon Apples	Healthy Spinach Lentil Soup	Choco Mug Cake
961	Ranch Potatoes	Mushroom Soup	Chocolate Cake
962	Quick & Easy Oatmeal	Spinach Soup	Chocolate Mousse
963	Creamy Mashed Potatoes	Hearty Beef Stew	Cinnamon Lemon Pears
964	Delicious Chocolate Oatmeal	Spinach Chickpea Stew	Cinnamon Pears
965	Hearty Polenta Porridge	Healthy Eggplant Stew	Coconut Custard

966	Peach Oatmeal	Squash Cauliflower Soup	Coconut Rice Pudding
967	Apple Cinnamon Oatmeal	Corn Soup	Delicious Pumpkin Pudding
968	Choco Banana Oatmeal	Carrot Pea Soup	Easy Egg Custard
969	Healthy Almond Oatmeal	Mexican Barbecue	Flavorful Carrot Halva
970	Spinach Frittata	Korean Beef Tacos	Hazelnuts Brownies
971	Broccoli Frittata	Delicious Italian Beef	Healthy Carrot Cake
972	Quinoa Porridge	Flavorful Barbacoa	Healthy Sweet Potato Rice Pudding
973	Creamy Walnut Grits	Asian Beef	Mini Choco Cake
974	Healthy Wheat Porridge	Tasty Steak Bites	Moist Pumpkin Brownie
975	Quinoa Pumpkin Porridge	Smoky Beef	Orange Strawberry Compote
976	Blueberry Oatmeal	Flank Steak	Peach Cobbler
977	Mushroom Frittata	Moist & Tender Ribs	Peanut Butter Brownies
978	Quick Brussels Sprouts	Spicy Beef Curry	Poached Pears
979	Oatmeal Porridge	Pork Tenderloin	Quinoa Pudding
980	Healthy Breakfast Porridge	Tasty Beef Chili	Saffron Rice Pudding
981	Strawberry Oatmeal	Chipotle Chili	Simple Raspberry Mug Cake
982	Berry Oatmeal	Veggie Beef Roast	Sliced Apples with Nuts
983	Perfect Breakfast Casserole	Meatballs	Sweet Tapioca Pudding
984	Delicious Breakfast Casserole	Mongolian Beef	Thai Black Rice Pudding
985	Sweet Potato Breakfast	Flavors Taco Meat	Vanilla Bread Pudding
986	Banana Peanut Butter Oats	Leg of Lamb	Vanilla Peanut Butter Fudge
987	Jalapeno Cheddar Grits	Flavors Lamb Shanks	Vermicelli Pudding
988	Fruit Compote	Perfect Dinner Lamb	Walnut Carrot Cake
989	Carrot Oatmeal	Flavorful Taco Mince	Yogurt Custard
990	Slow Cook Cherry Oatmeal	Delicious Lamb Curry	Yummy Strawberry Cobbler
991	Ham Cheese Breakfast Casserole	Eastern Lamb Stew	Saffron Rice Pudding
992	Cranberry Apple Breakfast Grains	Sweet & Sour Fish	Vanilla Bread Pudding
993	Sausage Casserole	Spicy Shrimp Noodles	Chocolate Mousse
994	Blueberry French Toast Casserole	Nutritious Salmon	Blueberry Cupcakes
995	Oat Millet Porridge	Vegetable Fish Curry	Moist Pumpkin Brownie
996	Baked Apples	Tuna Pasta	Mini Choco Cake
997	Quinoa Blueberry Bowl	Cajun Seafood Gumbo	Cinnamon Pears
998	Savory Barley	Lemon Pepper Salmon	Delicious Pumpkin Pudding
999	Fajita Casserole	Lemon Garlic Salmon	Easy Egg Custard
1000	Latte Oatmeal	Dill Salmon	Cinnamon Lemon Pears

Conclusion

Pressure cooking is one of the healthy cooking methods used around the world. Smart and advanced cooking equipment's make your daily cooking easy. In this book of recipes, we have to use advanced pressure-cooking equipment popularly known as instant pot. Instant pot not only pressure cooker it's a multifunctional cooking appliance which performs task of 7 different cooking appliances.

In this book you will find 450 healthy, delicious and tasty recipes. Each and every recipe is written by its preparation time, cooking time, ingredients require and step by step cooking instructions.